GCSE OCR Gateway
Core Science
Higher Revision Guide

This book is for anyone doing **GCSE OCR Gateway Core Science** at higher level. It covers everything you'll need for your year 10 exams.

GCSE Science is all about **understanding how science works**. And not only that — understanding it well enough to be able to **question** what you hear on TV and read in the papers.

But you can't do that without a fair chunk of **background knowledge**. Hmm, tricky.

Happily this CGP book includes all the **science facts** you need to learn, and shows you how they work in the **real world**. And in true CGP style, we've explained it all as **clearly and concisely** as possible.

It's also got some daft bits in to try and make the whole experience at least vaguely entertaining for you.

What CGP is all about

Our sole aim here at CGP is to produce the highest quality books — carefully written, immaculately presented and dangerously close to being funny.

Then we work our socks off to get them out to you — at the cheapest possible prices.

Contents

HOW SCIENCE WORKS

MODULE B1 — UNDERSTANDING OURSELVES

MODULE C1 — CARBON CHEMISTRY

MODULE P1 — ENERGY FOR THE HOME

Module B2 — Understanding Our Environment

Module C2 — Chemical Resources

Module P2 — Living for the Future

Published by CGP

From original material by Richard Parsons.

Editors:
Katie Braid, Joe Brazier, Emma Elder, Mary Falkner, Edmund Robinson, Lyn Setchell, Hayley Thompson, Jane Towle and Dawn Wright.

Contributors:
Mike Bossart, John Myers, Adrian Schmit.

ISBN: 978 1 84146 713 9

With thanks to Janet Cruse-Sawyer, Philip Dobson, Ian Francis, Glenn Rogers, Ann Shires, and Karen Wells for the proofreading.
With thanks to Jan Greenway, Laura Jakubowski and Laura Stoney for the copyright research.

Photo of Kwashiorkor sufferer on page 13 courtesy of Tom D Thacher, MD.

With thanks to Science Photo Library for permission to use the image on page 56.

Graph to show trend in atmospheric CO_2 concentration and global temperature on page 114 based on data by EPICA Community Members 2004 and Siegenthaler et al 2005.

Groovy website: www.cgpbooks.co.uk

Printed by Elanders Ltd, Newcastle upon Tyne.
Jolly bits of clipart from CorelDRAW®

The Scientific Process

You need to know a few things about how the world of science works — both for your exams and your controlled assessment. Investigate these next few pages and you'll be laughing all day long on results day.

Scientists Come Up with Hypotheses — Then Test Them

Hundreds of years ago, we thought demons caused illness.

1) Scientists try to explain things. Everything.
2) They start by observing or thinking about something they don't understand — it could be anything, e.g. planets in the sky, a person suffering from an illness, what matter is made of... anything.
3) Then, using what they already know (plus a bit of insight), they come up with a hypothesis — a possible explanation for what they've observed.
4) The next step is to test whether the hypothesis might be right or not — this involves gathering evidence (i.e. data from investigations).
5) To gather evidence the scientist uses the hypothesis to make a prediction — a statement based on the hypothesis that can be tested by carrying out experiments.
6) If the results from the experiments match the prediction, then the scientist can be more confident that the hypothesis is correct. This doesn't mean the hypothesis is true though — other predictions based on the hypothesis might turn out to be wrong.

Scientists Work Together to Test Hypotheses

Then we thought it was caused by 'bad blood' (and treated it with leeches).

1) Different scientists can look at the same evidence and interpret it in different ways. That's why scientists usually work in teams — they can share their different ideas on how to interpret the data they find.
2) Once a team has come up with (and tested) a hypothesis they all agree with, they'll present their work to the scientific community through journals and scientific conferences so it can be judged — this is called the peer review process.
3) Other scientists then check the team's results (by trying to replicate them) and carry out their own experiments to collect more evidence.
4) If all the experiments in the world back up the hypothesis, scientists start to have a lot of confidence in it.
5) However, if another scientist does an experiment and the results don't fit with the hypothesis (and other scientists can replicate these results), then the hypothesis is in trouble. When this happens, scientists have to come up with a new hypothesis (maybe a modification of the old explanation, or maybe a completely new one).

Scientific Ideas Change as New Evidence is Found

Now we know most illnesses are due to microorganisms.

1) Scientific explanations are provisional because they only explain the evidence that's currently available — new evidence may come up that can't be explained.
2) This means that scientific explanations never become hard and fast, totally indisputable fact. As new evidence is found (or new ways of interpreting existing evidence are found), hypotheses can change or be replaced.
3) Sometimes, an unexpected observation or result will suddenly throw a hypothesis into doubt and further experiments will need to be carried out. This can lead to new developments that increase our understanding of science.

You expect me to believe that — then show me the evidence...

If scientists think something is true, they need to produce evidence to convince others — it's all part of testing a hypothesis. One hypothesis might survive these tests, while others won't — it's how things progress. And along the way some hypotheses will be disproved — i.e. shown not to be true.

Evaluating Hypotheses and Scientific Information

In everyday life (and in your exams unfortunately) you'll encounter lots of scientific information. It's important that you know a few things about how to evaluate any evidence you're given.

Some Hypotheses are More Convincing Than Others

1) You might have to evaluate hypotheses that give different explanations for the same thing. Basically, this just means you need to say which one you think is better, and then explain why.
2) The most convincing hypotheses are based on reliable evidence (e.g. data that can be reproduced by others in independent experiments, see p. 1) — not opinions or old wives' tales.
3) Reliable evidence comes from controlled experiments in laboratories (where you can control variables to make it a fair test — see p. 4), studies (e.g. of a population), or observations (e.g. of animal behaviour).
4) Evidence that's based on samples that are too small doesn't have much more credibility than opinions. A sample should be representative of the whole population (i.e. it should share as many of the various characteristics in the population as possible) — a small sample just can't do that.

Scientific Information Isn't Always Very Good Quality

When you're given some scientific information, don't just believe it straight away — you need to think critically about what it's saying to work out how good the information really is.

1) Scientific information can be presented by a person who is biased.
2) When a person is biased, it means that they favour a particular interpretation of the evidence for a reason that's incorrect or unrelated to the scientific information.
3) This can be unintentional — the scientist might not realise they're being affected by something which makes them biased.
4) It can also be intentional — a scientist might give a particular interpretation on purpose because they have a personal reason for doing so.
5) A person who is intentionally biased might misrepresent the evidence — give the true facts, but present them in a way that makes them misleading. This might be to persuade you to agree with them...

EXAMPLE

Scientists say 1 in 2 people are of above average weight

Sounds like we're a nation of fatties. It's a scientific analysis of the facts, and almost certainly true.

But an average is a kind of 'middle value' of all your data. Some readings are higher than average (about half of them, usually). Others will be lower than average (the other half).

So the above headline (which made it sound like we should all lose weight) could just as accurately say:

Scientists say 1 in 2 people are of below average weight

6) A person who is intentionally biased might also give scientific information without any evidence to back it up. This might be because there's no evidence to support what they're saying, or it could be that the person is just ignoring the evidence that exists (e.g. because it contradicts what they're saying).
7) Information that isn't backed up with any evidence could just be an opinion — you've got no way of telling whether it's true or not.

EXAMPLE

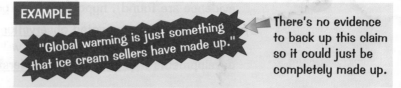

"Global warming is just something that ice cream sellers have made up."

There's no evidence to back up this claim so it could just be completely made up.

It's a scientific fact that the Moon's made of cheese...

Whenever you're given any kind of scientific information just stop for a second and ask yourself how convincing it really is — think about the evidence that's been used (if any) and the way that the information's been presented.

Scientific Development, Ethics and Risk

Scientific developments have a bit of a bumpy ride and yep, you guessed it, you need to know why this is.

Society Influences the Development of Science

1) You might think that scientific and technological developments are always a good thing. But society doesn't always agree about new developments.
2) Take embryo screening (which allows you to choose an embryo with particular characteristics). Different people have different opinions on it. For example:

THE GAZETTE
BONE MARROW BABY'S BROTHER SAVED
THE POST
BONE MARROW BABY BORN: WHAT RIGHTS DOES HE HAVE?

Some people say it's good... couples whose existing child needs a bone marrow transplant, but who can't find a donor, will be able to have another child selected for its matching bone marrow. This would save the life of their first child — and if they want another child anyway... where's the harm?
Other people say it's bad... they say it could have serious effects on the new child. In the above example the new child might feel unwanted — thinking they were only brought into the world to help someone else. And would they have the right to refuse to donate their bone marrow (as anyone else would)?

3) The question of whether something is morally or ethically right or wrong can't be answered by more experiments — there is no "right" or "wrong" answer.
4) In an ideal world, the best decision about any moral or ethical dilemma would have the best outcome for the majority of people involved.

Other Factors Can Affect Scientific Development Too

There are other factors that can influence the development of science and the way it's used:

Economic factors:
- Companies very often won't pay for research unless there's likely to be a profit in it.
- Society can't always afford to do things scientists recommend (e.g. investing heavily in alternative energy sources) without cutting back elsewhere.

Social factors: Decisions based on scientific evidence affect people — e.g. should fossil fuels be taxed more highly (to invest in alternative energy)? Should alcohol be banned (to prevent health problems)? Would the effect on people's lifestyles be acceptable...?

Cultural factors: Cultural feelings can sometimes affect whether research is carried out or given funding, e.g. some religious groups are against testing on human embryonic stem cells.

Scientific Development Has Benefits and Risks

1) Like most things, developments in scientific technology have both benefits and risks.

2) There often needs to be a balance between personal risk and the overall benefit to society. For example, building a nuclear power station poses a risk to the people who work there and those living nearby (because they may be exposed to radiation), but it will also supply a large section of society with a reliable source of electricity.
3) Scientists try to find ways of reducing the risks involved, e.g. introducing strict safety measures at the power station.

Scientific development — a nice quiet estate of labs on the edge of town...

As you can see, science isn't just about knowing your facts — you need to think about the factors that affect the development of science, the ethical issues raised and the benefits and risks that come with scientific development.

Planning Investigations

That's all the dull stuff about the world of science over — now onto the hands-on part. The next few pages show how practical investigations should be carried out — by both professional scientists and you.

To Make an Investigation a Fair Test You Have to Control the Variables

An important part of planning an investigation is making sure it's a fair test.

1) In a lab experiment you usually change one variable and measure how it affects the other variable.

> EXAMPLE: you might change only the temperature of an enzyme-controlled reaction and measure how it affects the rate of reaction.

2) To make it a fair test everything else that could affect the results should stay the same (otherwise you can't tell if the thing that's being changed is affecting the results or not — the data won't be reliable).

> EXAMPLE continued: you need to keep the pH the same, otherwise you won't know if any change in the rate of reaction is caused by the change in temperature, or the change in pH.

3) The variable that you change is called the independent variable.
4) The variable that's measured is called the dependent variable.
5) The variables that you keep the same are called control variables.
6) Because you can't always control all the variables, you often need to use a control experiment — an experiment that's kept under the same conditions as the rest of the investigation, but doesn't have anything done to it. This is so that you can see what happens when you don't change anything at all.

> EXAMPLE continued:
> Independent = temperature
> Dependent = rate of reaction
> Control = pH

The Equipment Used has to be Right for the Job

1) The measuring equipment you use has to be sensitive enough to accurately measure the chemicals you're using, e.g. if you need to measure out 11 ml of a liquid, you'll need to use a measuring cylinder that can measure to 1 ml, not 5 or 10 ml.
2) The smallest change a measuring instrument can detect is called its **RESOLUTION**. E.g. some mass balances have a resolution of 1 g and some have a resolution of 0.1 g.
3) You should also be able to explain why you've chosen each bit of kit.

Experiments Must be Safe

1) Part of planning an investigation is making sure that it's safe.
2) There are lots of hazards you could be faced with during an investigation, e.g. radiation, electricity, gas, chemicals and fire.
3) You should always make sure that you identify all the hazards that you might encounter.
4) You should also come up with ways of reducing the risks from the hazards you've identified.
5) One way of doing this is to carry out a risk assessment:

For an experiment involving a Bunsen burner, the risk assessment might be something like this:

> Hazard: Bunsen burner is a fire risk.
> Precautions:
> - Keep flammable chemicals away from the Bunsen.
> - Never leave the Bunsen unattended when lit.
> - Always turn on the yellow safety flame when not in use.

Hazard: revision boredom. Precaution: use CGP books

Wow, all this even before you've started the investigation — it really does make them run more smoothly though.

Getting the Data Right

There are a few things that can be done to make sure that you get the best results you possibly can.

Trial Runs Help Figure out the Range and Interval of Variable Values

1) Before you carry out an experiment, it's a good idea to do a trial run first — a quick version of your experiment.
2) Trial runs help you work out whether your plan is right or not — you might decide to make some changes after trying out your method.
3) Trial runs are used to figure out the range of variable values used (the upper and lower limit).
4) And they're used to figure out the interval (gaps) between the values too.

Enzyme-controlled reaction example from previous page continued:

- You might do trial runs at 10, 20, 30, 40 and 50 °C. If there was no reaction at 10 or 50 °C, you might narrow the range to 20-40 °C.
- If using 10 °C intervals gives you a big change in rate of reaction you might decide to use 5 °C intervals, e.g. 20, 25, 30, 35...

Data Should be as Reliable and Accurate as Possible

1) Reliable results are ones that can be consistently reproduced each time you do an experiment. If your results are reliable they're more likely to be true, so you can make valid conclusions from them.
2) When carrying out your own investigation, you can improve the reliability of your results by repeating the readings and calculating the mean (average, see next page). You should repeat readings at least twice (so that you have at least three readings to calculate an average result).
3) To make sure your results are reliable you can also take a second set of readings with another instrument, or get a different observer to cross check.
4) Checking your results match with secondary sources, e.g. studies that other people have done, also increases the reliability of your data.
5) You should also always make sure that your results are accurate. Really accurate results are those that are really close to the true answer.

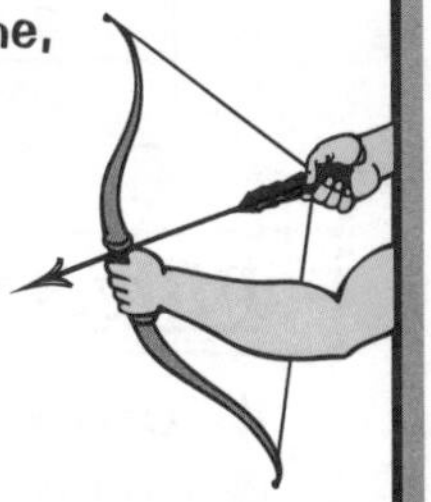

6) You can get accurate results by doing things like making sure the equipment you're using is sensitive enough (see previous page), and by recording your data to a suitable level of accuracy. For example, if you're taking digital readings of something, the results will be more accurate if you include at least a couple of decimal places instead of rounding to whole numbers.

You Can Check For Mistakes Made When Collecting Data

1) When you've collected all the results for an experiment, you should have a look to see if there are any results that don't seem to fit in with the rest.
2) Most results vary a bit, but any that are totally different are called anomalous results.
3) They're caused by human errors, e.g. by a whoopsie when measuring.
4) The only way to stop them happening is by taking all your measurements as carefully as possible.
5) If you ever get any anomalous results, you should investigate them to try to work out what happened. If you can work out what happened (e.g. you measured something wrong) you can ignore them when processing your results.

Reliable data — it won't ever forget your birthday...

All this stuff is really important — without good quality data an investigation will be totally meaningless. So give this page a read through a couple of times and your data will be the envy of the whole scientific community.

Processing, Presenting and Interpreting Data

The fun doesn't stop once you've collected your data — it then needs to be processed and presented...

Data Needs to be Organised

1) Data that's been collected needs to be organised so it can be processed later on.
2) Tables are dead useful for organising data.
3) When drawing tables you should always make sure that each column has a heading and that you've included the units.
4) Annoyingly, tables are about as useful as a chocolate teapot for showing patterns or relationships in data. You need to use some kind of graph or mathematical technique for that...

Test tube	Result (ml)	Repeat 1 (ml)	Repeat 2 (ml)
A	28	37	32
B	47	51	60
C	68	72	70

Data Can be Processed Using a Bit of Maths

1) Raw data generally just ain't that useful. You usually have to process it in some way.
2) A couple of the most simple calculations you can perform are the mean (average) and the range (how spread out the data is):

- To calculate the mean ADD TOGETHER all the data values and DIVIDE by the total number of values. You usually do this to get a single value from several repeats of your experiment.
- To calculate the range find the LARGEST number and SUBTRACT the SMALLEST number. You usually do this to check the accuracy and reliability of the results — the greater the spread of the data, the lower the accuracy and reliability.

Test tube	Result (ml)	Repeat 1 (ml)	Repeat 2 (ml)	Mean (ml)	Range
A	28	37	32	$(28 + 37 + 32) \div 3 = 32.3$	$37 - 28 = 9$
B	47	51	60	$(47 + 51 + 60) \div 3 = 52.7$	$60 - 47 = 13$
C	68	72	70	$(68 + 72 + 70) \div 3 = 70.0$	$72 - 68 = 4$

Different Types of Data Should be Presented in Different Ways

1) Once you've carried out an investigation, you'll need to present your data so that it's easier to see patterns and relationships in the data.
2) Different types of investigations give you different types of data, so you'll always have to choose what the best way to present your data is.

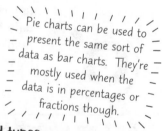

Pie charts can be used to present the same sort of data as bar charts. They're mostly used when the data is in percentages or fractions though.

Bar Charts

If the independent variable is categoric (comes in distinct categories, e.g. blood types, metals) you should use a bar chart to display the data. You also use them if the independent variable is discrete (the data can be counted in chunks, where there's no in-between value, e.g. number of people is discrete because you can't have half a person).

There are some golden rules you need to follow for drawing bar charts:

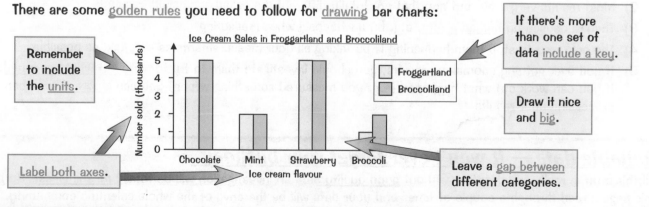

Remember to include the units.

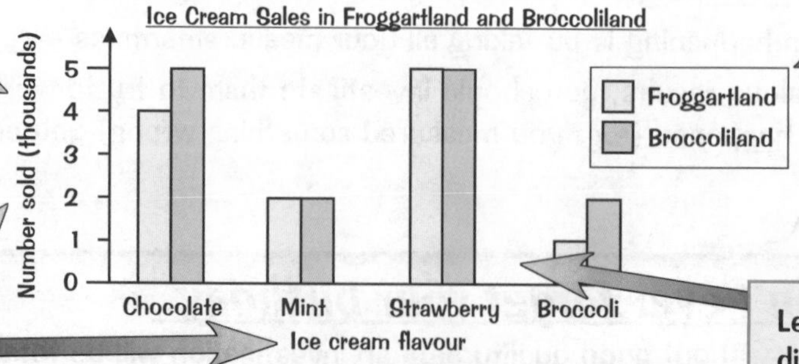

If there's more than one set of data include a key.

Draw it nice and big.

Label both axes.

Leave a gap between different categories.

Processing, Presenting and Interpreting Data

Line Graphs

If the independent variable is continuous (numerical data that can have any value within a range, e.g. length, volume, temperature) you should use a line graph to display the data.

Remember to include the units.

The dependent variable (the thing you measure) goes on the y-axis (the vertical one).

The independent variable (the thing you change) goes on the x-axis (the horizontal one).

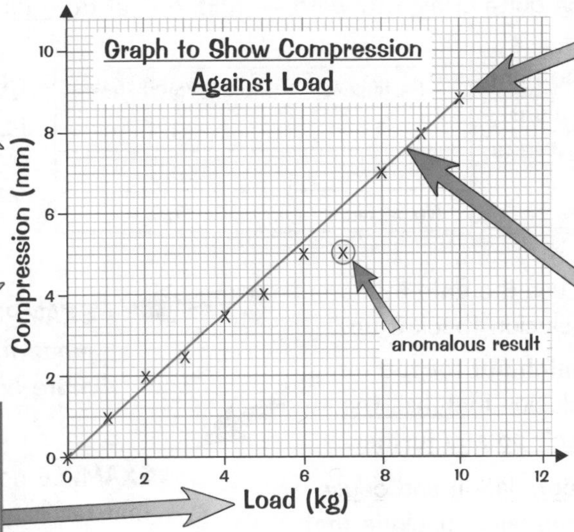

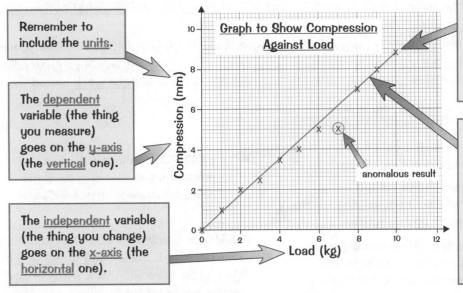

When plotting points, use a sharp pencil and make a neat little cross (don't do blobs).

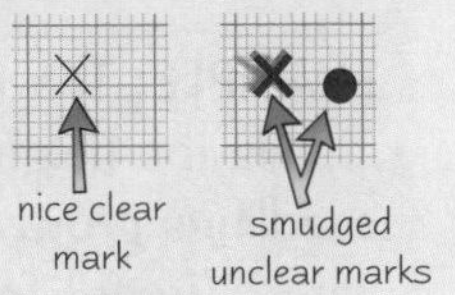

Don't join the dots up. You should draw a line of best fit (or a curve of best fit if your points make a curve). When drawing a line (or curve), try to draw the line through or as near to as many points as possible, ignoring anomalous results.

You can also use line graphs to process data a bit more. For example, if 'time' is on the x-axis, you can calculate the gradient (slope) of the line to find the rate of reaction:

1) Gradient = y ÷ x
2) You can calculate the gradient of the whole line or a section of it.
3) The rate would be in cm^3/s.

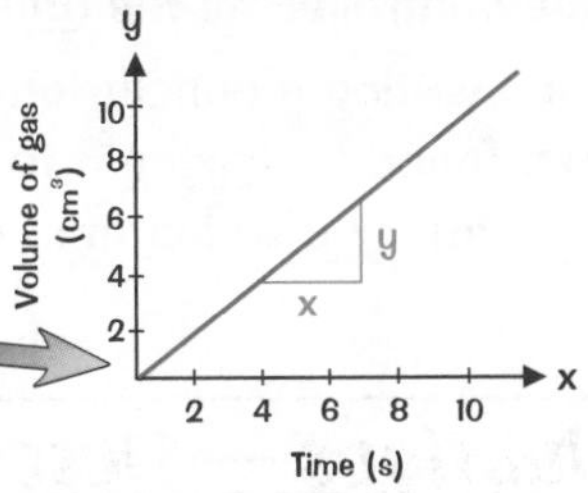

Line Graphs Can Show Relationships in Data

1) Unfortunately, when you're carrying out an investigation it's not enough to just present your data — you've got to analyse it to identify any patterns or relationships there might be.
2) Line graphs are great for showing relationships between two variables.
3) Here are the three different types of correlation (relationship) shown on line graphs:

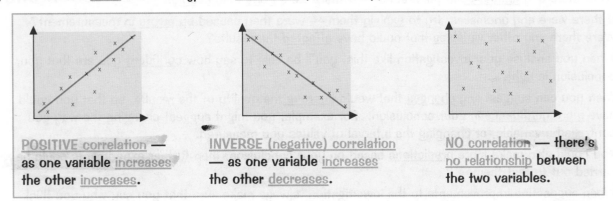

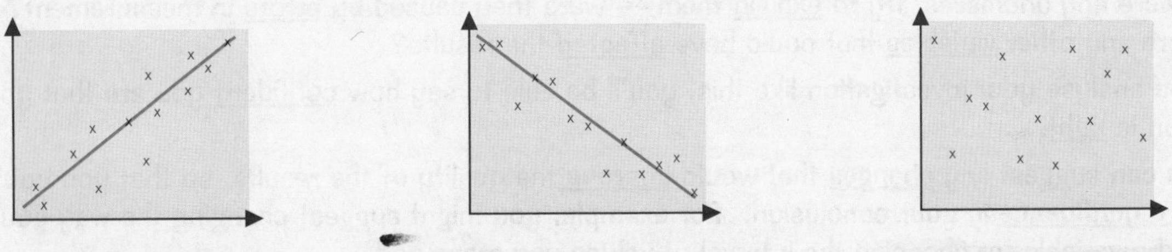

POSITIVE correlation — as one variable increases the other increases.

INVERSE (negative) correlation — as one variable increases the other decreases.

NO correlation — there's no relationship between the two variables.

4) You've got to be careful not to confuse correlation with cause though. A correlation just means that there's a relationship between two variables. It doesn't mean that the change in one variable is causing the change in the other (there might be other factors involved).

There's a positive correlation between age of man and length of nose hair...

Process, present, interpret... data's like a difficult child — it needs a lot of attention. Go on, make it happy.

Concluding and Evaluating

At the end of an investigation, the conclusion and evaluation are waiting. Don't worry, they won't bite.

A Conclusion is a Summary of What You've Learnt

1) Once all the data's been collected, presented and analysed, an investigation will always involve coming to a conclusion.
2) Drawing a conclusion can be quite straightforward — just look at your data and say what pattern you see.

EXAMPLE: The table on the right shows the heights of pea plant seedlings grown for three weeks with different fertilisers.

Fertiliser	Mean growth (mm)
A	13.5
B	19.5
No fertiliser	5.5

CONCLUSION: Fertiliser B makes pea plant seedlings grow taller over a three week period than fertiliser A.

3) However, you also need to use the data that's been collected to justify the conclusion (back it up).
4) There are some things to watch out for too — it's important that the conclusion matches the data it's based on and doesn't go any further.
5) Remember not to confuse correlation and cause (see previous page). You can only conclude that one variable is causing a change in another if you have controlled all the other variables (made it a fair test).
6) When writing a conclusion you should also explain what's been found by linking it to your own scientific knowledge (the stuff you've learnt in class).

EXAMPLE continued: Fertiliser B made the pea plants grow 6 mm more on average than fertiliser A.

EXAMPLE continued: You can't conclude that fertiliser B makes any other type of plant grow taller than fertiliser A — the results could be totally different. Also, you can't make any conclusions beyond the three weeks — the plants could drop dead.

Evaluations — Describe How it Could be Improved

An evaluation is a critical analysis of the whole investigation.

1) You should comment on the method — was the equipment suitable? Was it a fair test?
2) Comment on the quality of the results — was there enough evidence to reach a valid conclusion? Were the results reliable, accurate and precise?
3) Were there any anomalies in the results — if there were none then say so.
4) If there were any anomalies, try to explain them — were they caused by errors in measurement? Were there any other variables that could have affected the results?
5) When you analyse your investigation like this, you'll be able to say how confident you are that your conclusion is right.
6) Then you can suggest any changes that would improve the quality of the results, so that you could have more confidence in your conclusion. For example, you might suggest changing the way you controlled a variable, or changing the interval of values you measured.
7) You could also make more predictions based on your conclusion, then further experiments could be carried out to test them.
8) When suggesting improvements to the investigation, always make sure that you say why you think this would make the results better.

I'd value this E somewhere in the region of 250-300k
E

Evaluation — in my next study I will make sure I don't burn the lab down...

I know it doesn't seem very nice, but writing about where you went wrong is an important skill — it shows you've got a really good understanding of what the investigation was about. It's difficult for me — I'm always right.

Controlled Assessment

At some point you'll have to do the controlled assessment. Here's a bit about it, but make sure you can recite all the stuff we've covered in this section first — it'll really help you out.

There are Three Parts to the Controlled Assessment

1) Research and Collecting Secondary Data

For Part 1 you'll be given some material to introduce the task and a research question. You'll need to read this through and then:

1) Carry out research and collect secondary data (data that other people have collected, rather than data you collect yourself).
2) Show that you considered all the different sources you could have used (e.g. books, the Internet) and chose the ones that were most suitable. You also need to explain why you chose those sources.
3) Write a full list (bibliography) of all the sources you used.
4) Present all the data you collected in an appropriate way, e.g. using tables.

2) Planning and Collecting Primary Data

For Part 2 you'll be given a hypothesis to test and some more material to get your head around. You'll need to read this through and then:

1) Plan an experiment to test the hypothesis you've been given. You'll need to think about:
   - What equipment you're going to use (and why that equipment is right for the job).
   - What measurements you're going to take of the dependent variable.
   - How you're going to minimise errors so that your results are accurate and reliable.
   - What range of values you will use for the independent variable.
   - What interval you will use for the independent variable.
   - What variables you're going to control (and how you're going to do it).
   - How many times you're going to repeat the experiment.

There's lots of help on all of these things on pages 4-5.

2) Explain all the choices you made when planning the experiment.
3) Write a risk assessment for the experiment.
4) Carry out the experiment to collect primary data, taking any precautions from the risk assessment.
5) Present all the data you collected in an appropriate way, e.g. using tables.

3) Analysis and Evaluation

For Part 3 you'll have to complete a question paper which will ask you to do things like:

1) Process (e.g. using a bit of maths) and present (e.g. using graphs) both the primary and secondary data you collected in Part 1 and Part 2 in the most appropriate way.
2) Analyse and interpret the data to identify any patterns or relationships.
3) Compare your primary and secondary data to look for similarities and differences.
4) Write a conclusion based on your primary data and back it up with your own scientific knowledge. Say whether the secondary data you collected supports the conclusion.
5) Evaluate the methods you used to collect the data and the quality of the data that was collected.
6) Say how confident you are in your conclusion and make suggestions for how the investigation could be improved. You'll also need to say why your suggestions would be an improvement.

Read this through and your assessment will be well under control...

You could use this page like a tick list for the controlled assessment — to make sure you don't forget anything.

Fitness and Blood Pressure

If you've ever wondered what the docs on Casualty are on about when they say in excited voices that someone's blood pressure is "92 over 60" or something... well, you're about to find out.

Being Fit is Not the Same as Being Healthy

1) Make sure you know the difference between being fit and being healthy...

HEALTHY means being free of any infections or diseases, whereas being FIT is a measure of how well you can perform physical tasks.

2) Fitness is not a precise term and it can be measured in different ways.
3) Fitness profiles measure strength, speed, agility and flexibility, together with stamina.
4) Stamina is a good indication of cardiovascular efficiency (the ability of the heart to supply the muscles with oxygen). It can be tested by measuring oxygen uptake during exercise, and blood pressure.

Stamina is how long you can keep going.

Blood is Pumped Around Your Body Under Pressure

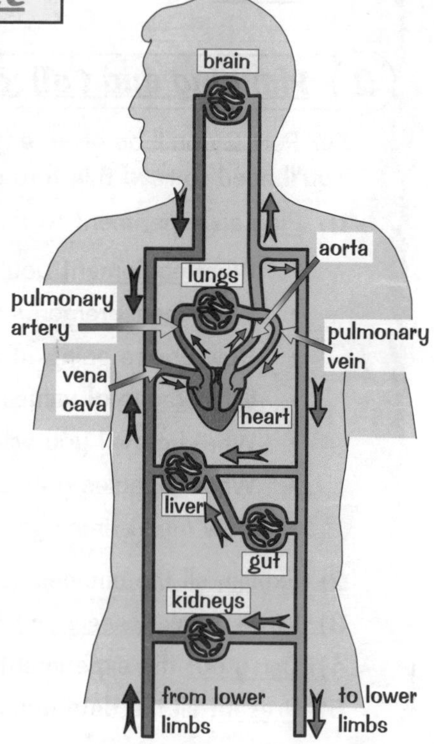

1) The blood is pumped around the body by the contractions of the heart. These contractions increase the pressure of the blood.
2) The blood leaves the heart and flows through arteries. These split into thousands of tiny capillaries, which take blood to every cell in the body. The blood then flows back to the heart through veins. The pressure gets lower as the blood flows through the system.
3) The blood pressure is at its highest when the heart contracts — this is the systolic pressure. When the heart relaxes, the pressure is at its lowest — this is the diastolic pressure.
4) Blood pressure is measured in mm of mercury (mmHg).
5) In a healthy person it shouldn't be higher than about 135 (systolic pressure) over about 85 (diastolic pressure).
6) There are other factors (apart from your heart contracting) that can increase your blood pressure:

- smoking
- being overweight
- drinking too much alcohol
- being under lots of stress for a long time

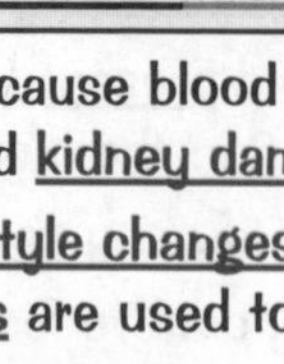

High or Low Blood Pressure Can Cause Health Problems

1) If the pressure of the blood is too high it can cause blood vessels to burst, and this can lead to strokes, brain damage and kidney damage.
2) High blood pressure can be decreased by lifestyle changes, e.g. eating a balanced diet, doing regular exercise, etc. In extreme cases, drugs are used to help correct the problem.
3) Low blood pressure is much less common than high blood pressure, but it can also cause problems. It causes poor circulation and tissues don't get all the food and oxygen they need. If your brain doesn't get enough food and oxygen you'll get dizzy and end up fainting.

My old P.E. teacher was really fit...

The exam might throw you a question asking you to evaluate the different ways of measuring someone's fitness. It might sound tricky, but all you need is a bit of common sense. Basically, the most effective method depends on the activity being carried out. For example, the best measure of fitness for a runner might be speed, whereas for a weight lifter it would be more useful to look at strength. Simple.

High Blood Pressure and Heart Disease

Smoking, in case you hadn't realised by now, is really quite BAD for you. Amongst other things, it's a major cause of high blood pressure — which can lead to all sorts of other health problems (see page 10).

Smoking Can Increase Blood Pressure

Cigarette smoke contains lots of nasty chemicals — some of which can increase blood pressure:

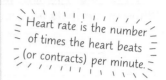

1) CARBON MONOXIDE — this combines with haemoglobin in red blood cells, which reduces the amount of oxygen they can carry. To make up for this (so that the tissues can get enough oxygen) heart rate has to increase. The heart contracts more frequently, which increases blood pressure.

Heart rate is the number of times the heart beats (or contracts) per minute.

2) NICOTINE — this increases heart rate. The heart contracts more often, increasing blood pressure.

A Poor Diet Can Lead to Heart Disease

1) Any disease that affects the heart is known as heart disease (clever). This includes things like heart attacks.
2) If your diet is high in saturated fat or salt, you may be more at risk of developing heart disease.

Saturated Fats Can Cause a Build Up of Cholesterol

1) Cholesterol is a fatty substance. Eating a diet high in saturated fat has been linked to high levels of cholesterol in the blood.
2) You need some cholesterol for things like making cell membranes. But if you get too much cholesterol it starts to build up in your arteries.
3) This forms plaques in the artery wall, which narrow the arteries. The plaques restrict the flow of blood, which can lead to a heart attack (see below).

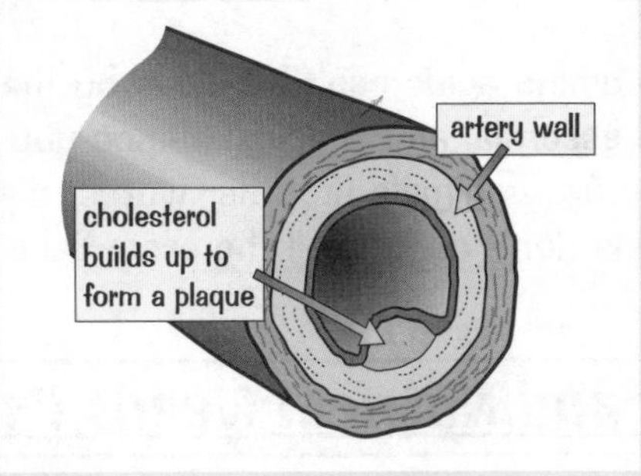

High Salt Levels Can Increase Blood Pressure

1) You need salt as part of a healthy diet. But eating too much salt can cause high blood pressure.
2) High blood pressure increases the risk of damage to the arteries — this damage can encourage the build up of plaques, which can lead to a heart attack.

Narrow Arteries Increase the Risk of a Heart Attack

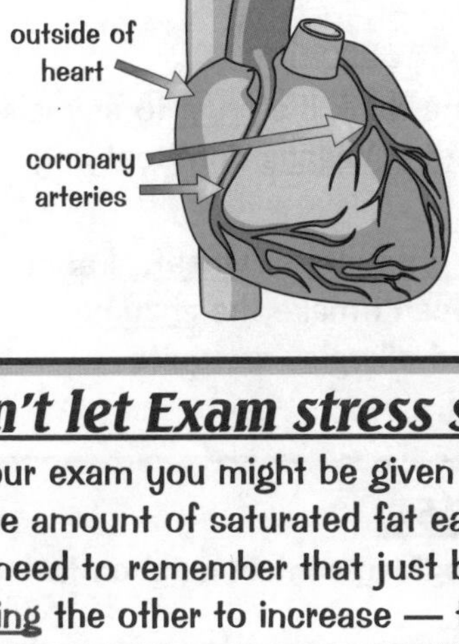

1) The heart muscle is supplied with blood by the coronary arteries.
2) If these become narrowed (e.g. due to plaques in the artery wall) blood flow to the heart is restricted and the heart muscle receives less oxygen.
3) A thrombosis (blood clot) also restricts blood flow.
4) If a thrombosis occurs in an already narrow coronary artery, blood flow to the heart might be blocked completely. If this happens, an area of heart muscle will be cut off from its oxygen supply.
5) This causes a heart attack.

Don't let Exam stress send your blood pressure through the roof...

In your exam you might be given some data to analyse. For example, they might give you a graph showing that as the amount of saturated fat eaten increases, so does the incidence of heart disease. With graphs like this you need to remember that just because both of the variables are increasing, it doesn't mean that one of them is causing the other to increase — there might only be a correlation between them (see page 7 for more on this).

Eating Healthily

As that doctor on the TV said this morning, food isn't just about energy — you need a balanced diet if you want to make sure that everything keeps working as it's supposed to.

A Balanced Diet Supplies All Your Essential Nutrients

A balanced diet gives you all the essential nutrients you need. The six essential nutrients are carbohydrates, proteins, fats, vitamins, minerals and water. You also need fibre (to keep the guts in good working order). Different nutrients are required for different functions in the body:

NUTRIENTS	FUNCTIONS
Carbohydrates	Carbohydrates (e.g. glucose) provide energy.
Fats	Fats provide energy, act as an energy store and provide insulation.
Proteins	Proteins are needed for growth and repair of tissue, and to provide energy in emergencies.
Vitamins and Minerals	Various functions: e.g. vitamin C is needed to prevent scurvy, and iron (a mineral) is needed to make haemoglobin for healthy blood.
Water	To prevent dehydration (where the body doesn't have enough water).

1) Carbohydrates are made up of simple sugars like glucose. They are stored in the liver as glycogen or converted to fats.
2) Fats are made up of fatty acids and glycerol. They can be stored under the skin and around organs as adipose tissue.
3) Proteins are made up of amino acids. They don't get stored.

Some amino acids can't be made by the body, so you have to get them from your diet — these are called essential amino acids. Since you can get all the essential amino acids by eating protein that comes from animals (in other words, meat), animal proteins are called first class proteins. Plant proteins don't contain all the essential amino acids — they're called second class proteins.

Energy and Nutrient Needs Vary Between People

A balanced diet isn't a set thing — it's different for everyone. The balance of the different nutrients a person needs depends on things like their age, gender and activity level.

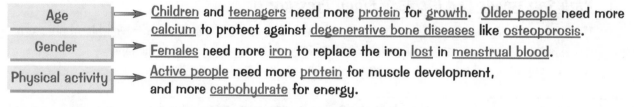

- Age → Children and teenagers need more protein for growth. Older people need more calcium to protect against degenerative bone diseases like osteoporosis.
- Gender → Females need more iron to replace the iron lost in menstrual blood.
- Physical activity → Active people need more protein for muscle development, and more carbohydrate for energy.

Some People Choose to Eat a Different Diet

Some people choose not to eat some foods for all sorts of reasons:

1) Religious reasons — e.g. Hindus don't eat cows because they believe they're sacred.
2) Personal reasons — vegetarians don't eat meat for various reasons — some think it's cruel to animals, some don't like the taste, some think it's healthier and some think it's trendy. Vegans don't eat any products from animals, e.g. milk, eggs and cheese.
3) Medical reasons — some people are intolerant to certain foods, e.g. dairy products or wheat. Eating them can make the person feel bloated and ill. This is often because they can't make the enzyme needed to digest that food properly. Some people are allergic to foods (nut allergies are quite common) — they get a severe reaction which can sometimes even be fatal.

I think the problem is that I've got an allergy to sprouts...

Having a food allergy can be a real pain. Just think how many random products have 'May contain nuts' on them. Some people carry a syringe of adrenaline to inject themselves with, just in case.

Diet Problems

You are what you eat, apparently. That makes me baked beans. But at least I'm not toast.

Eating Too Little Protein Can Cause Problems

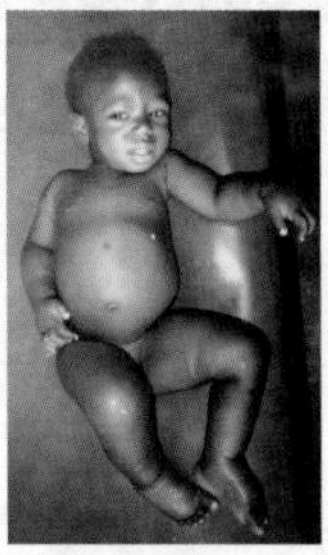

A kwashiorkor sufferer

Courtesy of Tom D. Thacher, MD.

1) Eating too little protein can cause a condition called kwashiorkor. A common symptom is a swollen stomach.
2) In developing countries lots of people have diets that are too low in protein. There are two main reasons for this:
   - Overpopulation means the demand for protein-rich food is greater than the amount that's available — so not everybody gets enough.
   - There isn't a lot of money to invest in agriculture — without the best farming techniques it's difficult to produce enough protein-rich food for everyone.
3) You can calculate a person's Estimated Average daily Requirement (EAR) of protein using this formula:

$$\text{EAR (g)} = 0.6 \times \text{body mass (kg)}$$

4) EAR is just an estimate though. It tells you how much protein the average person of a particular body mass should eat each day.
5) EAR varies with age, e.g. teenagers need to eat more protein than adults because they are still growing.
6) It also changes during and after pregnancy. Pregnant women need extra protein to help their baby grow. A woman who is breast feeding (lactating) needs extra protein in order to produce milk.

Eating Disorders Cause Problems too

1) Some psychological disorders, e.g. anorexia nervosa and bulimia nervosa, can also cause under-nutrition.
2) Anorexia nervosa leads to self-starvation. Bulimia nervosa involves bouts of binge eating, followed by self-induced vomiting. They're both usually caused by low self-esteem and a desire to be 'perfect' — sufferers have a poor self-image.
3) These disorders result in a poor diet, which can cause a host of other illnesses, e.g. liver failure, kidney failure, heart attacks, muscle wastage, low blood pressure and mineral deficiencies. Bulimia can lead to tooth decay (the acid in vomit eats away at the tooth enamel). Both disorders can be fatal.

Body Mass Index Indicates If You're Under- or Overweight

The Body Mass Index (BMI) is used as a guide to help decide whether someone is underweight, normal, overweight or obese. It's calculated from their height and weight:

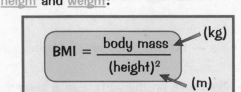

$$\text{BMI} = \frac{\text{body mass (kg)}}{(\text{height (m)})^2}$$

The table shows how BMI is used to classify people's weight.

Body Mass Index	Weight Description
below 18.5	underweight
18.5 - 24.9	normal
25 - 29.9	overweight
30 - 40	moderately obese
above 40	severely obese

BMI isn't always reliable. Athletes have lots of muscle, which weighs more than fat, so they can come out with a high BMI even though they're not overweight. An alternative to BMI is measuring % body fat.

Your EAR for revision = 4.7534 hours...

What a cheery page. Make sure you know exactly how to use those pesky equations. You could end up having to calculate BMI or EAR in the exam. Remember: EAR is an estimate and it varies from person to person.

Infectious Disease

There really are loads of things out to get you, and you really do have to fight attacks off every day.

Infectious Diseases are Caused by Pathogens

Pathogens are microorganisms that cause disease. There are four types:

1) fungi — e.g. athlete's foot is caused by fungi
2) bacteria — e.g. cholera is caused by bacteria
3) viruses — e.g. flu is caused by a virus
4) protozoa (single-celled organisms) — e.g. dysentery can be caused by protozoa.

The symptoms of an infectious disease are caused by cell damage or by toxins produced by the pathogens.

Malaria is an Example of an Infectious Disease

1) Malaria is caused by a protozoan. It's carried by mosquitoes, which are insects that feed on the blood of animals (including humans).
2) The protozoan is a parasite — an organism that lives off another organism (called a host) and often causes it harm (see page 78).
3) The mosquitoes are vectors, meaning they carry the disease without getting it themselves. They pick up the malarial parasite when they feed on an infected animal. Every time the mosquito feeds on another animal it infects it by inserting the parasite into the animal's blood vessels.
4) We know that mozzies carry malaria so we can target them to reduce the spread of infection:
   - The areas of water where mosquitoes lay their eggs can be drained or sprayed with insecticides.
   - Fish can be introduced into the water to eat mosquito larvae.
   - People can be protected from mosquitoes using insecticides and mosquito nets.

Your Immune System Deals with Pathogens

Once pathogens have entered your body they'll reproduce rapidly unless they're destroyed. That's the job of your immune system, and white blood cells are the most important part of it.

White blood cells travel around in your blood and crawl into every part of you, constantly patrolling for pathogens. When they come across an invading microorganism they have three lines of attack:

1) Consuming Them

White blood cells can engulf foreign cells and digest them.

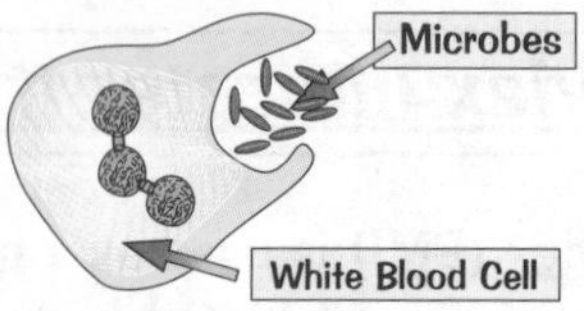

2) Producing Antitoxins

Antitoxins counter the effect of any poisons (toxins) produced by the invading pathogens.

3) Producing Antibodies

1) Every pathogen has unique molecules on the surface of its cells — no two pathogens have the same ones. These molecules are called antigens.
2) When your white blood cells come across a foreign antigen (like those on the surface of a bacterium) they'll start to produce proteins called antibodies, which lock on to and kill the new invading cells. The antibodies produced are specific to that pathogen — they won't lock on to other pathogens.
3) Antibodies are then produced rapidly and flow all round the body to kill all similar bacteria or viruses.
4) Some white blood cells stay around in the blood after the pathogen has been fought off — these are called memory cells. If the person is infected with the same pathogen again these cells will remember it and immediately make antibodies to kill it — the person is naturally immune to that pathogen.

If athletes get athlete's foot — do vicars get dog-cholera...?

White blood cells aren't the body's only defence. Your skin provides a tough layer that stops most pathogens getting in to begin with, and if you get a cut in it, clotting quickly seals it up again. Clever stuff.

Preventing and Treating Infectious Disease

An ounce of prevention is worth a pound of cure. That's what my mum says, anyhow.

Immunisation (Vaccination) Stops You Getting Infections

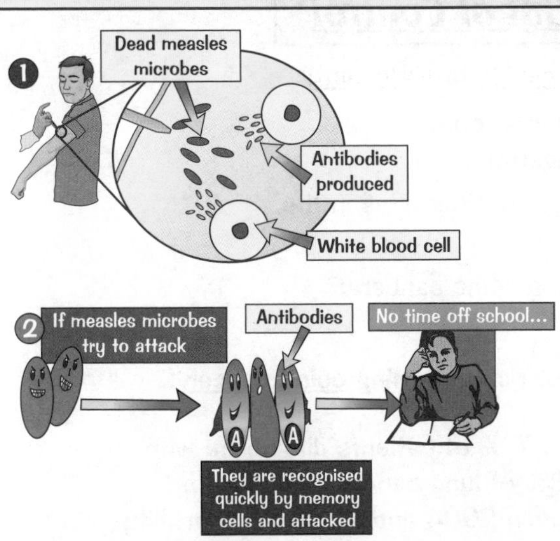

1) When you're infected with a new pathogen it can take your white blood cells a while to produce the antibodies to deal with it. In that time you can get very ill, or maybe even die.
2) To avoid this you can be immunised (vaccinated) against some diseases, e.g. polio or measles.
3) Immunisation involves injecting dead or inactive pathogens into the body. These carry antigens, so even though they're harmless they still trigger an immune response — your white blood cells produce antibodies to attack them.
4) Some of these white blood cells will remain in the blood as memory cells (see previous page) so if live pathogens of the same type ever appear, the antibodies to kill them will be produced immediately.

Immunisation is classed as active immunity:

- Active immunity is where the immune system makes its own antibodies after being stimulated by a pathogen. It includes becoming naturally immune (see previous page) and artificially immune (immunisation). Active immunity is usually permanent.
- Passive immunity is where you use antibodies made by another organism, e.g. antibodies are passed from mother to baby through breast milk. Passive immunity is only temporary.

There are Benefits and Risks Associated with Immunisation

1) Immunisation stops you from getting ill... a pretty obvious benefit.
2) And if most people are immunised the disease won't be able to spread as easily.
3) But there can be short-term side effects, e.g. swelling and redness at the site of injection and feeling a bit under the weather for a week or two afterwards.
4) You can't have some vaccines if you're already ill, especially if your immune system is weakened.
5) Some people think that immunisation can cause other disorders, e.g. one study suggested a link between the MMR (measles, mumps and rubella) vaccine and autism. Scientists now know it's perfectly safe, but for a few years many parents weren't willing to take the risk.

You Can Take Antibiotics to Get Rid of Some Infections

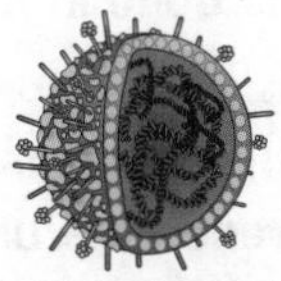

A horrid Flu Virus

1) Antibiotics are drugs that kill bacteria without killing your own body cells.
2) They're very useful for clearing up bacterial infections that your body is having trouble with, however they don't kill viruses.
3) Antivirals can be used to treat viral infections. Antivirals are drugs that stop viruses from reproducing.
4) Some bacteria are naturally resistant to (not killed by) certain antibiotics. Misuse of antibiotics (e.g. doctors overprescribing them or patients not finishing a course) has increased the rate of development of resistant strains. So nowadays you won't get antibiotics for a mild infection, only for something more serious. MRSA (the hospital 'superbug') is the best-known example of an antibiotic-resistant strain.

GCSEs are like antibiotics — you have to finish the course...

Science isn't just about doing an experiment, finding the answer and telling everyone about it — scientists often disagree. Not that long ago different scientists had different opinions on the MMR vaccine — and argued about its safety. Many different studies were done before scientists concluded it was safe.

Cancer and Drug Development

If you've ever thought you might be a hypochondriac, this page may not do you any favours. Still, at least you'll learn all about how drugs are developed.

Cancer is Caused by Body Cells Dividing Out of Control

This forms a tumour (a mass of cells). Tumours can either be benign or malignant:

1) **Benign** — This is where the tumour grows until there's no more room. The cells stay where they are. This type isn't normally dangerous.
2) **Malignant** — This is where the tumour grows and can spread to other sites in the body. Malignant tumours are dangerous and can be fatal.

Having a healthy lifestyle and diet can reduce your risk of getting some cancers:

1) Not smoking reduces your chances of getting lung cancer.
2) Eating less processed meat and more fibre may reduce your risk of getting colon cancer.

Different types of cancer have different survival rates, e.g. 77% of patients diagnosed with breast cancer survive for at least 5 years, whereas only 6% of lung cancer patients do. They also have different mortality (death) rates, e.g. between 2004 and 2006 the mortality rate for men with lung cancer was 53 per 100,000 of the male population, whereas the mortality rate for men with prostate cancer was only 29 per 100,000.

Drugs Developed to Treat Disease Need to be Tested

New drugs developed to treat any kind of disease need to be thoroughly tested before they can be used to make sure they're safe and that they work. This is the usual way that drugs are developed and tested:

Computer models are often used first of all — these simulate a human's response to a drug, so you don't need to test on live animals at this stage. They can identify promising drugs to be tested in the next stage, but it's not as accurate as actually seeing the effect on a live organism.

→ The drugs are then developed further by testing on human tissues. However, you can't use human tissue to test drugs that affect whole/multiple body systems, e.g. testing a drug for blood pressure must be done on a whole animal, i.e. one that has an intact circulatory system.

→ The last step is to develop and test the drug using animals. The law in Britain states that any new drug must be tested on two different live mammals. Some people think it's cruel to test on animals, but others believe this is the safest way to make sure a drug isn't dangerous before it's given to humans.

After the drug has been tested on animals it's tested on humans:

1) This is done in a study called a clinical trial.
2) There are two groups of patients. One is given the new drug, the other is given a placebo (a 'sugar pill' that looks like the real drug but doesn't do anything). This is done so scientists can see the actual difference the drug makes — it allows for the placebo effect (when the patient expects the treatment to work and so feels better, even though the treatment isn't doing anything).
3) Scientists sometimes test new drugs against the best existing treatment rather than a placebo. This tells them how well the new drug compares to what we already have.
4) Clinical trials are blind — the patient in the study doesn't know whether they're getting the drug or the placebo. In fact, they're often double blind — neither the patient nor the scientist knows until all the results have been gathered.

Double Blindman's Buff — now that's got to be fun...

In the exam they might give you data relating to the survival or mortality (death) rates of different types of cancer and ask you to interpret it. Shouldn't be a problem if you can read a graph.

Drugs: Use and Harm

Drugs (both the legal kind and the illegal kind) might be in the exam. So get reading.

Drugs Can be Beneficial or Harmful

1) Drugs are substances which alter the way the body works. Some drugs are medically useful, such as antibiotics (e.g. penicillin). But many drugs are dangerous if misused.
2) This is why you can buy some drugs over the counter at a pharmacy, but others are restricted so you can only get them on prescription — your doctor decides if you should have them.
3) Some people get addicted to drugs — this means they have a physical need for the drug, and if they don't get it they get withdrawal symptoms. It's not just illegal drugs that are addictive — many legal ones are as well, e.g. caffeine in coffee. Caffeine withdrawal symptoms include irritability and shaky hands.
4) Tolerance develops with some drugs — the body gets used to having it and so you need a higher dose to give the same effect. This can happen with both legal drugs (e.g. alcohol), and illegal drugs (e.g. heroin).
5) If someone's addicted to a drug but wants to get off it, rehabilitation can help — this is where you get help and support to try and overcome an addiction.

You need to know all about these drugs...

1) Depressants — e.g. alcohol, solvents and temazepam. These decrease the activity of the brain, which slows down the responses of the nervous system, causing slow reactions and poor judgement of speed and distances (which is why drink driving is dangerous).
2) Stimulants — e.g. nicotine, ecstasy, caffeine. These do the opposite of depressants — they increase the activity of the brain. This makes you feel more alert and awake. Stimulant drugs are often used to treat depression.

See page 20 for more detail on how stimulants and depressants work.

3) Painkillers — e.g. aspirin and paracetamol. Mild painkillers like aspirin work by reducing the number of 'painful' stimuli at the nerve endings near an injury.
4) Performance enhancers — e.g. anabolic steroids (testosterone, for example). These are sometimes taken by athletes. They help build muscle and allow the athletes to train harder. But they're banned by most sports organisations.
5) Hallucinogens — e.g. LSD. They distort what's seen and heard by altering the pathways that the brain sends messages along.

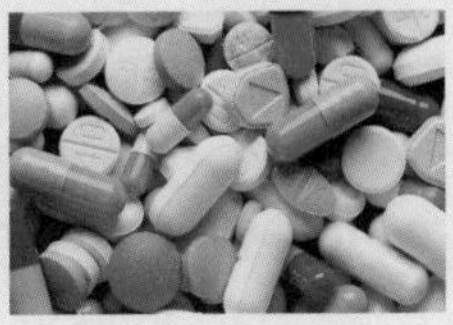

Some Drugs are Illegal

1) In the UK, illegal drugs are classified into three main categories — Classes A, B and C. Which class a drug is in depends on how dangerous it is — Class A drugs are the most dangerous.
   - CLASS A drugs include heroin, LSD, ecstasy and cocaine.
   - CLASS B drugs include cannabis and amphetamines (speed).
   - CLASS C drugs include anabolic steroids and tranquillisers.
2) Using or dealing Class A drugs is most serious — you could get a lengthy prison sentence. Being caught with Class C drugs will probably only get you a warning, although prison's still a possibility.
3) In all cases, supplying a drug to others usually results in a greater punishment than just using it yourself.

Drugs — they can cure you or kill you...

Many people take drugs of some kind, e.g. caffeine in coffee, headache tablets, alcohol, hay fever medicine or an inhaler for asthma. Most of these are okay if you're careful with them and don't go overboard. It's misuse that can get you into trouble (e.g. a paracetamol overdose can kill you). Read the packet.

Smoking and Alcohol

Everyone knows that drinking a lot and smoking don't do you much good. Sadly, it's unlikely that your exam question will ask you to say whether they're good or bad — it's the fiddly little details they'll want you to know.

Alcohol is a Depressant Drug

1) Alcohol's main effect is to reduce the activity of the nervous system — it's a depressant (see page 17).
2) The positive side of this is that it makes people feel less inhibited. (Many people think that alcohol in moderation helps people to socialise and relax with each other.)
3) However, alcohol is poisonous. Alcohol is broken down by enzymes in the liver and some of the products are toxic. If you drink too much alcohol over a long period of time these toxic products can cause the death of liver cells, forming scar tissue that stops blood reaching the liver — this is called cirrhosis. If the liver can't do its normal job of cleaning the blood, dangerous substances start to build up and damage the rest of the body.
4) Alcohol also causes dehydration, which can damage other cells in the body (including in the brain).
5) Being drunk leads to impaired judgement, poor balance, poor coordination, slurred speech, blurred vision and sleepiness. This is why you're not allowed to drive, fly a plane or operate heavy machinery when you're drunk.

There are legal alcohol limits...
For driving in the UK it's 80 milligrams of alcohol in 100 millilitres of blood.
For pilots it's 20 milligrams of alcohol per 100 millilitres of blood.

And there are also 'lifestyle guidelines'...
Doctors recommend drinking no more each week than 21 'units' of alcohol for a man, and 14 for a woman, where 1 unit is:
(i) half a pint of average strength beer,
(ii) 1 small glass of wine,
(iii) 1 standard pub measure of spirits, etc.

Smoking Causes All Sorts of Illnesses

Burning cigarettes produce nicotine, which is what makes smoking addictive. They also produce carbon monoxide, tar, and particulates — which can all cause illness and other problems. E.g.

1) Heart disease:

   Carbon monoxide reduces the oxygen carrying capacity of the blood. If the heart muscle doesn't receive enough oxygen it can lead to a heart attack (see page 11).

2) Lung, throat, mouth and oesophageal cancer:

   Tar from cigarette smoke collects in the lungs. It's full of toxic chemicals, some of which are carcinogens (cause cancer). Carcinogens make mutations in the DNA more likely. If this happens, cell division can go out of control and malignant tumours (see page 16) can form.

3) A smoker's cough and severe loss of lung function, which can lead to diseases like emphysema:

   Smoking damages the cilia on the epithelial tissue lining the trachea, bronchi and bronchioles (tubes in the lungs), which encourages mucus to be produced. But excess mucus can't be cleared because the cilia are damaged, so it sticks to air passages causing smoker's cough. The lungs also lose their elasticity, causing emphysema.

4) Low birth weight babies:

   Low oxygen in the blood of pregnant women (caused by carbon monoxide) can deprive the foetus of oxygen, leading to a small baby at birth.

The tar in cigarettes makes cilia black...

In the exam you might be asked to interpret data on the effects of smoking or alcohol, e.g. birth weights of babies born to mothers who smoke compared to those who don't, or the link between reaction time and alcohol level, etc. Don't panic — they'll give you any information you need to answer the question.

Receptors — The Eye

Your body has sense organs containing receptors that gather information about the world around you. My own personal favourite is the eye, which is sensitive to light and responsible for sight.

Learn the Eye with All Its Labels:

1) The cornea refracts (bends) light into the eye.
2) The iris controls how much light enters the pupil (the hole in the middle).
3) The lens also refracts light, focusing it onto the retina.
4) The retina is the light sensitive part and it's covered in receptors called rods and cones, which detect light.
5) Rods are more sensitive in dim light but can't sense colour.
6) Cones are sensitive to different colours but are not so good in dim light (red-green colour blindness is due to a lack of certain specialised cone cells).
7) The optic nerve carries impulses from the receptors to the brain.

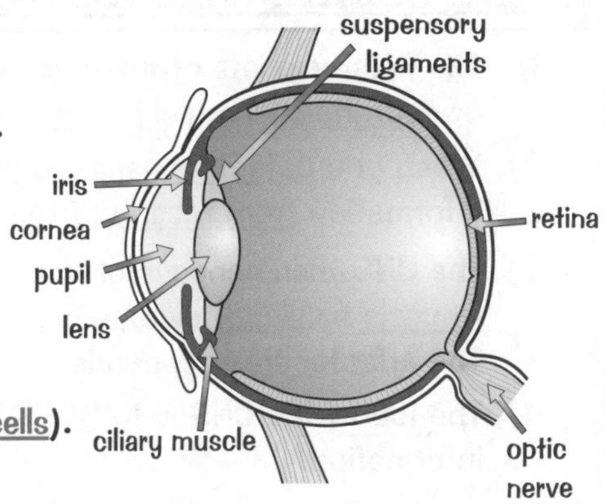

Focusing on Near and Distant Objects

The lens is elastic, so the eye can focus light by changing the shape of the lens — this is known as accommodation.

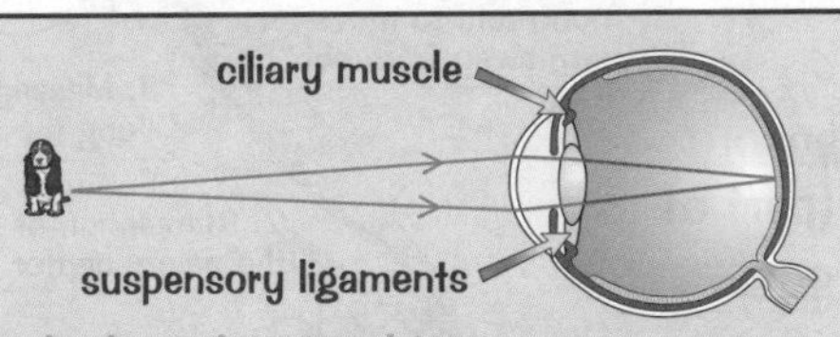

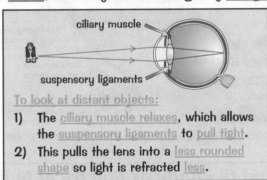

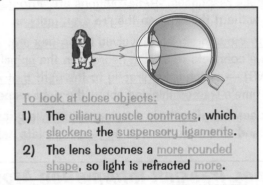

To look at distant objects:
1) The ciliary muscle relaxes, which allows the suspensory ligaments to pull tight.
2) This pulls the lens into a less rounded shape so light is refracted less.

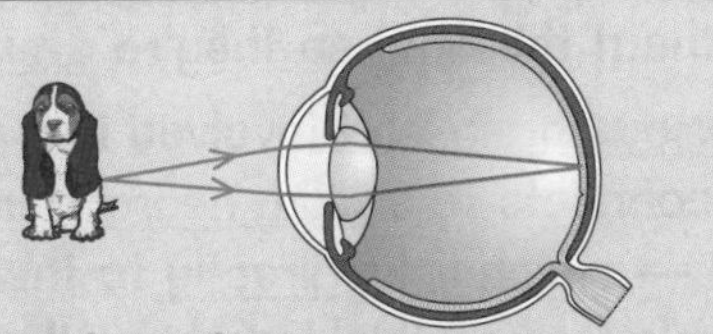

To look at close objects:
1) The ciliary muscle contracts, which slackens the suspensory ligaments.
2) The lens becomes a more rounded shape, so light is refracted more.

Some People are Long- or Short-sighted

Long-sighted people are unable to focus on near objects:
1) This occurs when the lens is the wrong shape and doesn't bend the light enough or the eyeball is too short.
2) The images of near objects are brought into focus behind the retina.
3) You can use glasses or contact lenses with a convex lens to correct it.

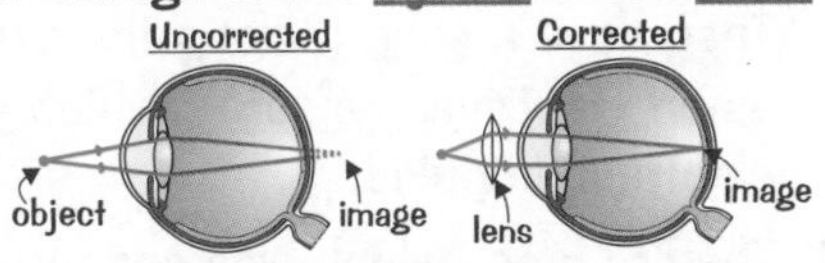

Short-sighted people are unable to focus on distant objects:
1) This occurs when the lens is the wrong shape and bends the light too much or the eyeball is too long.
2) The images of distant objects are brought into focus in front of the retina.
3) You can use glasses or contact lenses with a concave lens to correct it.

An alternative to glasses or contact lenses is to have corneal laser surgery.

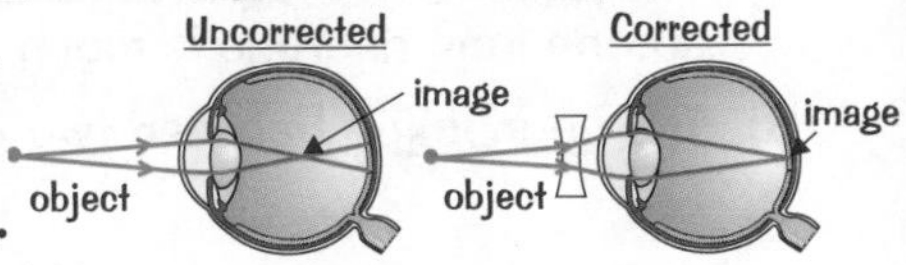

Binocular Vision Lets You Judge Depth

1) Some animals, including humans, have two eyes which work together — this is binocular vision.
2) When you look at an object, your brain compares the images seen by each eye.
3) The more similarities between the images, the further away the object.
4) This allows us to judge distances well, but gives us a narrow field of vision.

I think I'm a little long-sighted...

If you can read this you've got better eyesight than me!

To see how important binocular vision is, cover one eye and try pouring water into a glass at arm's length.

Neurones and Reflexes

Ever wondered how you can pull your hand away from a hot pan faster than you can say "Yowzers, that hurt"? It's all to do with reflex actions, so read on to find out more. Go on, you know you want to.

The Central Nervous System (CNS) Coordinates Information

1) The CNS consists of the brain and spinal cord. The nervous system is made up of the three types of neurone (nerve cell) — sensory neurones, relay neurones and motor neurones.
2) When you detect a change in your environment (a stimulus) your sensory neurones carry the information from receptors (e.g. light receptors in the back of the eye) to the CNS.
3) The CNS then sends information to an effector (muscle or gland) along a motor neurone. The effector then responds accordingly.
4) The job of the CNS is to COORDINATE the information.

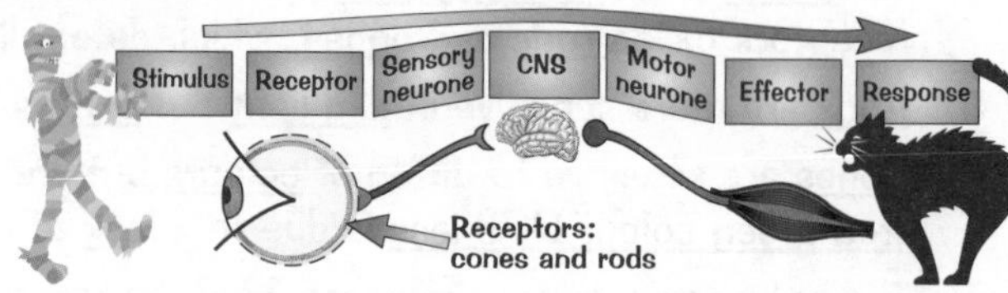

Reflex Actions Stop You Injuring Yourself

1) The nervous system uses electrical impulses to allow very quick responses. Reflex actions are automatic (done without thinking) so they're even quicker.
2) The conscious brain isn't involved in a reflex arc. The sensory neurone connects to a relay neurone in the spinal cord (part of the CNS) — which links directly to the right motor neurone, so no time's wasted thinking about the right response.
3) Reflex actions often have a protective role, e.g. snatching back your hand when you touch a burning hot plate happens almost before you realise you've done it.

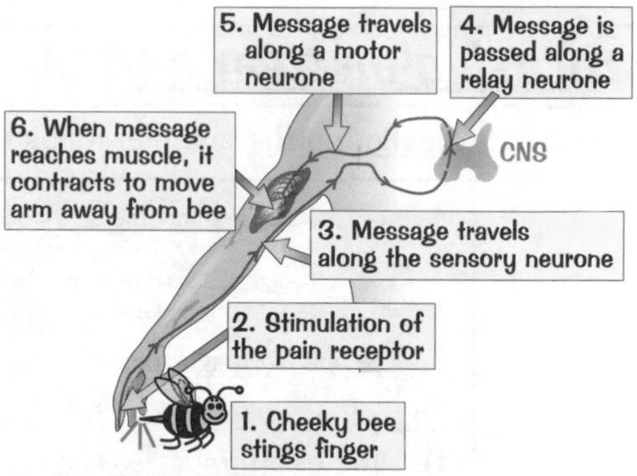

Neurones Transmit Information Around the Body as Electrical Impulses

1) The electrical impulse is passed along the axon of the cell.
2) Neurones have branched endings (dendrites) so they can connect with lots of other neurones.
3) They have a sheath along the axon that acts as an electrical insulator, which speeds up the electrical impulse.
4) They're long, which also speeds up the impulse (connecting with another neurone slows the impulse down, so one long neurone is much quicker than lots of short ones joined together).
5) The connection between two neurones is called a synapse. It's basically just a very tiny gap:

Here's a typical motor neurone:

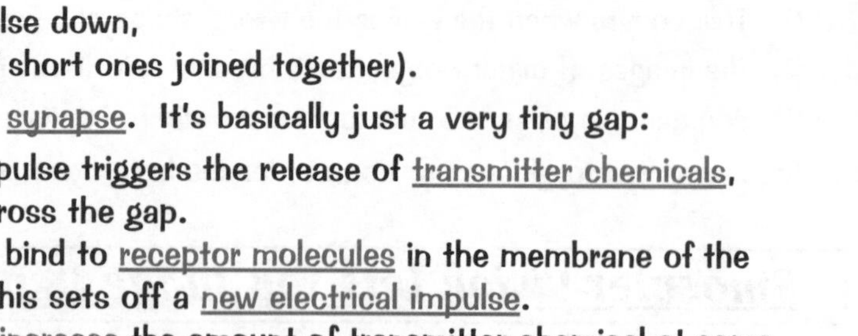

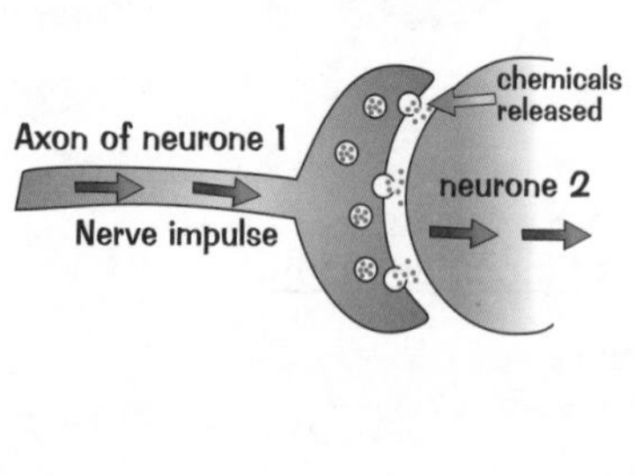

- The electrical impulse triggers the release of transmitter chemicals, which diffuse across the gap.
- These chemicals bind to receptor molecules in the membrane of the next neurone. This sets off a new electrical impulse.
- Stimulant drugs increase the amount of transmitter chemical at some synapses, which increases the frequency of impulses along neurone 2.
- Depressants bind with receptor molecules on the membrane of neurone 2, blocking the electrical impulse. This decreases brain activity.

Don't let the thought of exams play on your nerves...

Another example of a reflex is when the pupil in your eye constricts in bright light — it stops your eye getting damaged. Control of your posture happens automatically too — thanks to reflex arcs.

Homeostasis

Homeostasis involves balancing body functions to maintain a 'constant internal environment'. Smashing.

Homeostasis is Maintaining a Constant Internal Environment

Conditions in your body need to be kept steady so that cells can function properly. This involves balancing inputs (stuff going into your body) with outputs (stuff leaving). For example...

1) Levels of CO_2 — respiration constantly produces CO_2, which you need to get rid of.
2) Water content — you need to keep a balance between the water you gain (in drink, food, and from respiration) and the water you pee, sweat and breathe out.
3) Body temperature — you need to get rid of excess body heat when you're hot, but retain heat when the environment is cold.

A mechanism called negative feedback works automatically to help you keep all these things steady:

NEGATIVE FEEDBACK

Changes in the environment trigger a response that counteracts the changes — e.g. a rise in body temperature causes a response that lowers body temperature.

This means that the internal environment tends to stay around a norm, the level at which the cells work best.

This only works within certain limits — if the environment changes too much then it might not be possible to counteract it.

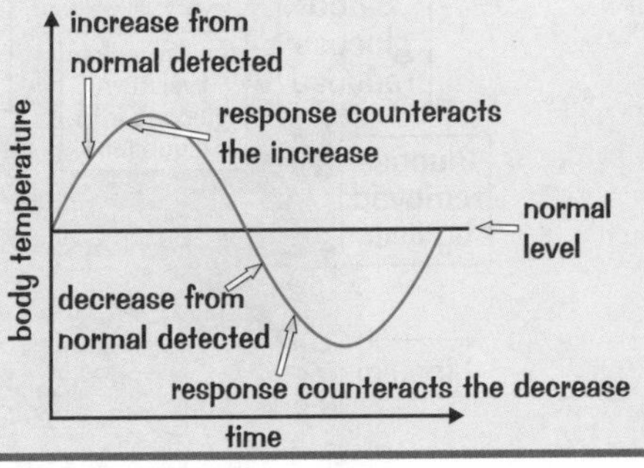

Body Temperature is Controlled by the Brain

All enzymes have an optimum temperature they work best at.
For enzymes in the human body it's about 37 °C.

1) There's a thermoregulatory centre in the brain which acts as your own personal thermostat.
2) It contains receptors that are sensitive to the blood temperature in the brain. It also receives impulses from the skin that provide information about skin temperature. The brain can respond to this information and bring about changes in the body's temperature using the nervous and hormonal systems to initiate temperature control mechanisms. For example:

When You're TOO HOT:

1) Hairs lie flat.
2) Lots of sweat is produced — when sweat evaporates it uses heat from the skin. This transfers heat from your skin to the environment, which cools you down.
3) Blood vessels close to the surface of the skin widen. This allows more blood to flow near the surface, so it can radiate more heat into the surroundings. This is called vasodilation.

If you're exposed to high temperatures you can get dehydrated and you could get heat stroke. This can kill you (see below).

When You're TOO COLD:

1) Hairs stand on end to trap an insulating layer of air which helps keep you warm.
2) Very little sweat is produced.
3) Blood vessels near the surface constrict (vasoconstriction) so that less heat can be transferred from the blood to the surroundings.
4) You shiver, and the movement generates heat in the muscles.

Your body temperature can drop to dangerous levels if you're exposed to very low temperatures for a long time — this is called hypothermia. If you don't get help quickly you can die.

If you do enough revision, you can avoid negative feedback...

If you're in really high temperatures for a long time you can get heat stroke — sweating stops because you're so dehydrated and there's a big rise in your body temperature. Your enzymes can't work properly and important reactions get disrupted — if you don't cool down you could collapse and die. Fortunately, good old British drizzle means that heat stroke needn't worry the majority of us. Lucky old us.

Controlling Blood Sugar Level

Blood sugar level is controlled as part of homeostasis, using the hormone insulin. Learn how it works.

Insulin Controls Blood Sugar Level

1) Eating foods containing carbohydrate puts glucose into the blood from the gut.
2) Normal respiration in cells removes glucose from the blood.
3) Vigorous exercise also removes a lot of glucose from the blood.
4) The level of glucose in the blood must be kept steady. Changes in blood glucose are monitored and controlled by the pancreas, using insulin...

Blood glucose level TOO HIGH — insulin is ADDED

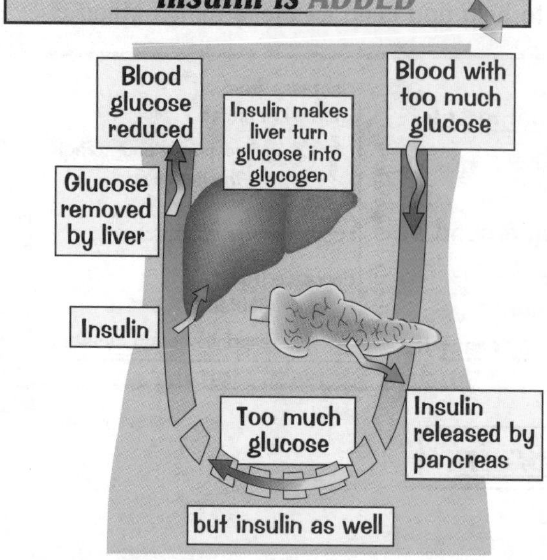

Blood glucose level TOO LOW — insulin is NOT ADDED

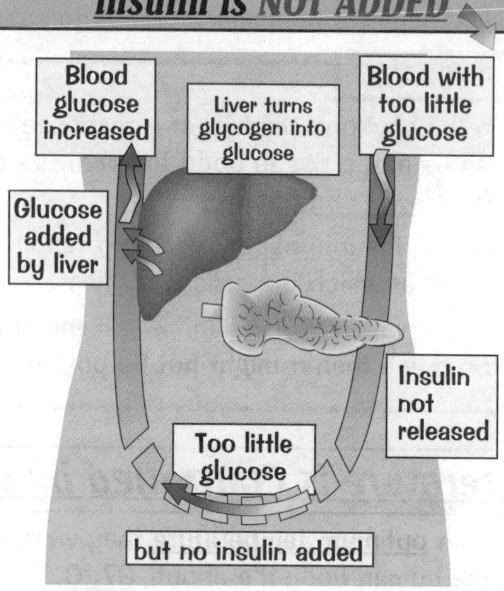

Glycogen can be stored in the liver until the blood sugar level is low again.

Insulin is a hormone. Hormones travel in the blood, so it can take quite a while for them to get to where they're needed in the body, i.e. their target organ. Electrical impulses sent along the nerves travel much faster. This means it takes the body longer to respond to a hormone than to a nervous impulse.

Having Diabetes Means You Can't Control Your Blood Sugar Level

Diabetes is a condition that affects your ability to control your blood sugar level. There are two types:

1) Type 1 diabetes is where the pancreas produces little or no insulin.
The result is that a person's blood glucose level can rise to a level that can kill them.

People with type 1 diabetes can partly control the condition by having a carefully controlled diet (see below), but they also need to inject insulin into the blood at mealtimes. This will make the liver remove the glucose as soon as it enters the blood from the gut, when the food is being digested. This stops the level of glucose in the blood from getting too high and is a very effective treatment. The amount of insulin that needs to be injected depends on the person's diet and how active they are.

2) Type 2 diabetes is where a person becomes resistant to insulin (their body's cells don't respond properly to the hormone). This can also cause blood sugar level to rise to a dangerous level.

Type 2 diabetes is usually just controlled by avoiding foods rich in simple carbohydrates, i.e. sugars (which cause glucose levels to rise rapidly).

My blood sugar feels low after all that — pass the biscuits...

This stuff can seem a bit confusing at first, but if you learn those two diagrams, it'll all start to get a lot easier. Don't forget that there are two types of diabetes — and different ways of controlling them.

Plant Hormones and Growth

Plants don't just grow randomly. Plant hormones make sure they grow in the right direction.

Auxins are Plant Growth Hormones

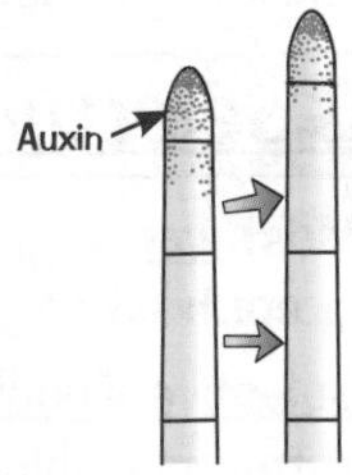

1) Auxins are plant hormones which control growth at the tips of shoots and roots. They move through the plant in solution (dissolved in water).
2) Auxin is produced in the tips and diffuses backwards to stimulate the cell elongation process which occurs in the cells just behind the tips.
3) Auxin promotes growth in the shoot, but actually inhibits growth in the root.
4) Auxins are involved in the growth responses of plants to light (phototropism) and gravity (geotropism).

Auxins Change the Direction of Root and Shoot Growth

SHOOTS ARE POSITIVELY PHOTOTROPIC (grow towards light)

1) When a shoot tip is exposed to light, it accumulates more auxin on the side that's in the shade than the side that's in the light.
2) This makes the cells grow (elongate) faster on the shaded side, so the shoot bends towards the light.

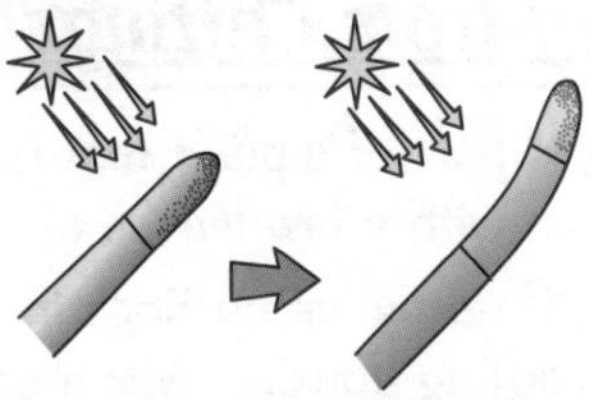

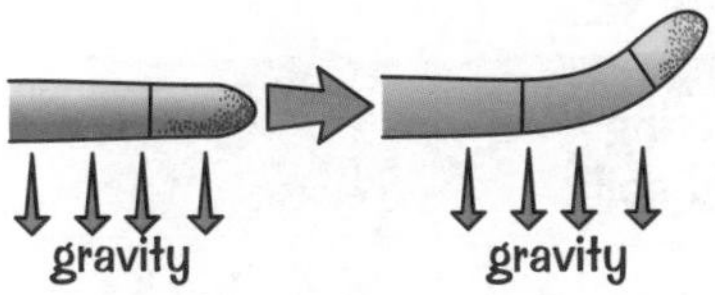

SHOOTS ARE NEGATIVELY GEOTROPIC (grow away from gravity)

1) When a shoot is growing sideways, gravity produces an unequal distribution of auxin in the tip, with more auxin on the lower side.
2) This causes the lower side to grow faster, bending the shoot upwards.

ROOTS ARE POSITIVELY GEOTROPIC (grow towards gravity)

1) A root growing sideways will also have more auxin on its lower side.
2) But in a root the extra auxin inhibits growth. This means the cells on top elongate faster, and the root bends downwards.

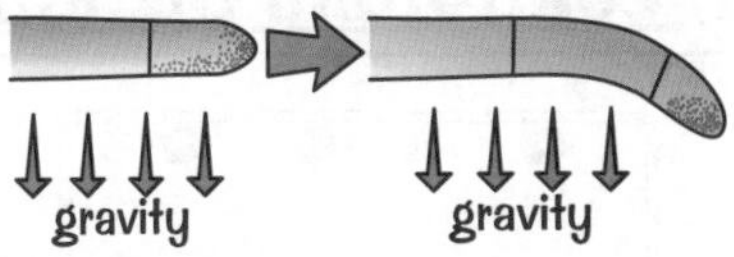

ROOTS ARE NEGATIVELY PHOTOTROPIC (grow away from light)

1) If a root starts being exposed to some light, more auxin accumulates on the more shaded side.
2) The auxin inhibits cell elongation on the shaded side, so the root bends downwards, back into the ground.

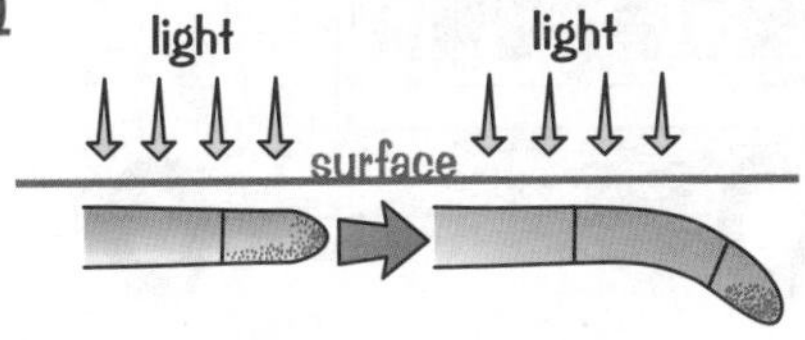

Experiments Have Shown How Auxins Work

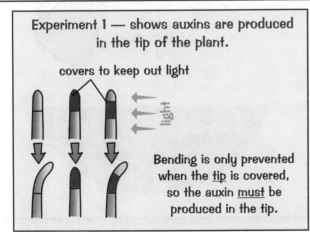

Experiment 1 — shows auxins are produced in the tip of the plant.

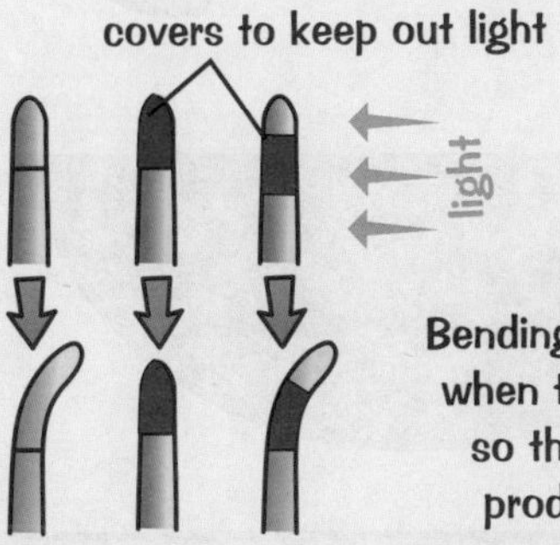

Bending is only prevented when the tip is covered, so the auxin must be produced in the tip.

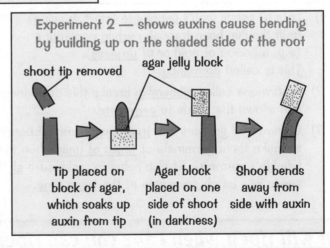

Experiment 2 — shows auxins cause bending by building up on the shaded side of the root

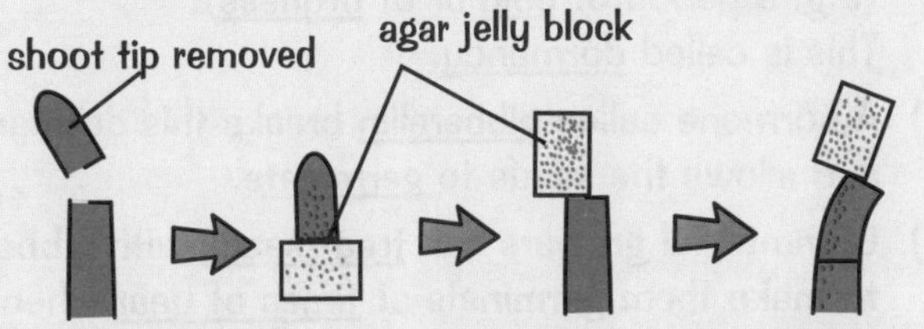

Tip placed on block of agar, which soaks up auxin from tip → Agar block placed on one side of shoot (in darkness) → Shoot bends away from side with auxin

A plant auxin to a bar — 'ouch'...

Shoots grow towards light and roots grow towards gravity — that's not too hard to remember, now, is it.

Commercial Use of Plant Hormones

Plant hormones can be extracted, or artificial copies can be made. They can then be used to do all kinds of useful things, including killing weeds, growing cuttings and ripening fruit.

1) As Selective Weedkillers

1) Most weeds growing in fields of crops or in a lawn are broad-leaved, in contrast to grasses and cereals which have very narrow leaves.
2) Selective weedkillers have been developed from plant growth hormones which only affect the broad-leaved plants.
3) They totally disrupt their normal growth patterns, which soon kills them, whilst leaving the grass and crops untouched.

2) Growing from Cuttings with Rooting Powder

1) A cutting is part of a plant that has been cut off it, like the end of a branch with a few leaves on it.
2) Normally, if you stick cuttings in the soil they won't grow, but if you add rooting powder, which contains a plant growth hormone, they will produce roots rapidly and start growing as new plants.
3) This enables growers to produce lots of clones (exact copies) of a really good plant very quickly.

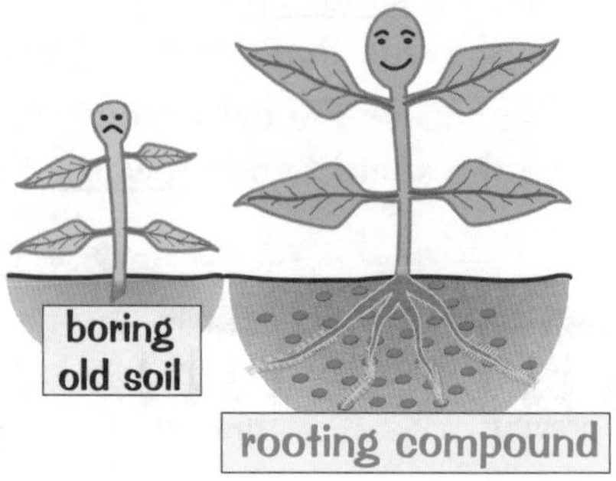

3) Controlling the Ripening of Fruit

1) Plant hormones can be used to delay the ripening of fruits — either while they are still on the plant, or during transport to the shops.
2) This allows the fruit to be picked while it's still unripe (and therefore firmer and less easily damaged).
3) Ripening hormone is then added and the fruit will ripen on the way to the supermarket and be perfect just as it reaches the shelves.

4) Controlling Dormancy

1) Lots of seeds won't germinate (start growing) until they've been through certain conditions (e.g. a period of cold or of dryness). This is called dormancy.
2) A hormone called gibberellin breaks this dormancy and allows the seeds to germinate.
3) Commercial growers can treat seeds with gibberellin to make them germinate at times of year when they wouldn't normally. It also helps to make sure all the seeds in a batch germinate at the same time.

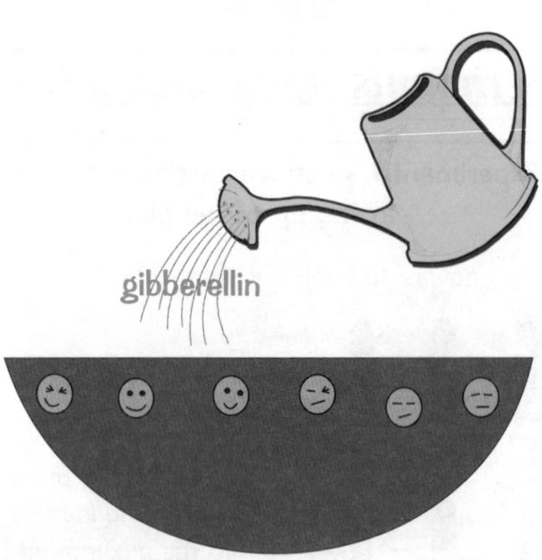

You will ripen when I SAY you can ripen — and NOT BEFORE...

If you want some fruit to ripen, put it into a paper bag with a banana. The banana releases a ripening hormone called ethene which causes the fruit to ripen. Bad apples also release lots of ethene. Unfortunately this means if you've got one bad apple in a barrel, you'll soon have lots of bad apples.

Genes and Chromosomes

This page is a bit tricky, but it's dead important that you get to grips with all the stuff on it — because you're going to hear a lot more about it over the next few pages...

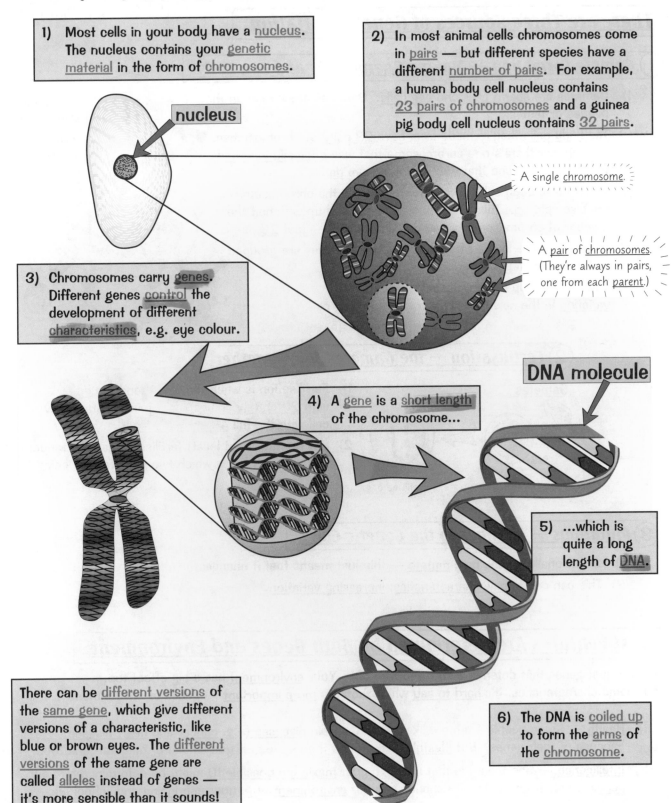

1) Most cells in your body have a nucleus. The nucleus contains your genetic material in the form of chromosomes.

2) In most animal cells chromosomes come in pairs — but different species have a different number of pairs. For example, a human body cell nucleus contains 23 pairs of chromosomes and a guinea pig body cell nucleus contains 32 pairs.

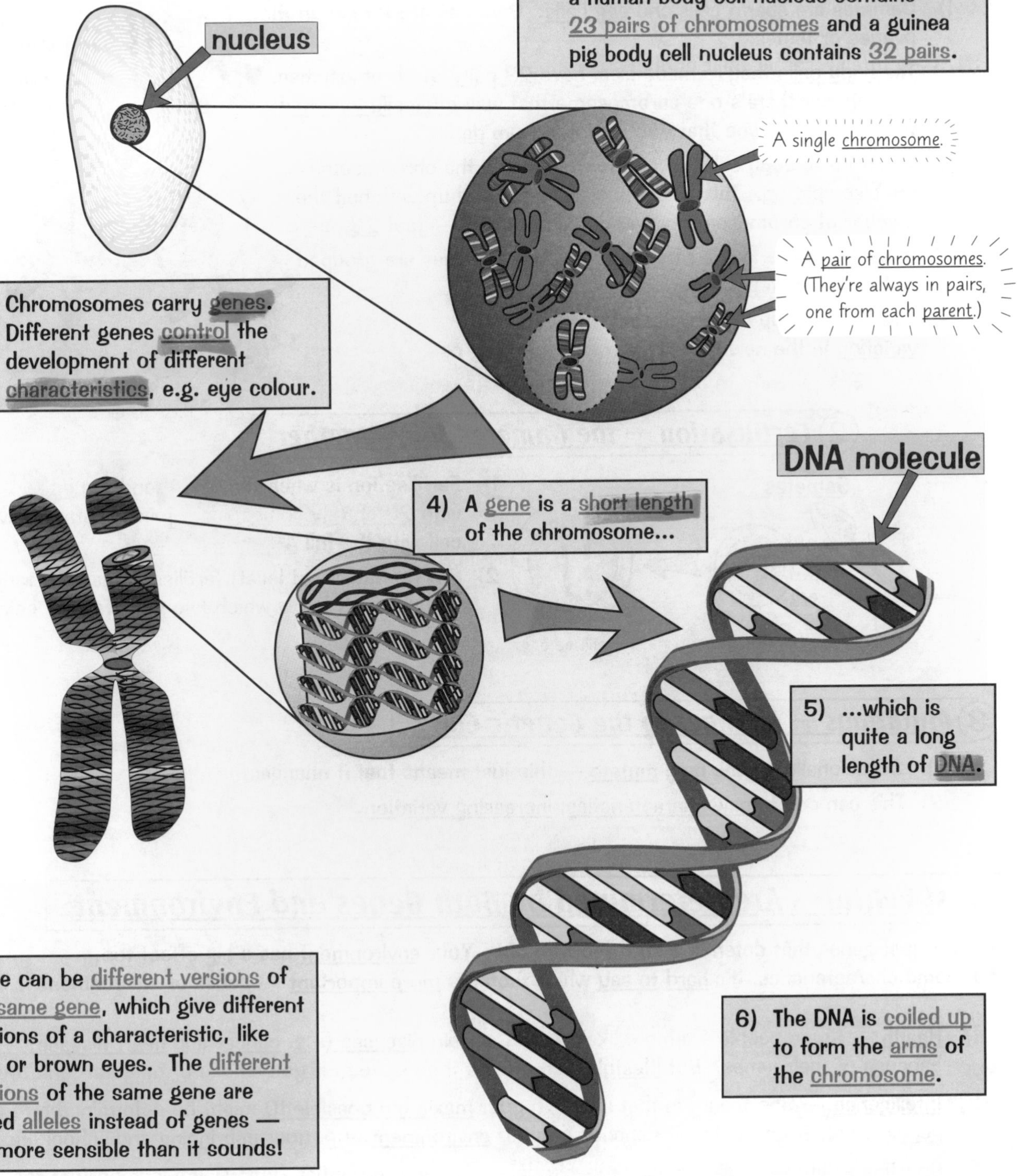

3) Chromosomes carry genes. Different genes control the development of different characteristics, e.g. eye colour.

4) A gene is a short length of the chromosome...

5) ...which is quite a long length of DNA.

6) The DNA is coiled up to form the arms of the chromosome.

There can be different versions of the same gene, which give different versions of a characteristic, like blue or brown eyes. The different versions of the same gene are called alleles instead of genes — it's more sensible than it sounds!

It's hard being a DNA molecule, there's so much to remember...

This is the bare bones of genetics, so you definitely need to understand everything on this page or you'll find the rest of this topic dead hard. The best way to get all of these important facts engraved in your mind is to cover the page, scribble down the main points and sketch out the diagrams...

Genetic Variation

Everyone (except identical twins) has different genes to everyone else. There are a few reasons why, so stick with me. If that wasn't enough, the environment also affects how we turn out. Sheesh.

There are Three Sources of Genetic Variation

1) Gamete Formation — Making Sperm Cells and Egg Cells

1) Gametes are sperm cells and egg cells. Gametes are formed in the ovaries or testes.
2) The body cells they're made from have 23 pairs of chromosomes. In each pair there's one chromosome that was originally inherited from mum, and one that was inherited from dad.
3) When these body cells split to form gametes the chromosomes are also split up. This means that gametes end up with half the number of chromosomes of a normal body cell — just 23.
4) In each gamete, some of your dad's chromosomes are grouped with some from your mum.
5) This shuffling up of chromosomes leads to variation in the new generation.

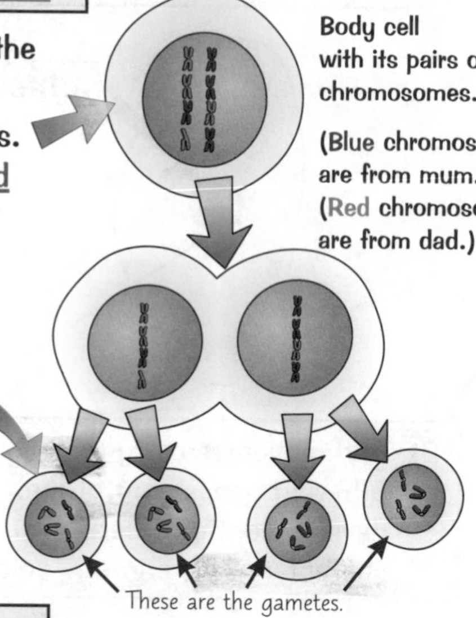
Body cell with its pairs of chromosomes.
(Blue chromosomes are from mum.)
(Red chromosomes are from dad.)
These are the gametes.

2) Fertilisation — the Gametes Join Together

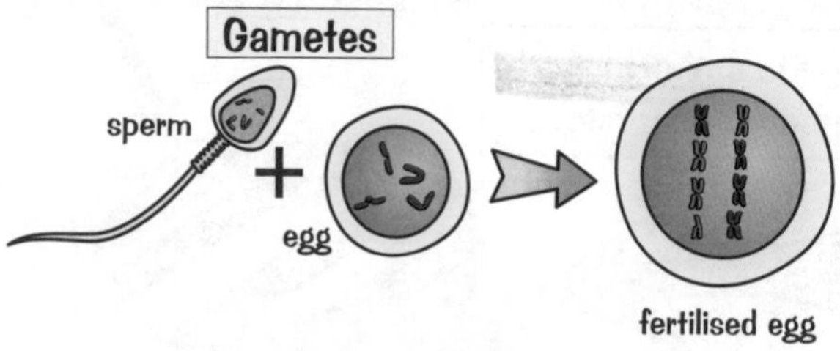
Gametes
sperm
egg
fertilised egg

1) Fertilisation is when the sperm and the egg, with 23 chromosomes each, join to form a new cell with the full 46 chromosomes.
2) But (in nature, at least) fertilisation is a bit random — you don't know which two gametes are going to join together.

3) Mutations — Changes to the Genetic Code

1) Occasionally a gene may mutate — this just means that it changes.
2) This can create new characteristics, increasing variation.

Most Features Are Determined by Both Genes and Environment

It's not just genes that determine how you turn out. Your environment has a big effect too. For some characteristics, it's hard to say which factor is more important — genes or environment...

1) Health — Some people are more likely to get certain diseases (e.g. cancer and heart disease) because of their genes. But lifestyle also affects the risk, e.g. if you smoke or only eat junk food.
2) Intelligence — One theory is that although your maximum possible IQ might be determined by your genes, whether you get to it depends on your environment, e.g. your upbringing and school life.
3) Sporting ability — Again, genes probably determine your potential, but training is important too.

So if you weren't picked for netball — blame your parents...

So in sexual reproduction a mixture of chromosomes is randomly shuffled into gametes.
Then a random gamete fuses with another random gamete at fertilisation (oh, the romance of it all).

Genetic Diagrams

In the exam they could ask about the inheritance of <u>any</u> kind of characteristic that's controlled by a <u>single gene</u>. Luckily, the basic idea's always the same, whatever the gene...

Genetic Diagrams Show the Possible Genes of Offspring

1) <u>Alleles</u> are <u>different versions</u> of the <u>same gene</u>.
2) Most of the time you have <u>two</u> of each gene (i.e. two alleles) — one from each parent.
3) If the alleles are different you have instructions for two different versions of a characteristic (e.g. blue eyes or brown eyes), but you only show one version of the two (e.g. brown eyes). The version of the characteristic that appears is caused by the <u>dominant allele</u>. The other allele is said to be <u>recessive</u>. The recessive allele is only expressed if there's <u>no dominant allele</u> present.
4) In genetic diagrams <u>letters</u> are used to represent <u>genes</u>. <u>Dominant</u> alleles are always shown with a <u>capital letter</u>, and <u>recessive</u> alleles with a <u>small letter</u>.
5) If you're <u>homozygous</u> for a trait you have <u>two alleles the same</u> for that particular gene, e.g. CC or cc. If you're <u>heterozygous</u> for a trait you have <u>two different alleles</u> for that particular gene, e.g. Cc.
6) Your <u>genetic makeup</u> (i.e. the alleles you have for a particular gene) is known as your <u>genotype</u>. The <u>characteristics</u> that these alleles produce (e.g. brown eyes) is known as your <u>phenotype</u>.

You Need to be Able to Interpret, Explain and Construct Them

Imagine you're cross-breeding <u>hamsters</u>, and that some have a normal, boring disposition while others have a leaning towards crazy acrobatics. And suppose you know the behaviour is due to one gene...

Let's say that the allele which causes the crazy nature is <u>recessive</u> — so use a '<u>b</u>'.
And normal (boring) behaviour is due to a <u>dominant allele</u> — call it '<u>B</u>'.

1) For an organism to display a <u>recessive</u> characteristic, <u>both</u> its alleles must be <u>recessive</u> — so a crazy hamster must have the alleles 'bb' (i.e. it must be homozygous for this trait).
2) However, a <u>normal hamster</u> could be BB (homozygous) or Bb (heterozygous), because the dominant allele (B) <u>overrules</u> the recessive one (b).
3) Here's what happens if you breed from two <u>heterozygous</u> hamsters:

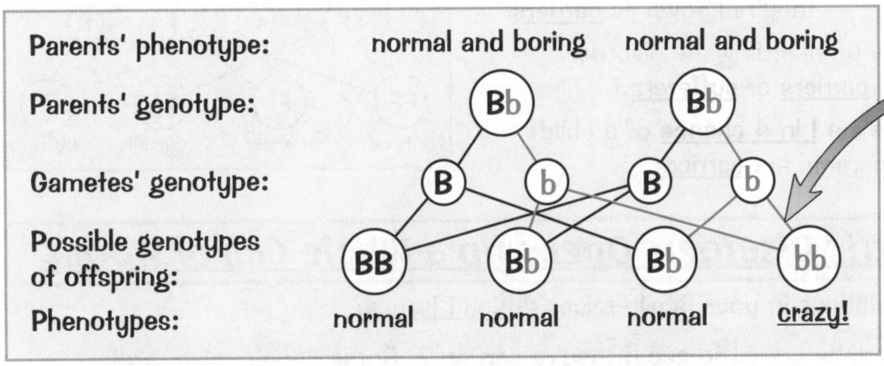

The lines show <u>all</u> the <u>possible</u> ways the parents' alleles <u>could</u> combine. Remember, only <u>one</u> of these possibilities would <u>actually happen</u> for any one offspring.

When you breed two organisms together to look at a characteristic that's controlled by one gene, it's called a MONOHYBRID CROSS.

There's a <u>75% chance</u> of having a normal, boring hamster, and a <u>25% chance</u> of a crazy one. (To put that another way... you'd expect a <u>3:1 ratio</u> of normal:crazy hamsters.)

4) This is a genetic diagram too — it shows exactly the same thing as the one above. Diagrams like these are called <u>Punnett squares</u>.

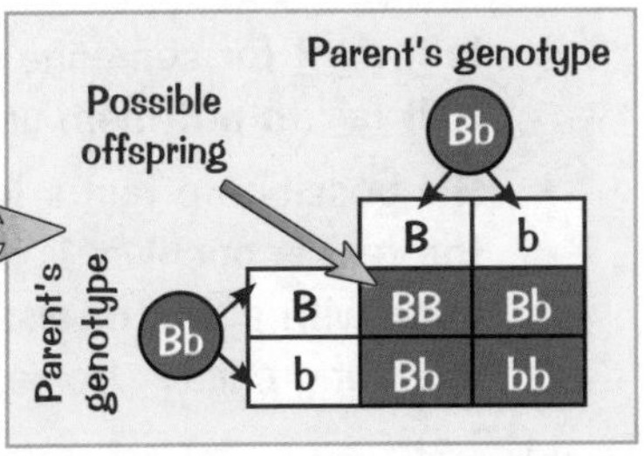

It's not just hamsters that have the wild and scratty allele...

...my sister definitely has it too. Remember, '<u>results</u>' like this are only <u>probabilities</u>. It doesn't mean it'll actually happen. (If you have my luck, you'll end up trying to contain a mini-riot of nine lunatic baby hamsters.)

Sex Inheritance and Genetic Disorders

There's a lot to learn about genes and inheritance. This is the last page though, I promise.

Your Chromosomes Control Whether You're Male or Female

There are 23 matched pairs of chromosomes in every human body cell. The 23rd pair are labelled XY. They're the two chromosomes that decide whether you turn out male or female.

All men have an X and a Y chromosome: XY
The Y chromosome causes male characteristics.

All women have two X chromosomes: XX
The XX combination causes female characteristics.

This is true for all mammals, but not for some other organisms, e.g. plants.

There's an Equal Chance of Having a Boy or a Girl...

...and there's a genetic diagram to prove it.

Even though we're talking about inheriting chromosomes here and not single genes, the genetic diagram still works the same way.

When you plug all the letters into the diagram, it shows that there are two XX results and two XY results, so there's the same probability of getting a boy or a girl.

Don't forget that this 50:50 ratio is only a probability. If you had four kids they could all be boys.

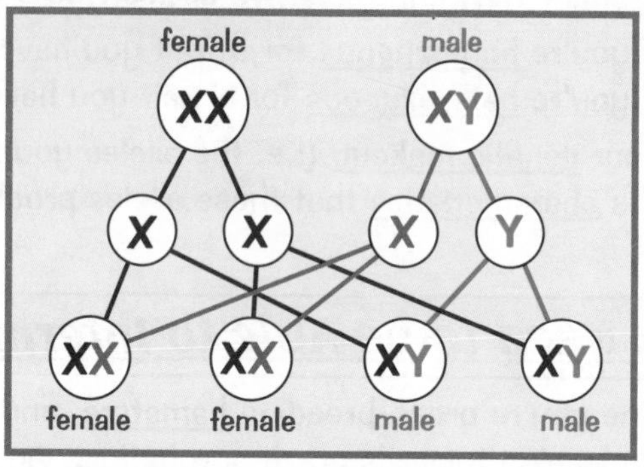

Genetic (Inherited) Disorders are Caused by Faulty Genes

Here's an example: cystic fibrosis is a genetic disorder that causes the body to produce a lot of thick, sticky mucus in the air passages and in the pancreas.

1) The allele which causes cystic fibrosis is a recessive allele, 'f', carried by about 1 person in 25.
2) Because it's recessive, people with only one copy of the allele won't have the disorder — they're known as carriers.
3) For a child to have a chance of inheriting the disorder, both parents must be either carriers or sufferers.
4) As the diagram shows, there's a 1 in 4 chance of a child having the disorder if both parents are carriers.

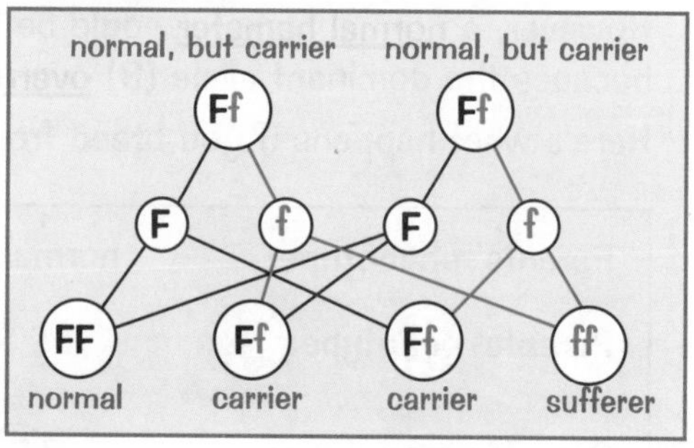

Knowing About Genetic Disorders Opens Up a Whole Can of Worms

Knowing there are inherited conditions in your family raises difficult issues:

- Should all family members be tested to see if they're carriers? Some people might prefer not to know, but is this fair on any partners or future children they might have?
- Is it right for someone who's at risk of passing on a genetic condition to have children? Is it fair to put them under pressure not to, if they decide they want children?
- It's possible to test a foetus for some genetic conditions while it's still in the womb. But if the test is positive, is it right to terminate the pregnancy? The family might not be able to cope with a sick or disabled child, but why should that child have a lesser right to life than a healthy child? Some people think abortion is always wrong under any circumstances.

What do you get when you cross a snowman with a vampire?

...frostbite. There are lots of other genetic disorders — e.g. red-green colour blindness and sickle cell anaemia. To work out the chance of any inherited disorders being passed on, follow the same method.

Revision Summary for Module B1

That was a long section, but kind of interesting, I reckon. These questions will show what you know and what you don't... if you get stuck, have a look back to remind yourself. But before the exam, make sure you can do all of them without any help — that's the only way you'll know you're ready.

1) What's the difference between 'fit' and 'healthy'? Can you be one without being the other?
2)* Below are the blood pressure measurements of a group of smokers and a group of non-smokers.

Group A	Person 1	Person 2	Person 3	Person 4	Person 5	Person 6
Systolic pressure (mm Hg)	126	100	110	110	114	112
Diastolic pressure (mm Hg)	84	72	60	78	66	68

Group B	Person 1	Person 2	Person 3	Person 4	Person 5	Person 6
Systolic pressure (mm Hg)	138	150	122	118	120	116
Diastolic pressure (mm Hg)	100	100	80	78	84	68

a) Is Group A likely to be smokers or non-smokers? Explain your answer.
b) How many of the smokers would be considered to have high blood pressure?
c) What would you advise these smokers to do to help reduce their blood pressure?

3) Explain one way that smoking can increase blood pressure.
4) How do narrow arteries increase the risk of a heart attack?
5) Explain why plant proteins are called 'second class proteins'.
6) Explain what causes the condition called kwashiorkor.
Why is this condition more common in developing countries?
7) Explain how psychological disorders can cause under-nutrition.
8) What is the meaning of the term 'parasite'?
9) Explain how antibodies destroy pathogens.
10) Explain how immunisation stops you getting infections.
11) Explain the difference between benign and malignant tumours.
12) What is a double blind clinical trial?
13) What effect does a stimulant have on brain activity? Give two examples of stimulants.
14) Describe how drinking too much alcohol can damage your liver.
15) Explain why smoking can give you a 'smoker's cough'.
16) Describe the path of light through the eye.
17) Describe the path taken by a reflex arc.
18) Draw a diagram of a typical motor neurone, labelling all its parts.
19) Explain how negative feedback helps to maintain a constant internal environment.
20) Describe how body temperature is reduced when you're too hot.
21) Explain how insulin controls blood sugar levels.
22) What is the difference between how type 1 and type 2 diabetes are usually controlled?
23) What are auxins?
24) Shoots are negatively geotropic. How are auxins responsible for this?
25) Give three ways that plant growth hormones are used commercially.
26) How many pairs of chromosomes are there in most human body cells?
27) What is an allele?
28) Name three sources of genetic variation.
29) Why is your ability at sport determined by both your genes and your environment?
30)* Draw a genetic diagram for a cross between a man with blue eyes (bb) and a woman who has green eyes (Bb). The gene for blue eyes (b) is recessive.
31) Which chromosomes determine your gender? Draw a genetic diagram showing that there's an equal chance of a baby being a boy or a girl.

* Answers on page 132

Atoms, Molecules and Compounds

Here we go then... atoms are the building blocks that everything is made from. Atoms can join up with other atoms to make molecules. Molecules containing different types of atoms make up compounds.

Atoms Have a Positive Nucleus with Orbiting Electrons

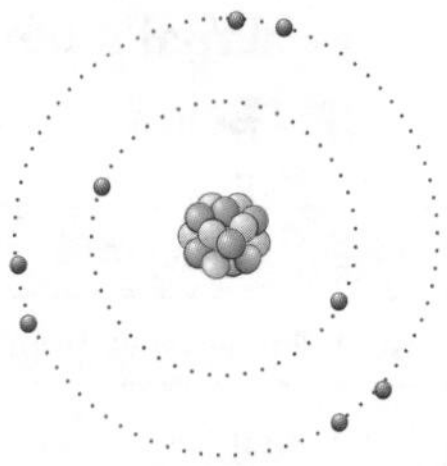

Atoms are really tiny. They're too small to see, even with a microscope. They have a nucleus which is positively charged, and electrons which are negatively charged. The electrons move around the nucleus in layers known as shells.

Atoms can form bonds to make molecules or compounds. It's the electrons that are involved in making bonds. Sometimes an atom loses or gains one or more electrons and this gives it a charge (positive if it loses an electron, and negative if it gains one).

Charged atoms are known as ions. If a positive ion meets a negative ion they'll be attracted to one another and join together. This is called an ionic bond.

See pages 41-42 for more about bonding.

The other main type of bond is called a covalent bond — atoms in a covalent bond share a pair of electrons.

You Need to Know About Displayed and Molecular Formulas

You need to be able to say how many atoms of each type there are in a substance when you're given its formula. Here are some examples:

This is called a molecular formula. It shows the number and type of atoms in a molecule.

This is called a displayed formula. It shows the atoms and the covalent bonds in a molecule as a picture.

CH_4

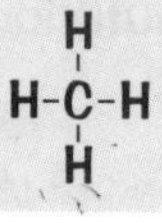

Methane contains 1 carbon atom and 4 hydrogen atoms.

H_2O

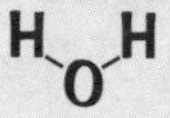

Water contains 2 hydrogen atoms and 1 oxygen atom.

Don't panic if the molecular formula has brackets in it. They're easy too.

$CH_3(CH_2)_2CH_3$

The 2 after the bracket means that there are 2 lots of CH_2. So altogether there are 4 carbon atoms and 10 hydrogen atoms.

Drawing the displayed formula of the compound is a good way to count up the number of atoms.

Do it a bit at a time.

$CH_3(CH_2)_2CH_3$

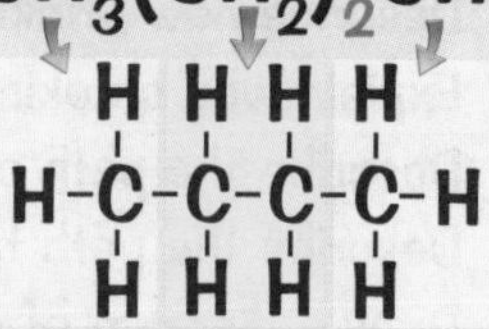

In the exam they might give you a displayed formula and ask you to write down the molecular formula. Easy — just count up the number of each type of atom and write it as above, e.g. CH_4, H_2O, etc. Even better... you can write $CH_3(CH_2)_2CH_3$ as C_4H_{10}. It just doesn't get any easier. Not in Chemistry.

You Need to Remember Some Formulas

One formula, two formulas, or even two formulae.

Here are some formulas. Learn them now. There are only eight, and you'll have come across most of them already. You'll need to learn others later, but these'll be a good start.

1) Carbon dioxide — CO_2
2) Hydrogen — H_2
3) Water — H_2O
4) Hydrochloric acid — HCl
5) Carbon monoxide — CO
6) Oxygen — O_2
7) Sodium carbonate — Na_2CO_3
8) Sulfuric acid — H_2SO_4

Some chemicals have slightly more interesting names...

With so many chemicals around, you'd think there might be some interesting names... And so there are. There's windowpane (C_9H_{12}). And angelic acid ($CH_3CHC(CH_3)COOH$). There's the mineral that's named after the mineralogist Wilfred Welsh, which goes by the name of welshite ($Ca_2SbMg_4FeBe_2Si_4O_{20}$). And if you think that diethyl azodicarboxylate is a bit much, you can just call it DEAD. Better than boring names like 'ethene'.

Chemical Equations

If you're going to get anywhere in chemistry you need to know about chemical equations...

Chemical Changes are Shown Using Chemical Equations

One way to show a chemical reaction is to write a word equation. It's not as quick as using chemical symbols and you can't tell straight away what's happened to each of the atoms, but it's dead easy.
Here's an example — you're told that methane burns in oxygen giving carbon dioxide and water.
So here's the word equation:

The molecules on the left-hand side of the equation are called the reactants (because they react with each other).

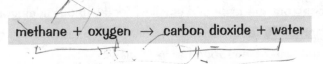

methane + oxygen → carbon dioxide + water

The molecules on the right-hand side are called the products (because they've been produced from the reactants).

Symbol Equations Show the Atoms on Both Sides

Chemical changes can be shown in a kind of shorthand using symbol equations. Symbol equations just show the formulas of the reactants and products...

magnesium	+	oxygen	→	magnesium oxide
2Mg	+	O_2		2MgO

You'll have spotted that there's a '2' in front of the Mg and the MgO. The reason for this is explained below...

Symbol Equations Need to be Balanced

1) There must always be the same number of atoms on both sides — they can't just disappear.
2) You balance the equation by putting numbers in front of the formulas where needed. Take this equation for reacting sulfuric acid with sodium hydroxide:

$$H_2SO_4 + NaOH \rightarrow Na_2SO_4 + H_2O$$

The formulas are all correct but the numbers of some atoms don't match up on both sides.
You can't change formulas like H_2SO_4 to H_2SO_5. You can only put numbers in front of them:

Method: Balance Just One Type of Atom at a Time

The more you practise, the quicker you get, but all you do is this:

1) Find an element that doesn't balance and pencil in a number to try and sort it out.
2) See where it gets you. It may create another imbalance, but if so, pencil in another number and see where that gets you.
3) Carry on chasing unbalanced elements and it'll sort itself out pretty quickly.

I'll show you: In the equation above you'll notice we're short of H atoms on the RHS (Right-Hand Side).

1) The only thing you can do about that is make it $2H_2O$ instead of just H_2O:

$$H_2SO_4 + NaOH \rightarrow Na_2SO_4 + 2H_2O$$

2) But that now gives too many H atoms and O atoms on the RHS, so to balance that up you could try putting 2NaOH on the LHS (Left-Hand Side):

$$H_2SO_4 + 2NaOH \rightarrow Na_2SO_4 + 2H_2O$$

3) And suddenly there it is! Everything balances. And you'll notice the Na just sorted itself out.

They can ask you in the exam to balance symbol equations using formulas that have bits in brackets — like $CH_3(CH_2)_2CH_3$ on the last page. Don't worry about that, just make sure you're clear before you start how many of each type of atom there are — in this case it's 4 carbons and 10 hydrogens.

It's all about getting the balance right...

Balancing equations isn't as scary as it looks — you just plug numbers in until it works itself out. Get some practice in — you'll see. You can balance equations with displayed formulas in exactly the same way. Just make sure there are the same number of each type of atom on both sides — dead easy.

Emulsifiers

All sorts of natural and synthetic additives get put in food, generally to improve quality or shelf life. Emulsifiers are additives which make oil and water mix well together — so your peanut butter doesn't separate.

Additives Make Food Last Longer and Look and Taste Better

Additives are added to lots of our foods to improve their flavour, colour or to make them last longer.

1) Food colours make food look more appetising.
2) Flavour enhancers bring out the taste and smell of food without adding a taste of their own.
3) Antioxidants help to preserve food.
4) Emulsifiers help oil and water blend together in foods like salad cream and ice cream — see below.

Emulsifiers Help Oil and Water Mix

1) You can mix an oil with water to make an emulsion.
2) Emulsions are made up of lots of droplets of one liquid suspended in another liquid.
3) Oil and water naturally separate into two layers with the oil floating on top of the water — they don't "want" to mix. Emulsifiers help to stop the two liquids in an emulsion from separating out.
4) Mayonnaise, low-fat spread and ice cream are foods which contain emulsifiers.
5) Emulsifiers are molecules with one part that's attracted to water and another part that's attracted to oil or fat.
6) The bit that's attracted to water is called hydrophilic and the bit that's attracted to oil is called hydrophobic:

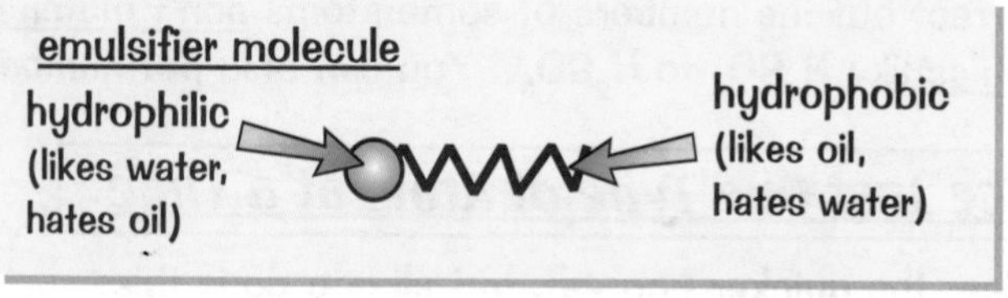

7) The hydrophilic end of each emulsifier molecule bonds to water molecules.
8) The hydrophobic end of each emulsifier molecule bonds to oil molecules.
9) When you shake oil and water together with a bit of emulsifier, the oil forms droplets, surrounded by a coating of emulsifier... with the hydrophilic bit facing outwards.
10) Other oil droplets are repelled by the hydrophilic bit of the emulsifier, while water molecules latch on. So the emulsion won't separate out. Clever.

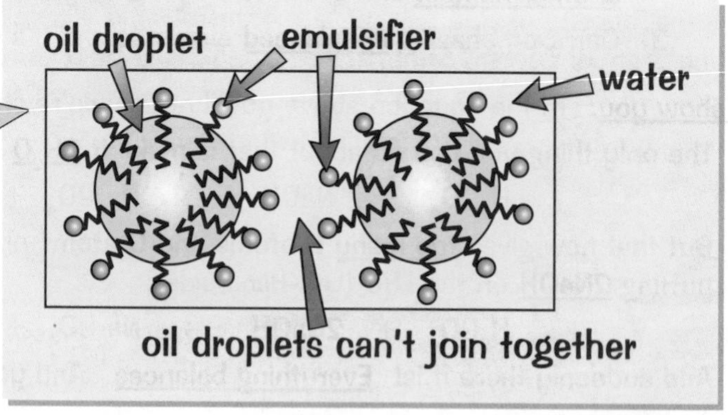

Add me to food and it'll disappear...

Some people don't like the idea of additives like emulsifiers in their food, so a lot of food manufacturers now make additive-free products. There is, as yet, no additive-free exam though. So you'll need to learn this page — the words, diagrams, hydrophilic and hydrophobic bits and all. Lovely jubbly.

Cooking and Chemical Change

This is a page about irreversible chemical changes. When you cook things, the chemical structure of the substance changes, and it can't change back. (In my case, cooking and burning are similar processes.)

Some Foods Have to be Cooked

There are loads of different ways to cook food — e.g. boiling, steaming, frying, grilling and cooking in an oven or a microwave.

1) Many foods have a better taste and texture when cooked.
2) Some foods are easier to digest once they're cooked (e.g. potatoes, flour). See below for why.
3) The high temperatures involved in cooking also kill off those nasty little microbes that cause disease — this is very important with meat.
4) Some foods are poisonous when raw, and must be cooked to make 'em edible — e.g. red kidney beans contain a poison that's only destroyed by at least 10 minutes boiling (and 2 hours cooking in total).

Cooking Causes Chemical Changes

Note: not all chemical changes are irreversible — but if there is an irreversible change, you know there's definitely been a chemical change.

Cooking food produces new substances. That means a chemical change has taken place. Once cooked, you can't change it back. The cooking process is irreversible.

e.g. Eggs and Meat

Eggs and meat are good sources of protein. Protein molecules change shape when you heat them. The energy from cooking breaks some of the chemical bonds in the protein and this allows the molecule to take a different shape. This gives the food a more edible texture. The change is irreversible. It's called denaturing.

e.g. Potatoes

Potatoes are plants, so each potato cell is surrounded by a rigid cell wall made of cellulose. Humans can't digest cellulose, so it's difficult for us to get to the contents of the cells. Cooking the potato ruptures (breaks down) the cell walls. It also makes the starch grains inside the cells swell up and spread out. These changes make the potato softer and more flexible, and much easier to digest.

Baking Powder Undergoes a Chemical Change When Heated

1) When you heat baking powder, it undergoes thermal decomposition.
2) Thermal decomposition is when a substance breaks down into simpler substances when heated. Many thermal decompositions are helped along by a catalyst. (Thermal decomposition is different from a lot of reactions you'll come across, since there's only one substance to start with.)
3) Baking powder contains the chemical sodium hydrogencarbonate. You need to know the word and symbol equations for its thermal decomposition:

The word equation is:	sodium hydrogencarbonate →	sodium carbonate	+ carbon dioxide	+ water
The symbol equation is:	$2NaHCO_3$ →	Na_2CO_3	+ CO_2	+ H_2O

4) Baking powder is used in baking cakes — the carbon dioxide produced makes the cake rise.
5) You can check that it is actually carbon dioxide that has been formed by using a chemical test:

Carbon dioxide can be detected using limewater — CO_2 turns limewater cloudy when it's bubbled through.

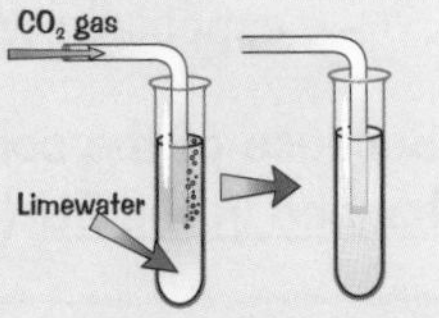

You'll need to learn this page for your eggsam...

Cooking is a kind of chemistry — when you cook something, you're bringing about chemical change. The changes are irreversible, as you'll know if you've ever tried to unscramble an egg.

Perfumes

Some things smell nice, some don't... it's all down to the chemicals a substance contains.

Perfumes Can be Natural or Artificial

1) Chemicals that smell nice are used as perfumes and air fresheners. Esters are often used as perfumes as they usually smell quite pleasant.
2) Esters are pretty common in nature. Loads of common fruity smells (like apples) and flowery smells (like jasmine) contain natural esters.
3) Esters can also be manufactured synthetically to use as perfumes or flavourings, e.g. there are esters (or combinations of esters) that smell of lavender, oranges, cinnamon and so on.

Esters are Made by Esterification

A carboxylic acid is an acid built around one or more carbon atoms.

1) You can make an ester by heating a carboxylic acid with an alcohol. (This is an example of esterification.)
2) An acid catalyst is usually used (e.g. concentrated sulfuric acid).

Acid + Alcohol → Ester + Water ← You need to learn this equation.

Method: Mix 10 cm^3 of a carboxylic acid such as ethanoic acid with 10 cm^3 of an alcohol such as ethanol. Add 1 cm^3 of concentrated sulfuric acid to this mixture and warm gently for about 5 minutes. Tip the mixture into 150 cm^3 of sodium carbonate solution (to neutralise the acids) and smell carefully (by wafting the smell towards your nose). The fruity-smelling product is the ester.

Perfumes Need Certain Properties

You can't use any old chemical with a smell as a perfume. You need a substance with certain properties:

1) Easily evaporates — or else the perfume particles won't reach your nose and you won't be able to smell it... bit useless really.
2) Non-toxic — it mustn't seep through your skin and poison you.
3) Doesn't react with water — or else it would react with the water in sweat.
4) Doesn't irritate the skin — or else you couldn't apply it directly to your neck or wrists. If you splash on any old substance you risk burning your skin.
5) Insoluble in water — if it was soluble in water it would wash off every time you got wet.

New Perfumes and Cosmetics Have to be Tested

1) Companies are always developing new cosmetic products to sell to us. Before they're released to the shops, they need to be tested thoroughly to make sure they're safe to use.
2) But some tests are carried out using animals, which is a bit controversial.
3) People have different opinions about whether it's OK to test cosmetic products on animals.

- Some think it's worth testing cosmetic products on animals first to check they won't damage humans.
- Others claim that it's wrong to cause suffering to animals just to test the safety of a cosmetic — especially when the results of the animal tests might not be conclusive.

4) Because of the concerns about animal welfare, testing cosmetics on animals has now been banned in the EU (except for a few tests which are still allowed).

My dog's got no nose — how does he smell? (Answer below)

Perfume needs to smell nice, but not everyone agrees on what smells nice. Perfume also needs to be safe, but not everyone agrees on the best way to test for this. That's life for you.

Like I said, he's got no nose, so he can't smell.

Kinetic Theory and Forces Between Particles

You can explain a lot of things (including perfumes) if you get your head round this lot.

States of Matter — Depend on the Forces Between Particles

All stuff is made of particles (molecules, ions or atoms) that are constantly moving, and the forces between these particles can be weak or strong, depending on whether it's a solid, liquid or a gas.

Solids

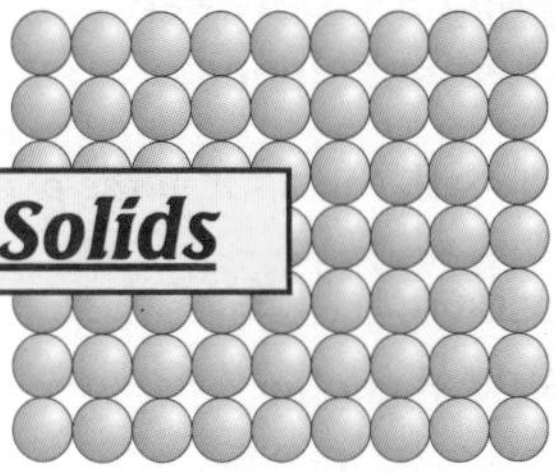

1) There are strong forces of attraction between particles, which holds them in fixed positions in a very regular lattice arrangement.
2) The particles don't move from their positions, so all solids keep a definite shape and volume, and don't flow like liquids.
3) The particles vibrate about their positions — the hotter the solid becomes, the more they vibrate (causing solids to expand slightly when heated).

If you heat the solid (give the particles more energy), eventually the solid will melt and become liquid.

Liquids

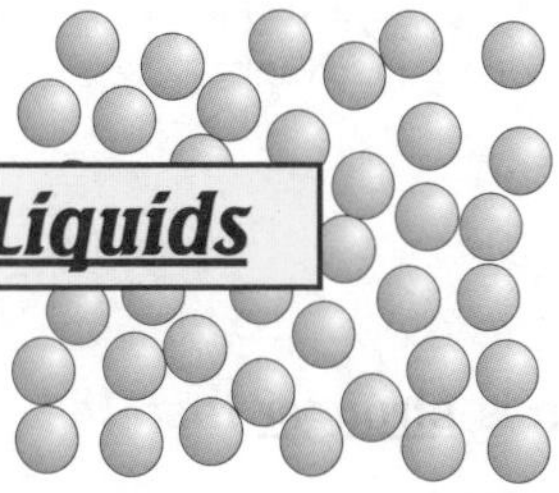

1) There is some force of attraction between the particles. They're free to move past each other, but they do tend to stick together.
2) Liquids don't keep a definite shape and will flow to fill the bottom of a container. But they do keep the same volume.
3) The particles are constantly moving with random motion. The hotter the liquid gets, the faster they move. This causes liquids to expand slightly when heated.

If you now heat the liquid, eventually it will boil and become gas.

Gases

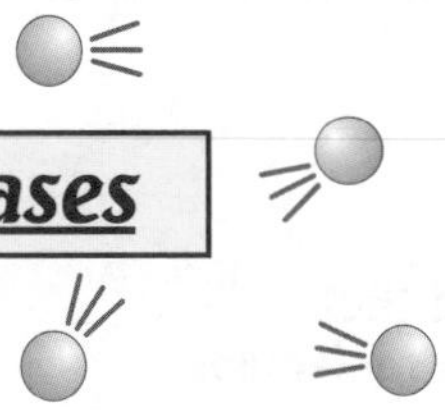

1) There's next to no force of attraction between the particles — they're free to move. They travel in straight lines and only interact when they collide.
2) Gases don't keep a definite shape or volume and will always fill any container. When particles bounce off the walls of a container they exert a pressure on the walls.
3) The particles move constantly with random motion. The hotter the gas gets, the faster they move. Gases either expand when heated, or their pressure increases.

How We Smell Stuff — Volatility's the Key

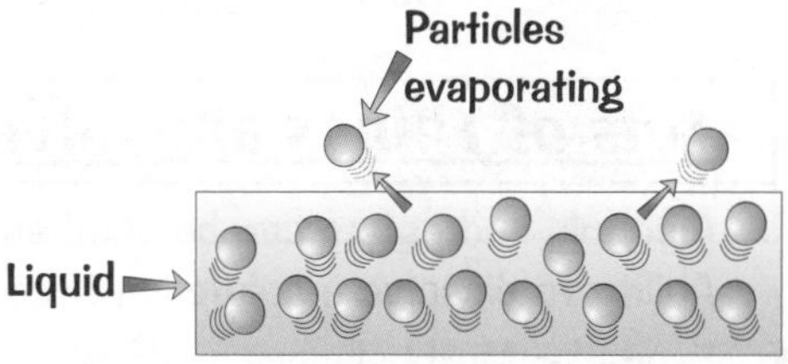

1) When a liquid is heated, the heat energy goes to the particles, which makes them move faster.
2) Some particles move faster than others.
3) Fast-moving particles at the surface will overcome the forces of attraction from the other particles and escape. This is evaporation.
4) How easily a liquid evaporates is called its volatility.

So... the evaporated particles are now drifting about in the air, the smell receptors in your nose pick up the chemical — and hey presto — you smell it.

Perfumes need to be quite volatile so that they can evaporate enough for you to smell them.
The particles in liquid perfumes only have a very weak attraction between them. It's easy for the particles to overcome this and escape — so you only need a very little heat energy to make the perfume evaporate.

Eau de sweaty sock — thankfully not very volatile...

Take another smelly chemical — petrol. The molecules in petrol are held together (otherwise it wouldn't be a liquid), but they must be constantly escaping (evaporating) in order for you to smell it. That's why you shouldn't have naked flames at a petrol station... the vapour from the pumps could catch fire.

Solutions

Solutions are all around you — e.g. sea water, bath salts... And inside you even — e.g. instant coffee...

A Solution is a Mixture of Solvent and Solute

When you add a solid (the solute) to a liquid (the solvent) the bonds holding the solute molecules together sometimes break and the molecules then mix with the molecules in the liquid — forming a solution. This is called dissolving. Whether the bonds break depends on how strong the attractions are between the molecules within each substance and how strong the attractions are between the two substances.

Here's some definitions you need to know:

Learn this definition of a solution — they might ask you for it in the exam.

1) Solution – is a mixture of a solute and a solvent that does not separate out.
2) Solute – is the substance being dissolved.
3) Solvent – is the liquid it's dissolving into.
4) Soluble – means it will dissolve.
5) Insoluble – means it will NOT dissolve.
6) Solubility – a measure of how much will dissolve.

E.g. brine is a solution of salt and water — if you evaporated off the solvent (the water), you'd see the solute (the salt) again.

Water is a very common solvent.

Nail Varnish is Insoluble in Water...

Nail varnish doesn't dissolve in water. This is for two reasons:

1) The molecules of nail varnish are strongly attracted to each other. This attraction is stronger than the attraction between the nail varnish molecules and the water molecules.
2) The molecules of water are strongly attracted to each other. This attraction is stronger than the attraction between the water molecules and the nail varnish molecules.

Because the two substances are more attracted to themselves than each other, they don't form a solution.

...but Soluble in Acetone

Nail varnish dissolves in acetone — more commonly known as nail varnish remover. This is because the attraction between acetone molecules and nail varnish molecules is stronger than the attractions holding the two substances together.

So the solubility of a substance depends on the solvent used.

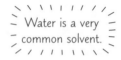

Acetone is also called propanone.

Lots of Things are Solvents

Alcohols and esters can be used as solvents, and so can lots of other weird and wacky organic molecules. Ability to dissolve a solute isn't the only consideration though... some solvents are horribly poisonous.

Example: Mothballs are made of a substance called naphthalene. Imagine you've trodden a mothball into your carpet. Choose one of the solvents from the table to clean it up.

Solvent	Solubility of naphthalene	Boiling point	Other properties
water	0 g/100 g	100 °C	safe
methanol	9.7 g/100 g	65 °C	flammable
ethyl acetate	18.5 g/100 g	77 °C	flammable
dichloromethane	25.0 g/100 g	40 °C	extremely toxic

Looking at the data, water wouldn't be a good choice because it doesn't dissolve the naphthalene. Dichloromethane would dissolve it easily, but it's very toxic. Of the two solvents left, ethyl acetate dissolves more naphthalene (so you won't need as much). Ethyl acetate is best (just don't set light to it).

Learn this page, it's the only solution...

If you ever spill bright pink nail varnish (or any other colour for that matter) on your carpet, go easy with the nail varnish remover. If you use too much, the nail varnish dissolves in the remover, forming a solution which can go everywhere — and you end up with an enormous bright pink stain... aaagh.

Paints and Pigments

You might just think of paint as brightly coloured stuff — but there's a lot of chemistry that goes into making your bedroom walls lime green.

Pigments Give Paints Their Colours

1) Paint usually contains the following bits: solvent, binding medium and pigment.
2) The pigment gives the paint its colour.
3) The binding medium is a liquid that carries the pigment bits and holds them together. When the binding medium goes solid it sticks the pigments to the surface you've painted.
4) The solvent is the stuff that thins the paint and makes it easier to spread.

Paints are Colloids

1) A colloid consists of really tiny particles of one kind of stuff dispersed in (mixed in with) another kind of stuff. They're mixed in, but not dissolved.
2) The particles can be bits of solid, droplets of liquid or bubbles of gas.
3) Colloids don't separate out because the particles are so small. They don't settle out at the bottom.

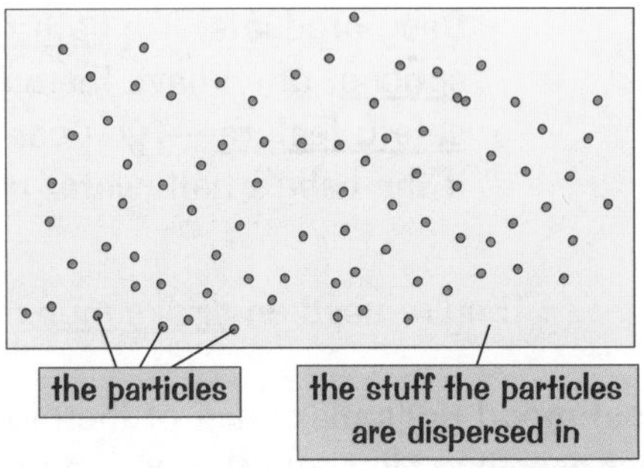

4) A paint is a colloid where particles of a pigment (usually a solid) are dispersed through a liquid.

Some Paints are Water-based and Some are Oil-based

When you're painting (whether it's a bedroom wall or a work of art) you usually apply paint in a thin layer. The paint dries as the solvent evaporates. (A thin layer dries a heck of a lot quicker than a thick layer.)

Depending on the type of job you're doing, you might choose a water-based paint or an oil-based paint.

1) Emulsion paints are water-based. The solvent used in these paints is water, and the binding medium is usually an acrylic or vinyl acetate polymer.
2) A water-based emulsion dries when the solvent evaporates, leaving behind the binder and pigment as a thin solid film. A thin layer of emulsion paint dries quite quickly.
3) Emulsion paints are fast-drying and don't produce harmful fumes — so they're ideal for painting things like inside walls.

1) Traditional gloss paint and artists' oil paints are oil-based. This time, the binding material is oil, and the solvent is an organic compound that'll dissolve oil.
2) Oil paints dry in two stages. First the solvent evaporates, and then the oil is oxidised by oxygen in the air before it turns solid. (So they tend to take longer to dry than water-based paints.)
3) Oil paints are glossy, waterproof and hard-wearing, but the solvents used to make them often produce harmful fumes. They're best used for painting things like outside doors and metalwork.

Some modern gloss paints are water-based.

The world was black and white before the 1950s — I saw it on TV...

There are heaps of different types of paint — and some are more suitable for certain jobs than others. Like if you're repainting your car, watercolours are definitely not the way to go. And likewise if you painted your little sister's face with gloss paint, your mum would probably ground you for a year.

Special Pigments

If you thought the science behind brightly coloured paint was clever, wait till you read about the pigments on this page. They can change colour and even **glow in the dark...**

Thermochromic Pigments Change Colour When Heated

1) Thermochromic pigments change colour or become transparent when heated or cooled.
2) Different pigments change colour at different temperatures, so a mixture of different pigments can be used to make a colour-coded temperature scale. These are used to make basic thermometers that you stick on your forehead to take your temperature.

There are lots of other cunning uses for thermochromic pigments:

Thermochromic pigments are used in fancy electric kettles that change colour as the water boils.

Baby products, like bath toys and baby spoons, often have them added as a safety feature — you can tell at a glance if the baby's bath water or food is too hot.

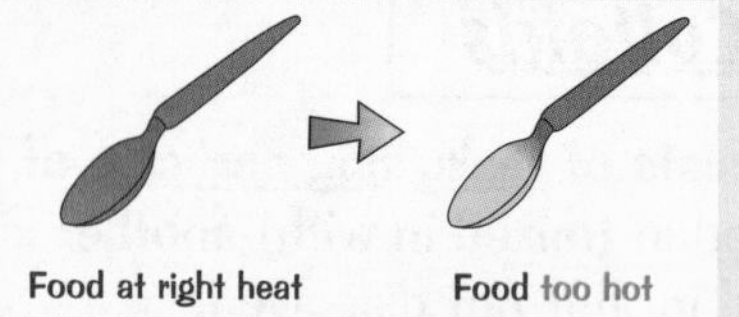

They're used on drinks mugs to warn you when the contents are too hot to drink.

Most mood rings make use of thermochromic pigments — the middle of the ring contains heat sensitive pigments that change colour depending on the temperature of your finger.

(And you thought it was all to do with how **calm** or how **passionate** you were...)

You can mix thermochromic pigments with paints too:

1) Thermochromic pigments can be mixed with acrylic paint, giving a wide range of colour changes. For example, mixing a blue thermochromic pigment that loses its colour above 27 °C with a yellow acrylic paint would give a paint that's green below 27 °C and yellow above 27 °C.

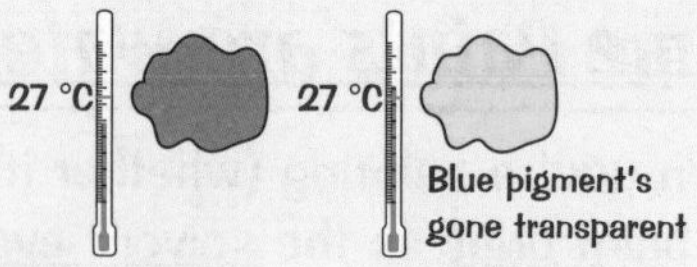

2) These paints are used on novelty mugs. For example, some mugs have a design that changes colour when a hot drink's poured into them.
   Other mugs use a thermochromic pigment that becomes transparent when heated. A picture underneath the paint is only visible when a hot drink is poured in.

Phosphorescent Pigments Glow in the Dark

1) Phosphorescent pigments absorb natural or artificial light and store the energy in their molecules. This energy is released as light over a period of time — from a few seconds to a couple of hours.
2) An obvious use is a watch or clock with glow-in-the-dark hands.
3) Other uses include traffic signs, emergency exit signs, toys and novelty decorations.
4) Glow-in-the-dark watches used to be made with radioactive paints. These paints would glow for years without needing to be "charged up" by putting 'em in the light. Unfortunately, a lot of them weren't very safe, and could give quite a dose of atomic radiation. Phosphorescent pigments were developed as a much safer alternative.

Thermochromic pigments — the truth behind mood rings...

For a brief spell in the early 1990s colour-changing T-shirts were reeeeally cool. Although I was never quite sure why you'd want to show the world just how hot and sweaty your armpits were. Glow-in-the-dark erasers too... I mean... when do you ever need to rub out mistakes in the dark?

Polymers

Plastics are made up of lots of molecules joined together. They're like long chains.

Plastics are Long-Chain Molecules Called Polymers

1) Polymers are formed when lots of small molecules called monomers join together. This reaction is called polymerisation — and it usually needs high pressure and a catalyst.
2) Plastics are polymers. They're usually carbon based and their monomers are often alkenes — see page 42.

Addition Polymers are Made From Unsaturated Monomers

1) The monomers that make up addition polymers have a double covalent bond.
2) Molecules with at least one double covalent bond between carbon atoms are called unsaturated compounds. Molecules with no double bond between carbon atoms are saturated compounds.
3) Lots of unsaturated monomer molecules (alkenes) can open up their double bonds and join together to form polymer chains.

This is called addition polymerisation.

The 'n' just means there can be any number of monomers.

Ethene becoming polyethene (or polythene) is the easiest example:

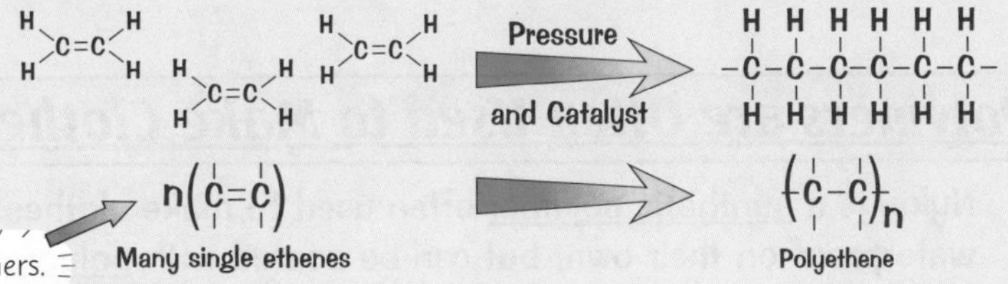

1) Drawing the displayed formula of an addition polymer from the displayed formula of its monomer is easy. Join the carbons together in a row with no double bonds between them, stick a pair of brackets around the repeating bit, and put an 'n' after it (to show that there are lots of monomers).

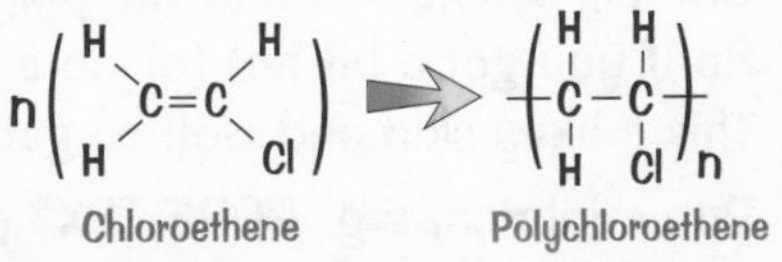

2) The name of the polymer comes from the type of monomer it's made from — you just stick the word "poly" in front of it. So propene becomes polypropene, etc.
3) To get from the displayed formula of the polymer to the displayed formula of the monomer, just do the reverse. Draw out the repeating bit of the polymer, get rid of the two bonds going out through the brackets and put a double bond between the carbons.

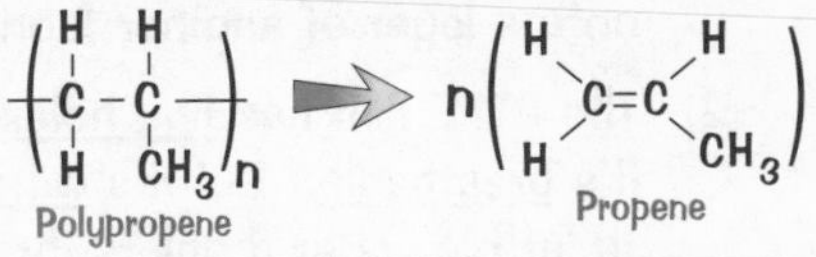

Forces Between Molecules Determine the Properties of Plastics

Strong covalent bonds hold the atoms together in polymer chains. But it's the forces between the different chains that determine the properties of the plastic.

Weak Forces:

If the plastic is made up of long chains that are held together by weak intermolecular forces, then the chains will be free to slide over each other. This means that the plastic can be stretched easily, and will have a low melting point.

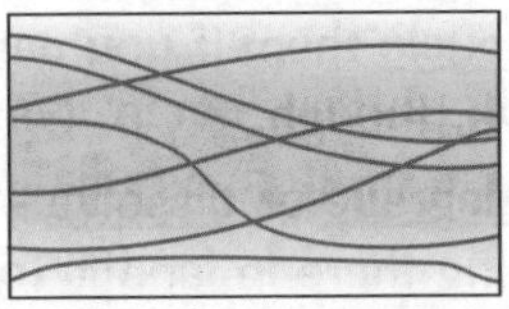

Strong Forces:

Some plastics have stronger bonds between the polymer chains — these might be covalent bonds between the chains, or cross-linking bridges. These plastics have higher melting points, are rigid and can't be stretched, as the crosslinks hold the chains firmly together.

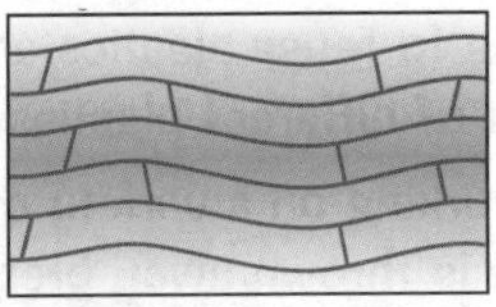

Revision — it's all about stringing lots of facts together...

Which monomer a polymer is made from affects the properties of the plastic, which also affects what the plastic can be used for (more about the uses of plastics on page 40 by the way). For this page, you need to be completely sure about what a monomer is, and how polymers are made.

Polymers and Their Uses

Plastics are fantastically useful. You can make novelty football pencil sharpeners and all sorts.

Polymers' Properties Decide What They're Used For

Different polymers have different physical properties — some are stronger, some are stretchier, some are more easily moulded, and so on. These different physical properties make them suited for different uses.

- Strong, rigid polymers such as high density polyethene are used to make plastic milk bottles.
- Light, stretchable polymers such as low density polyethene are used for plastic bags and squeezy bottles. Low density polyethene has a low melting point, so it's no good for anything that'll get very hot.

- PVC is strong and durable, and it can be made either rigid or stretchy. The rigid kind is used to make window frames and piping. The stretchy kind is used to make synthetic leather.
- Polystyrene foam is used in packaging to protect breakable things, and it's used to make disposable coffee cups (the trapped air in the foam makes it a brilliant thermal insulator).

Polymers are Often Used to Make Clothes

1) Nylon is a synthetic polymer often used to make clothes. Fabrics made from nylon are not waterproof on their own, but can be coated with polyurethane to make tough, hard-wearing and waterproof outdoor clothing which also keeps UV light out.
2) One big problem is that the polyurethane coating doesn't let water vapour pass through it. So if you get a bit hot (or do a bit of exercise), sweat condenses on the inside. This makes skin and clothes get wet and uncomfortable — the material isn't breathable.
3) Some fabrics, e.g. GORE-TEX® products, have all the useful properties of nylon/polyurethane ones, but are also breathable. If you sweat in breathable material, water vapour can escape — so no condensation.

1) GORE-TEX® fabrics are made by laminating a thin film of a plastic called expanded PTFE onto a layer of another fabric, such as polyester or nylon. This makes the PTFE sturdier.
2) The PTFE film has tiny holes which let water vapour through — so it's breathable. But it's waterproof, since the holes aren't big enough to let big water droplets through and the PTFE repels liquid water.
3) This material is great for outdoorsy types — they can hike without getting rained on or soaked in sweat.

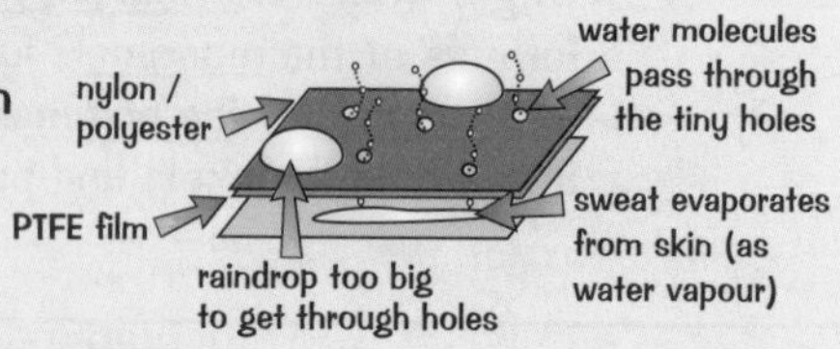

Non-biodegradable Plastics Cause Disposal Problems

1) Most polymers aren't "biodegradable" — they're not broken down by micro-organisms, so they don't rot. This property is actually kind of useful until it's time to get rid of your plastic.
2) It's difficult to get rid of plastics — if you bury them in a landfill site, they'll still be there years later. Landfill sites fill up quickly, and they're a waste of land. And a waste of plastic.
3) When plastics are burnt, some of them release gases such as acidic sulfur dioxide and poisonous hydrogen chloride and hydrogen cyanide. So burning's out, really. Plus it's a waste of plastic.
4) The best thing is to reuse plastics as many times as possible and then recycle them if you can. Sorting out lots of different plastics for recycling is difficult and expensive, though.
5) Chemists are working on a variety of ideas to produce polymers that biodegrade or dissolve — that way any plastic that is thrown away breaks down or dissolves rather than sitting there in landfill for ages.

Disposal problems — you should go and see a doctor...

If you're making a product, you need to pick your plastic carefully. It's no good trying to make a kettle out of a plastic that melts at 50 °C — you'll end up with a messy kitchen, a burnt hand and no cuppa. You'd also have a bit of difficulty trying to wear clothes made of brittle, un-bendy plastic.

Hydrocarbons — Alkanes

Hydrocarbons look like simple enough chemicals — just carbon and hydrogen. But different types of hydrocarbon molecules can have all sorts of different properties — and we use them for loads of things.

Hydrocarbons Only Contain Hydrogen and Carbon Atoms

A hydrocarbon is any compound that is formed from carbon and hydrogen atoms only. So $C_{10}H_{22}$ (decane, an alkane) is a hydrocarbon, but $CH_3COOC_3H_7$ (an ester) is not — it's got oxygen atoms in it.

Hydrocarbons are really useful chemicals — fuels like petrol and diesel are hydrocarbons, and lots of plastics are made from hydrocarbons too.

Covalent Bonds Hold Atoms in a Molecule Together

1) All the atoms in hydrocarbon molecules are held together by covalent bonds. These covalent bonds are very strong. They form when atoms 'share' electrons.
2) This way both atoms get a full outer shell — which is an atom's main aim in life.
3) Each covalent bond provides one extra shared electron for each atom. And each atom involved has to make enough covalent bonds to fill up its outer shell. So carbon atoms always want to make a total of 4 bonds, while hydrogen atoms only want to make 1.

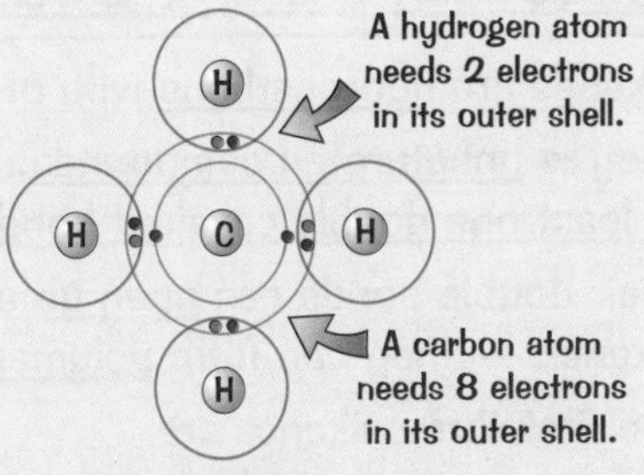

Methane (CH_4)

Alkanes Have All C–C Single Bonds

1) Alkanes are the simplest type of hydrocarbon you can get. They're just chains of carbon atoms with two or three hydrogen atoms attached to each one (three if the carbon's at the end of the chain, two if it's in the middle).
2) Alkanes are saturated compounds — this means they contain only single covalent bonds between their carbon atoms. (They don't have any double bonds that can open up and join onto things.)
3) You can tell the difference between an alkane and an alkene by adding the substance to bromine water — an alkane won't decolourise the bromine water (there's more about this on the next page).
4) Alkanes won't form polymers — same reason again, no double bonds to open up.
5) The first four alkanes are methane (natural gas), ethane, propane and butane.

Methane: CH_4

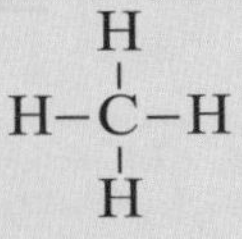

(natural gas)

Ethane: C_2H_6

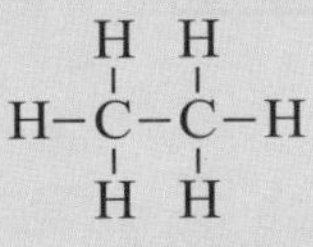

Propane: C_3H_8

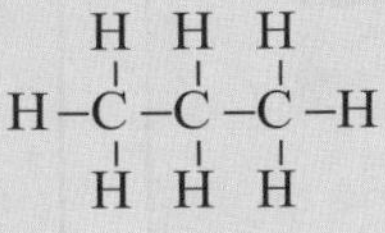

Butane: C_4H_{10}

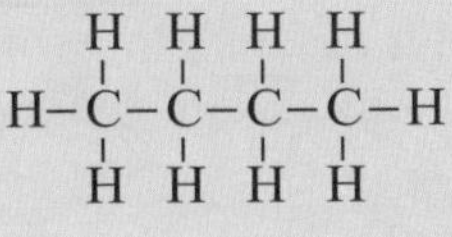

All alkanes have the formula: C_nH_{2n+2}

The 'a' bit of these names is important because it's telling you that the molecules don't contain any double bonds. If they did, it would be an 'e' instead — like the alkenes on the next page.

Alkane anybody who doesn't learn this lot properly...

Covalent bonds are so sweet — the little atoms sharing their electrons. Heartwarming. Now warm your brain to match by learning what an alkane is — keep drawing out the structures of the examples on this page until you get the hang of the basic pattern. They're important molecules in the modern world because they make good fuels.

Hydrocarbons — Alkenes

Alkenes are another type of hydrocarbon. They're different from alkanes because they have double bonds...

Covalent Bonds can be Single or Double Bonds

1) A single covalent bond is formed when two atoms share a pair of electrons so that both can have a full outer shell (see p.41).
2) Sometimes, to fill up their outer shells, two atoms will share two pairs of electrons instead of just one pair.
3) By doing this the atoms form a double bond.
4) Carbon atoms can do this — each bond still provides one extra shared electron for each atom, but this time there are two bonds between the carbons.

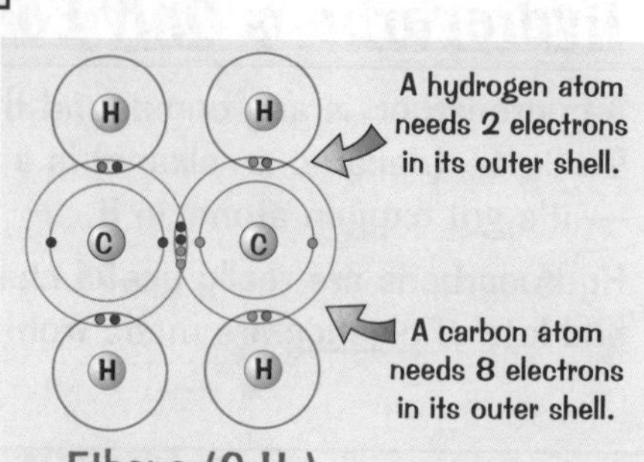

H
C
A hydrogen atom needs 2 electrons in its outer shell.
A carbon atom needs 8 electrons in its outer shell.

Ethene (C_2H_4)

Alkenes Have a C=C Double Bond

1) Alkenes are hydrocarbons with one or more double bonds between carbon atoms.
2) They're unsaturated compounds. An unsaturated compound is just one that contains at least one double covalent bond.
3) Their double bonds can open up and join onto things. This makes alkenes much more reactive than alkanes — they can form polymers by opening up their double bonds to 'hold hands' in a long chain.
4) The first three alkenes are ethene, propene and butene:

These all have an 'e' in the middle of their names to show that they do contain a double bond.

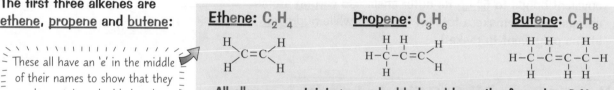

Ethene: C_2H_4 **Propene**: C_3H_6 **Butene**: C_4H_8

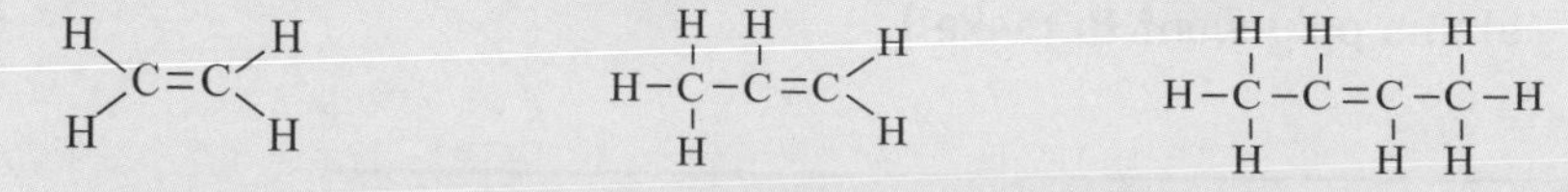

All alkenes containing one double bond have the formula: C_nH_{2n}

Alkenes React with Bromine Water

1) Bromine water is a bright orange solution that contains bromine (well, obviously), Br_2.
2) It's really reactive — if there are any double bonds around, they'll spring open and react with the bromine. When this happens the orange colour disappears from the solution — the bromine water is decolourised.
3) You can use this to test whether what you've got is an alkene or not. You just take a sample of your hydrocarbon, mix it with bromine water, and shake:

If it's a saturated compound, like an alkane, no reaction will happen and it'll stay bright orange.

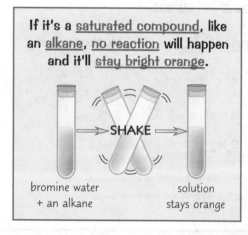

SHAKE

bromine water + an alkane — solution stays orange

If it's an alkene an addition reaction will take place. The bromine will add to the double bond, making a colourless dibromo compound — so the bromine water is decolourised.

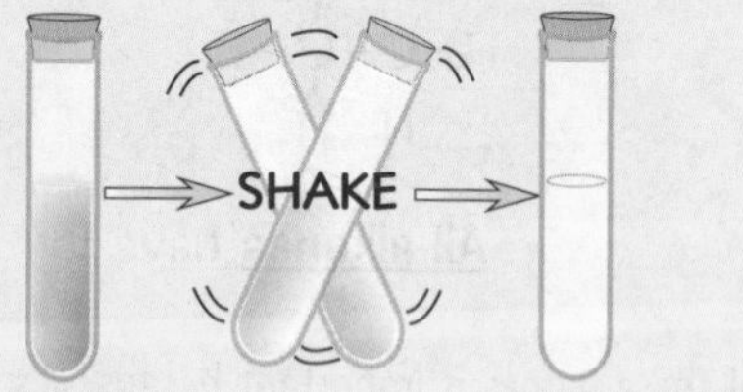

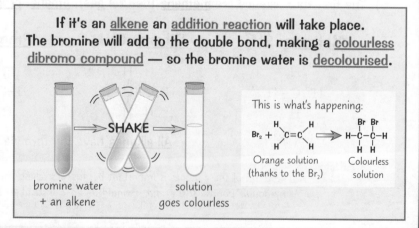

SHAKE

bromine water + an alkene — solution goes colourless

This is what's happening:

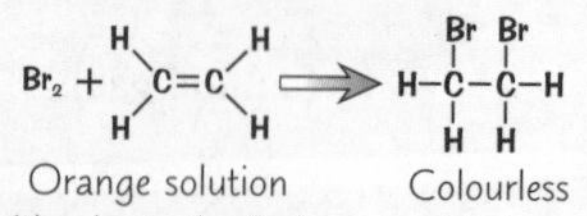

Orange solution (thanks to the Br_2) → Colourless solution

The name's bond — double covalent bond...

Just one double bond, that's all it takes, and you go from a boring, stable old alkane to a reactive alkene, forming polymers at the drop of a (metaphorical) hat and making bromine water change colour. Amazing.

Fractional Distillation of Crude Oil

Fossil fuels like coal, oil and gas are called non-renewable fuels as they take so long to make that they're being used up much faster than they're being formed. They're finite resources — one day they'll run out.

Crude Oil is Separated into Different Hydrocarbon Fractions

1) Crude oil is formed from the buried remains of plants and animals — it's a fossil fuel. Over millions of years, with high temperature and pressure, the remains turn to crude oil, which can be drilled up.
2) Crude oil is a mixture of lots of different hydrocarbons. Remember that hydrocarbons are chains of carbon atoms (e.g. alkanes and alkenes) of various lengths.
3) The different compounds in crude oil are separated by fractional distillation. The oil is heated until most of it has turned into gas. The gases enter a fractionating column (and the liquid bit, bitumen, is drained off at the bottom). In the column there's a temperature gradient (i.e. it's hot at the bottom and gets gradually cooler as you go up).
4) The longer hydrocarbons have high boiling points. They turn back into liquids and drain out of the column early on, when they're near the bottom. The shorter hydrocarbons have lower boiling points. They turn to liquid and drain out much later on, near to the top of the column where it's cooler.
5) You end up with the crude oil mixture separated out into different fractions. Each fraction contains a mixture of hydrocarbons with similar boiling points.

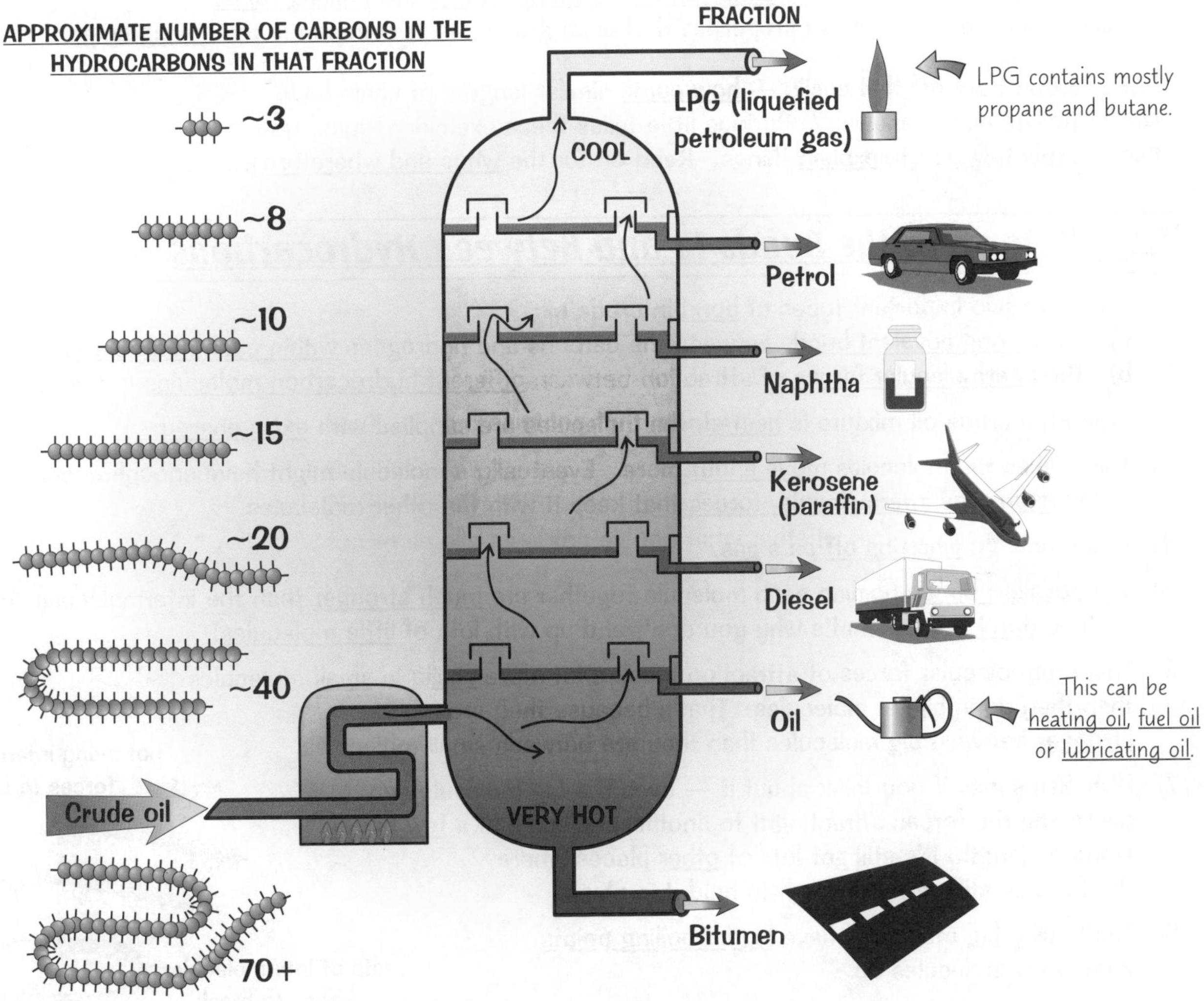

How much petrol is there in crude oil? Just a fraction...

In the exam, you could be given a diagram of the fractional distillation column and asked to add labels, or say where on the column a certain fraction (like petrol or diesel) would drain off. This means you need to learn the diagram properly — don't just glance at it and assume you know it. Cover the page up and test yourself.

Hydrocarbon Properties — Bonds

The examiners seem quite keen that you know why long hydrocarbon chains boil at a higher temperature than short hydrocarbon chains. If that's what they want, then you'd best give it to them...

Hydrocarbon Properties Change as the Chain Gets Longer

As the size of the hydrocarbon molecule increases:

1) The boiling point increases.
2) It gets less flammable (doesn't set on fire so easily).
3) It gets more viscous (doesn't flow so easily).
4) It gets less volatile (i.e. doesn't evaporate so easily).

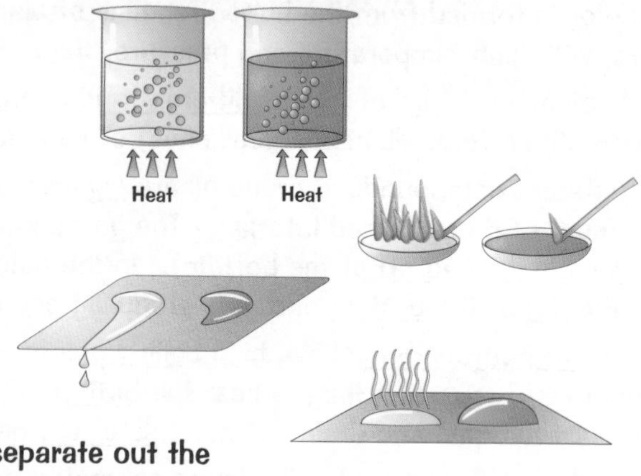

That's how fractional distillation works — you can separate out the random mixture of all kinds of hydrocarbons into groups (fractions) that have similar chain lengths and so similar properties. Then you can use them for various useful things like powering vehicles, heating homes and making roads. It works because one of those properties that each group has in common is the boiling point.

But you don't get off that easily — how come similar lengths of chain have similar boiling points anyway? Curious little fellas these examiner types, you know, expecting you to explain things. Read on for the whys and wherefores...

It's All Down to the Bonds In and Between Hydrocarbons

1) There are two important types of bond in crude oil:
   a) The strong covalent bonds between the carbons and hydrogens within each hydrocarbon molecule.
   b) The intermolecular forces of attraction between different hydrocarbon molecules in the mixture.
2) When the crude oil mixture is heated, the molecules are supplied with extra energy.
3) This makes the molecules move about more. Eventually a molecule might have enough energy to overcome the intermolecular forces that keep it with the other molecules.
4) It can now go whizzing off as a gas.
5) The covalent bonds holding each molecule together are much stronger than the intermolecular forces, so they don't break. That's why you don't end up with lots of little molecules.
6) The intermolecular forces of attraction break a lot more easily in small molecules than they do in bigger molecules. That's because they are much stronger between big molecules than they are between small molecules.
7) It makes sense if you think about it — even if a big molecule can overcome the forces attracting it to another molecule at a few points along its length, it's still got lots of other places where the force is still strong enough to hold it in place.
8) That's why big molecules have higher boiling points than small molecules do.

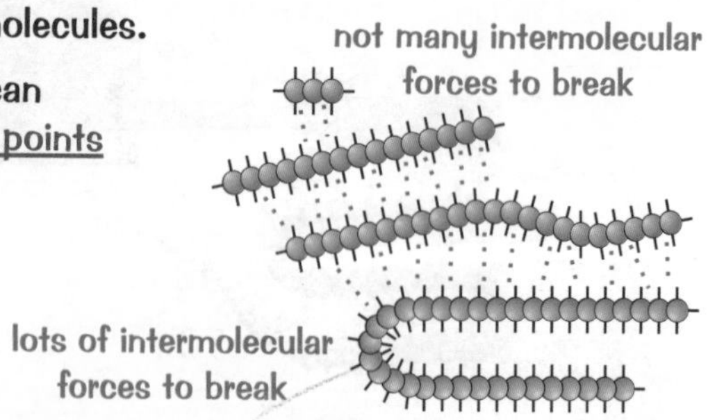

Positively boiling over with chemistry fun...

One minute it's all petrol and kerosene, the next it's all molecules and forces and covalent bonds. That's the way with chemistry. If you can scribble down a reasonable version of the stuff about intermolecular bonds and boiling point, you'll get the marks. Which is what it's all about.

Cracking

Crude oil fractions from fractional distillation are split into smaller molecules — this is called cracking.
It's dead important — otherwise we might not have enough fuel for cars and planes and things.

Cracking is Splitting Up Long-Chain Hydrocarbons

1) Cracking turns long alkane molecules into smaller alkane and alkene molecules (which are much more useful).

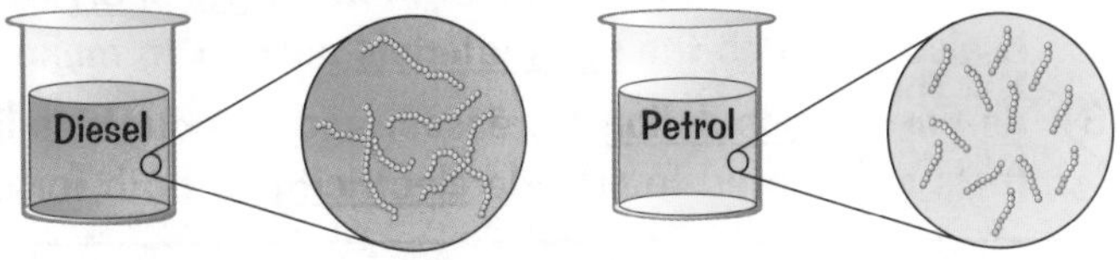

2) It's a form of thermal decomposition, which is when one substance breaks down into at least two new ones when you heat it.
This means breaking strong covalent bonds, so you need lots of heat and a catalyst.
3) A lot of the longer molecules produced from fractional distillation are cracked into smaller ones because there's more demand for products like petrol and kerosene (jet fuel) than for diesel or lubricating oil.
4) Cracking also produces lots of alkene molecules, which can be used to make polymers (mostly plastics).

Conditions Needed for Cracking: Hot, Plus a Catalyst

1) Vaporised hydrocarbons are passed over powdered catalyst at about 400 °C – 700 °C.
2) Aluminium oxide is the catalyst used. The long-chain molecules split apart or "crack" on the surface of the bits of catalyst.

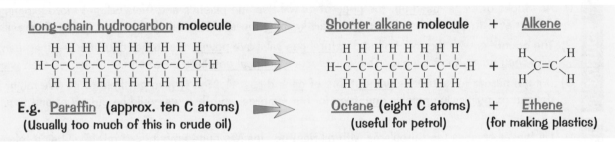

Long-chain hydrocarbon molecule → Shorter alkane molecule + Alkene

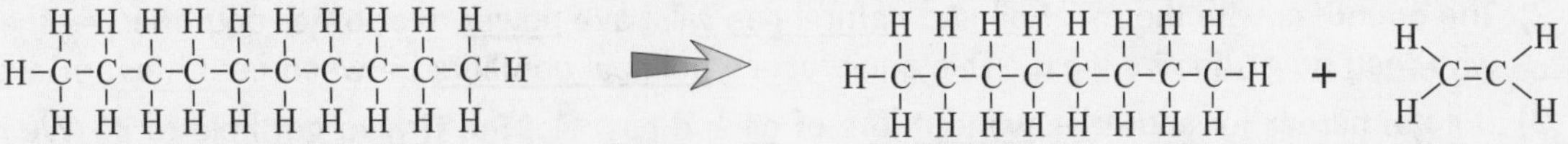

E.g. Paraffin (approx. ten C atoms) (Usually too much of this in crude oil) → Octane (eight C atoms) (useful for petrol) + Ethene (for making plastics)

3) You can use the apparatus shown below to crack liquid paraffin in the lab:

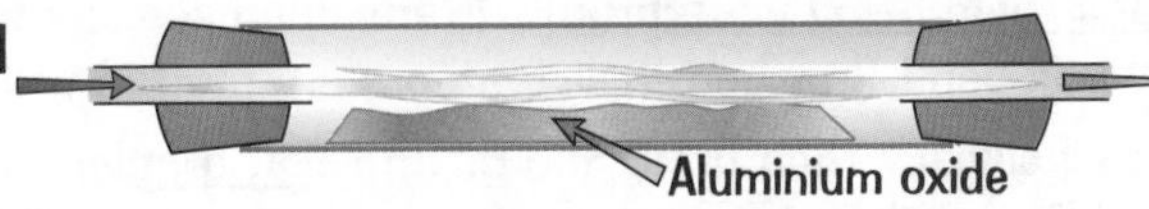

You'll probably get other products too — it all depends on what exactly is in your paraffin.

Cracking Helps Match Supply and Demand

The examiner might give you a table like the one below to show the supply and demand for various fractions obtained from crude oil. You could be asked which fraction is more likely to be cracked to provide us with petrol and diesel (demand for petrol and diesel is greater than the amount in crude oil).

Fraction	Approx % in crude oil	Approx % demand
LPG	2	4
Petrol and naphtha	16	27
Kerosene	13	8
Diesel	19	23
Oil and bitumen	50	38

OK, you could use the kerosene fraction to supply the extra petrol and the oil and bitumen fraction to supply the extra diesel.
Or you could crack the oil and bitumen to supply both the extra petrol and the extra diesel. This might be cleverer, as there's a lot more oil/bitumen.

Don't crack up, it's not that bad...

Cracking helps an oil refinery to match its supply of useful products, like petrol, with the demand for them. It also produces short chain alkenes that can be used to make plastics. Remember, you can crack any long hydrocarbon chain into smaller chains, but you can't make longer chains from shorter ones by cracking (duh...).

Use of Fossil Fuels

Nothing as amazingly useful as crude oil would be without its problems. No, that'd be too good to be true.

Crude Oil Provides Important Fuels for Modern Life

1) Crude oil provides the energy needed to do lots of vital things — generating electricity, heating homes...
2) Oil provides the fuel for most modern transport — cars, trains, planes, the lot.
   It also provides the raw materials needed to make various chemicals, including plastics.
3) As Earth's population increases, and as countries like India and China become more developed, more fossil fuels are burned to provide electricity — both for increased home use and to run manufacturing industries.

But It Will Run Out Eventually... Eeek

Crude oil supplies are limited and non-renewable. New reserves are sometimes found, and new technology means we can get to oil that was once too difficult to extract. But one day we'll just run out.

However long the oil lasts, it's a good idea to start thinking about alternative energy sources now — like using nuclear or wind power to generate electricity, ethanol to power cars, and solar energy to heat water. (These alternatives aren't without their own problems, but we need them to be ready when the oil runs out.)

Some people think we should stop using oil for fuel (where we have alternatives) and keep it for making plastics and other chemicals. This could lead to conflict for resources between the fuel and chemical industries.

Oil Can Cause Political and Environmental Problems

POLITICAL

1) As stocks of oil get used up, the price of oil will rise and plastics and fuels will get more expensive. Countries with big stocks of oil might start keeping more of it for their own use, rather than selling it.
2) The countries with the most oil and natural gas will have power over other countries — they can choose who they do or don't supply. This could cause political conflicts between countries, or even wars.
3) It'll get harder for countries without lots of oil and gas, like the UK, to get hold of it. We might have to depend on politically unstable countries for our supplies, and then we could be cut off at any time.

ENVIRONMENTAL

1) Oil tanker crashes (and problems with oil rigs) can lead to huge amounts of crude oil being released into the sea. Oil floats on water and the action of waves and tides spreads it out into big oil slicks.
2) Oil covers sea birds' feathers, and stops them being waterproof. Water then soaks into their downy feathers, and they die of cold. Also, birds can't fly when their feathers are matted with oil.
3) Detergents are often used to clean up oil slicks. They break the oil into tiny droplets, making it easier to disperse. But some detergents harm wildlife — they can be toxic to marine creatures like fish and shellfish.

There's Lots to Consider When Choosing the Best Fuel

1) Energy value (i.e. amount of energy) — funnily enough, this isn't always as important as it may seem.
2) Availability — there's not much point in choosing a fuel you can't get hold of easily.
3) Storage — if a fuel is flammable or explosive then it might be difficult to store it safely.
4) Cost — some fuels are expensive, but still good value in terms of energy content etc.
5) Toxicity — some fuels are toxic, and some produce poisonous fumes when they burn.
6) Ease of use — whether it lights easily, whether you can move it safely.
7) Pollution — e.g. will you be adding to acid rain and the greenhouse effect...

EXAMPLE: You're at home and there's a power cut. You want a cup of tea. The only fuels you have are candles or meths (in a spirit burner). Which would you use to boil the water?

Even though a candle has more energy per gram, you'd probably choose meths because it's quicker and cleaner.

Fuel	Energy per gram	Rate of energy produced	Flame
Meths	28 kJ	15 kJ per minute	Clean
Candle	50 kJ	8 kJ per minute	Smoky

Oil not be impressed if you don't bother learning this...

We use lots of oil — we're dependent on it for loads of things. So we could be in a proper pickle when it runs out...

Burning Fuels

A fuel is a substance that reacts with oxygen to release useful energy.

Complete Combustion Happens When There's Plenty of Oxygen

The complete combustion of any hydrocarbon in oxygen will produce only carbon dioxide and water as waste products, which are both quite clean and non-poisonous.

hydrocarbon + oxygen ⟹ carbon dioxide + water (+ energy)

1) Many gas heaters release these waste gases into the room, which is perfectly OK. As long as the gas heater is working properly and the room is well ventilated there's no problem.
2) This reaction, when there's plenty of oxygen, is known as complete combustion. It releases lots of energy and only produces those two harmless waste products.
3) When there's plenty of oxygen and combustion is complete, the gas burns with a clean blue flame.
4) You need to be able to give a balanced symbol equation for the complete combustion of a simple hydrocarbon fuel when you're given its molecular formula. It's pretty easy — here's an example:

Lots of CO_2 isn't ideal, but the alternatives are worse (see below).

$$CH_4 + 2O_2 \rightarrow 2H_2O + CO_2 \text{ (+ energy)}$$

You've just got to make sure you end up with the same number of Cs, Hs and Os on either side of the arrow.

You can show a fuel burns to give CO_2 and H_2O...

The water pump draws gases from the burning hexane through the apparatus. Water collects inside the cooled U-tube and you can show that it's water by checking its boiling point. The limewater turns milky, showing that carbon dioxide is present.

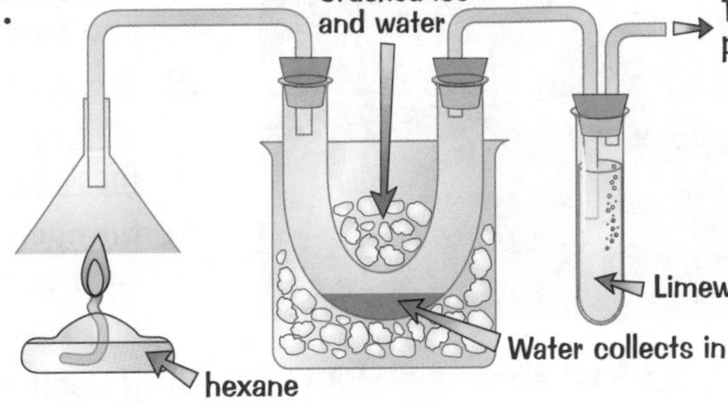

Incomplete Combustion of Hydrocarbons is NOT Safe

1) If there isn't enough oxygen the combustion will be incomplete. This gives carbon monoxide and carbon as waste products, and produces a smoky yellow flame.

hydrocarbon + oxygen ⟹ carbon dioxide + water + carbon monoxide + carbon (+ energy)

2) The carbon monoxide is a colourless, odourless and poisonous gas and it's very dangerous. Every year people are killed while they sleep due to faulty gas fires and boilers filling the room with deadly carbon monoxide (CO) and nobody realising — this is why it's important to regularly service gas appliances. The black carbon given off produces sooty marks — a clue that the fuel is not burning fully.
3) So basically, you want lots of oxygen when you're burning fuel — you get more heat energy given out, and you don't get any messy soot or poisonous gases.

You need to be able to write a balanced symbol equation for incomplete combustion too, e.g.

$$4CH_4 + 6O_2 \rightarrow C + 2CO + CO_2 + 8H_2O \text{ (+ energy)}$$

This is just one possibility. The products depend on the quantity of the reactants present...

... E.g. you could also have: $2CH_4 + 3O_2 \rightarrow 2CO + 4H_2O$ — the important thing is that the equation is balanced.

Blue flame good, yellow flame bad...

This is why people should get their gas appliances serviced every year, and get carbon monoxide detectors fitted. Carbon monoxide really can kill people in their sleep — scary stuff. Don't let that scare you off from learning everything that's on this page — any of it could come up in the exam.

The Evolution of the Atmosphere

The atmosphere wasn't always like it is today. It's gradually evolved over billions of years and we have evolved with it. All very slowly. Here's one theory for how the first 4.5 billion years have gone:

Phase 1 — Volcanoes Gave Out Steam and CO_2

1) The Earth's surface was originally molten for many millions of years. Any atmosphere boiled away.
2) Eventually it cooled and a thin crust formed, but volcanoes kept erupting, releasing gases from inside the Earth. This 'degassing' released mainly carbon dioxide, but also steam and ammonia.
3) When things eventually settled down, the early atmosphere was mostly CO_2 and water vapour (the water vapour later condensed to form the oceans). There was very little oxygen.

Holiday report: Not a nice place to be. Take strong walking boots and a good coat.

Phase 2 — Green Plants Evolved and Produced Oxygen

Holiday Report: A bit slimy underfoot. Take wellies and a lot of suncream.

1) A lot of the early CO_2 dissolved into the oceans.
2) Green plants evolved over most of the Earth. As they photosynthesised, they removed CO_2 and produced O_2.
3) Thanks to the plants the amount of O_2 in the air gradually built up and much of the CO_2 eventually got locked up in fossil fuels and sedimentary rocks (more about this on p.49).
4) Nitrogen gas (N_2) was put into the atmosphere in two ways — it was formed by ammonia reacting with oxygen, and was released by denitrifying bacteria.
5) N_2 isn't very reactive. So the amount of N_2 in the atmosphere increased, because it was being made but not broken down.

Phase 3 — Ozone Layer Allows Evolution of Complex Animals

1) The build-up of oxygen in the atmosphere killed off early organisms that couldn't tolerate it.
2) But it did allow the evolution of more complex organisms that made use of the oxygen.
3) The oxygen also created the ozone layer (O_3), which blocked harmful rays from the Sun and enabled even more complex organisms to evolve.
4) There is virtually no CO_2 left now.

Holiday report: A nice place to be. Get there before the crowds ruin it.

Today's Atmosphere is Just Right for Us

The present composition of Earth's atmosphere is:

78% nitrogen, 21% oxygen and 0.035% carbon dioxide

There are also: 1) Varying amounts of water vapour,
2) And noble gases (mainly argon).

4 billion years ago, it was a whole other world...

It's amazing how much the atmosphere of Planet Earth has changed. The climate change that we're all talking about nowadays is small beer in comparison (though it's massively important to us of course).

The Carbon Cycle

There's a scientific consensus that human activities are changing the proportion of carbon dioxide in the atmosphere — and that that's going to have massive effects on life on Earth. You need to understand the science behind the scary headlines, and to do that you first need to understand the carbon cycle.

Carbon is Constantly Being Recycled

Carbon is the key to the greenhouse effect — it exists in the atmosphere as carbon dioxide gas, and is also present in many other greenhouse gases (e.g. methane).

1) The carbon on Earth moves in a big cycle — the diagram below is a pretty good summary.
2) Respiration, combustion and decay of plants and animals add carbon dioxide to the air and remove oxygen.
3) Photosynthesis does the opposite — it removes carbon dioxide and adds oxygen.
4) These processes should all balance out. However, humans have upset the natural carbon cycle, which has affected the balance of gases in the atmosphere.

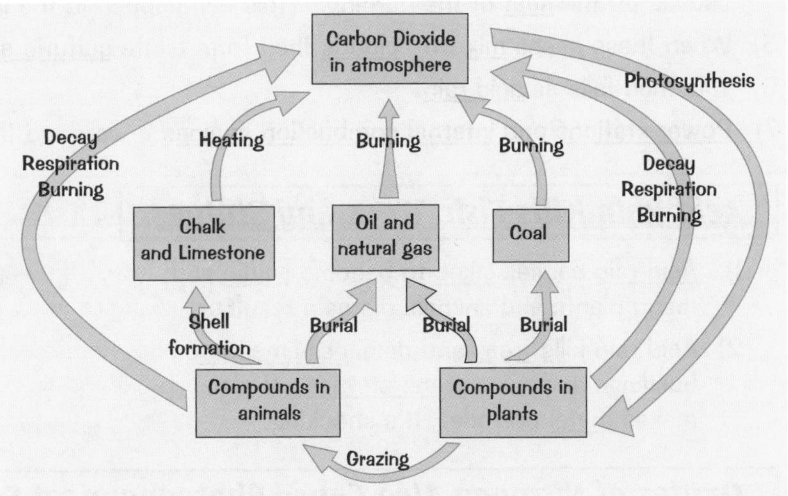

Human Activity Affects the Composition of Air

1) The human population is increasing. This means there are more people respiring — giving out more carbon dioxide. But that's not the half of it...
2) More people means that more energy is needed for lighting, heating, cooking, transport and so on. And people's lifestyles are changing too. More and more countries are becoming industrialised and well-off. This means the average energy demand per person is also increasing (since people have more electrical gadgets at home, more people have cars, and more people travel on planes, etc.).
   This increased energy consumption comes mainly from the burning of fossil fuels, which releases more carbon dioxide.

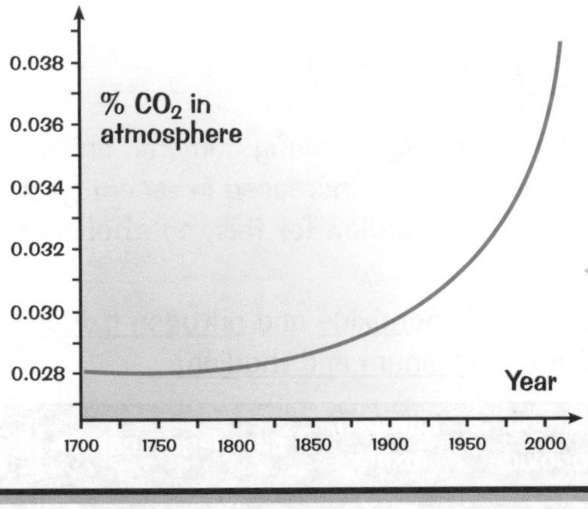

3) More people also means more land is needed to build houses and grow food. This space is often made by chopping down trees — this is called deforestation. But plants are the main things taking carbon dioxide out of the atmosphere (as they photosynthesise) — so fewer plants means less carbon dioxide is taken out of the atmosphere.
4) The graph shows how CO_2 levels in the atmosphere have risen over the last 150 years.

Eeeek — the carbon cycle's got a puncture...

For each person on a one-way flight from London to New York, a whopping 600 kg of carbon dioxide is added to the air. If you feel bad about the amount of carbon dioxide that flying off on your holidays releases, you can balance it by paying for trees to be planted. There are companies that'll tell you just how many trees need to be planted to balance the carbon dioxide released by your flight.

Air Pollution and Acid Rain

Increasing carbon dioxide is causing climate change. But CO_2 isn't the only gas released when fossil fuels burn — you also get other nasties like oxides of nitrogen, sulfur dioxide and carbon monoxide.

Acid Rain is Caused by Sulfur Dioxide and Oxides of Nitrogen

1) When fossil fuels are burned they release mostly CO_2 (a big cause of global warming).
2) But they also release other harmful gases — especially sulfur dioxide and various nitrogen oxides.
3) The sulfur dioxide (SO_2) comes from sulfur impurities in the fossil fuels.
4) However, the nitrogen oxides are created from a reaction between the nitrogen and oxygen in the air, caused by the heat of the burning. (This can happen in the internal combustion engines of cars.)
5) When these gases mix with clouds they form dilute sulfuric acid and dilute nitric acid.
6) This then falls as acid rain.
7) Power stations and internal combustion engines in cars are the main causes of acid rain.

Acid Rain Kills Fish, Trees and Statues

1) Acid rain causes lakes to become acidic and many plants and animals die as a result.
2) Acid rain kills trees and damages limestone buildings and ruins stone statues. It also makes metal corrode. It's shocking.

Oxides of Nitrogen Also Cause Photochemical Smog

Photochemical smog is a type of air pollution caused by sunlight acting on oxides of nitrogen.
These oxides combine with oxygen in the air to produce ozone (O_3).
Ozone can cause breathing difficulties, headaches and tiredness.
(Don't confuse ground-level ozone with the useful ozone layer high up in the atmosphere.)

Carbon Monoxide is a Poisonous Gas

1) Carbon monoxide (CO) can stop your blood doing its proper job of carrying oxygen around the body.
2) A lack of oxygen in the blood can lead to fainting, a coma or even death.
3) Carbon monoxide is formed when petrol or diesel in car engines is burnt without enough oxygen — this is incomplete combustion (see page 47 for more details).

It's Important That Atmospheric Pollution is Controlled

1) The build-up of all these pollutants can make life unhealthy and miserable for many humans, animals and plants. The number of cases of respiratory illnesses (e.g. asthma) has increased in recent years — especially among young people. Many people blame atmospheric pollution for this, so efforts are being made to improve things.
2) Catalytic converters on motor vehicles reduce the amount of carbon monoxide and nitrogen oxides getting into the atmosphere. The catalyst is normally a mixture of platinum and rhodium.

   It helps unpleasant exhaust gases from the car react to make things that are less immediately dangerous (though more CO_2 is still not exactly ideal).

$$\text{carbon monoxide} + \text{nitrogen oxide} \rightarrow \text{nitrogen} + \text{carbon dioxide}$$

$$2CO + 2NO \rightarrow N_2 + 2CO_2$$

Revision and pollution — the two bugbears of modern life...

Eeee.... cars and fossil fuels — they're nowt but trouble. But at least this topic is kind of interesting, what with its relevance to everyday life and all. Just think... you could see this kind of stuff on TV.

Revision Summary for Module C1

Okay, if you were just about to turn the page without doing these revision summary questions, then stop. What kind of an attitude is that... Is that really the way you want to live your life... running, playing and having fun... Of course not. That's right. Do the questions. It's for the best all round.

1)* A molecule has the molecular formula $CH_3(CH_2)_4CH_3$. How many H and C atoms does it contain?
2)* Write down the displayed formula for a molecule with the molecular formula C_3H_8.
3) Write down the symbol equation for magnesium reacting with oxygen.
4)* Balance this equation which shows sodium reacting with water: $Na + H_2O \rightarrow NaOH + H_2$.
5) Define the word 'hydrophobic'.
6) What is an emulsifier? Briefly explain how an emulsifier does its job.
7) Explain why we don't eat uncooked potatoes.
8) Give the word equation for the thermal decomposition of baking powder (sodium hydrogencarbonate).
9) Esterification produces an ester and water — what are the reactants?
10) Give three properties that a substance must have in order to make a good perfume.
11) A substance keeps the same volume, but changes its shape according to the container it's held in. Is it a solid, a liquid or a gas? How strong are the forces of attraction between its particles?
12) What does it mean if a liquid is said to be very volatile?
13) In salt water, what is: a) the solute, b) the solution?
14) Explain why nail varnish doesn't dissolve in water.
15) Paint is a colloid — what is a colloid?
16) How does oil paint dry?
17) What are thermochromic pigments? Give four uses for them.
18) What makes glow-in-the-dark watches glow in the dark?
19) Name the monomer that's used to make polythene.
20) Plastic bags stretch and melt easily. Are the forces between the polymer chains weak or strong?
21) Give one disadvantage of burning plastics and one disadvantage of burying them.
22) Give the general formula for an alkene containing one double bond.
23) Describe a test you can do to tell whether a particular hydrocarbon is an alkene.
24) True or false: in a fractionating column the shortest hydrocarbons leave the column at the bottom.
25) Give three ways that the properties of hydrocarbons change as they increase in size.
26) Why can small hydrocarbon molecules change state from liquid to gas more easily than big ones?
27) What is cracking used for?
28) What two conditions are needed for cracking to happen, and why?
29) Explain why the amount of fossil fuels being used is increasing all the time.
30) Explain why having few oil and gas reserves might become a problem for a country like the UK.
31) How might an oil slick harm sea birds?
32) Give four factors which affect the choice of fuel for a job.
33) Give two advantages of complete combustion over incomplete combustion.
34)* Write down a balanced symbol equation for the incomplete combustion of ethane (C_2H_6).
35) 3 billion years ago, the Earth's atmosphere was mostly CO_2. Where did this CO_2 come from?
36) Today, there's mostly O_2 and N_2 in the Earth's atmosphere. What process produced the O_2? What two processes produced the N_2?
37) Sketch and label a diagram of the carbon cycle.
38) What kind of air pollution makes limestone buildings and statues look worn?
39) Name a poisonous gas that catalytic converters help to remove from car exhausts.

* Answers on page 132.

Moving and Storing Heat

When it starts to get a bit nippy, on goes the heating to warm things up a bit.
Heating is all about the transfer of energy. Here are a few useful definitions to begin with.

Heat is a Measure of Energy

1) When a substance is heated, its particles gain kinetic energy (KE). This energy makes the particles in a gas or a liquid move around faster. In a solid, the particles vibrate more rapidly.
This is what eventually causes solids to melt and liquids to boil.
2) This energy is measured on an absolute scale. (This means it can't go lower than zero, because there's a limit to how slow particles can move.) The unit of heat energy is the joule (J).

Temperature is a Measure of Hotness

1) Temperature is a measure of the average kinetic energy of the particles in a substance.
The hotter something is, the higher its temperature, and the higher the average KE of its particles.
2) Temperature is usually measured in °C (degrees Celsius), but there are other temperature scales, like °F (degrees Fahrenheit). These are not absolute scales as they can go below zero.

Energy tends to flow from hot objects to cooler ones. E.g. warm radiators heat the cold air in your room — they'd be no use if heat didn't flow.

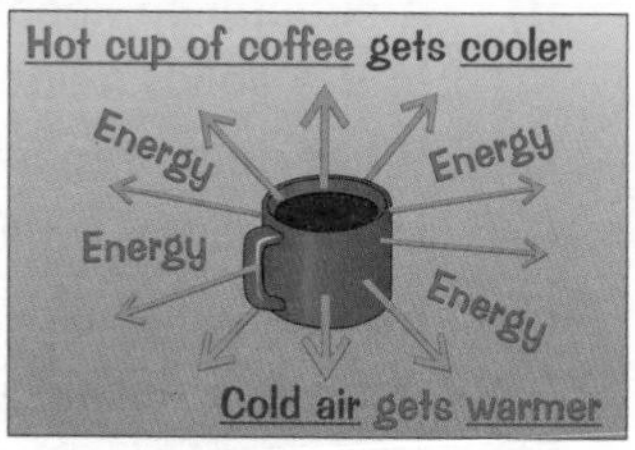

If there's a DIFFERENCE IN TEMPERATURE between two places, then ENERGY WILL FLOW between them.

The greater the difference in temperature, the faster the rate of cooling will be.
E.g. a hot cup of coffee will cool down quicker in a cold room than in a warm room.

Specific Heat Capacity Tells You How Much Energy Stuff Can Store

1) It takes more heat energy to increase the temperature of some materials than others.
E.g. you need 4200 J to warm 1 kg of water by 1 °C, but only 139 J to warm 1 kg of mercury by 1 °C.
2) Materials which need to gain lots of energy to warm up also release loads of energy when they cool down again. They can 'store' a lot of heat.
3) The measure of how much energy a substance can store is called its specific heat capacity.
4) Specific heat capacity is the amount of energy needed to raise the temperature of 1 kg of a substance by 1 °C. Water has a specific heat capacity of 4200 J/kg/°C.
5) The specific heat capacity of water is high. Once water's heated, it stores a lot of energy, which makes it good for central heating systems. Also, water's a liquid so it can easily be pumped around a building.
6) You'll have to do calculations involving specific heat capacity. This is the equation to learn:

Energy = Mass × Specific Heat Capacity × Temperature Change

EXAMPLE: How much energy is needed to heat 2 kg of water from 10 °C to 100 °C?
ANSWER: Energy needed = 2 × 4200 × 90 = 756 000 J

Flick to the inside front cover for more on formula triangles.

If you're not working out the energy, you'll have to rearrange the equation, so this formula triangle will come in dead handy.
You cover up the thing you're trying to find. The parts of the formula you can still see are what it's equal to.

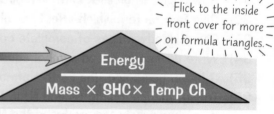

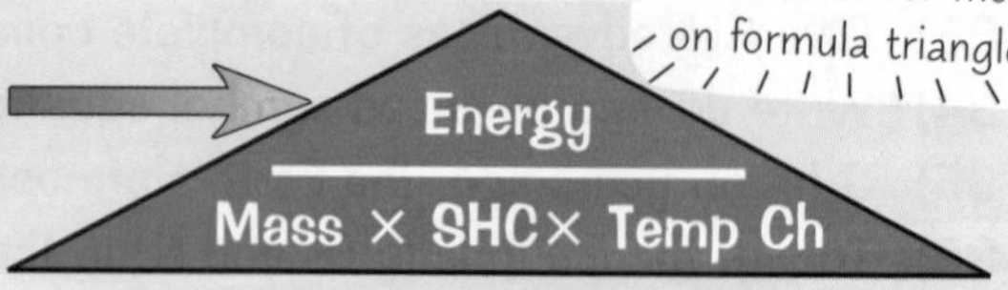

EXAMPLE: An empty 200 g aluminium kettle cools down from 115 °C to 10 °C, losing 19 068 J of heat energy. What is the specific heat capacity of aluminium?

Remember — you need to convert the mass to kilograms first.

ANSWER: $\text{SHC} = \dfrac{\text{Energy}}{\text{Mass} \times \text{Temp Change}} = \dfrac{19\,068}{0.2 \times 105} = 908\ \text{J/kg/°C}$

I wish I had a high specific fact capacity...

There are two reasons why water's used in central heating systems — it's a liquid and it has a high specific heat capacity. This makes water good for cooling systems too. Water can absorb a lot of energy and carry it away.

Melting and Boiling

If you heat up a pan of water on the stove, the water never gets any hotter than 100 °C. You can carry on heating it up, but the temperature won't rise. How come, you say? It's all to do with latent heat...

You Need to Put In Energy to Break Intermolecular Bonds

1) When you heat a liquid, the heat energy makes the particles move faster. Eventually, when enough of the particles have enough energy to overcome their attraction to each other, big bubbles of gas form in the liquid — this is boiling.
2) It's similar when you heat a solid. Heat energy makes the particles vibrate faster until eventually the forces between them are overcome and the particles start to move around — this is melting.
3) When a substance is melting or boiling, you're still putting in energy, but the energy's used for breaking intermolecular bonds rather than raising the temperature — there are flat spots on the heating graph.

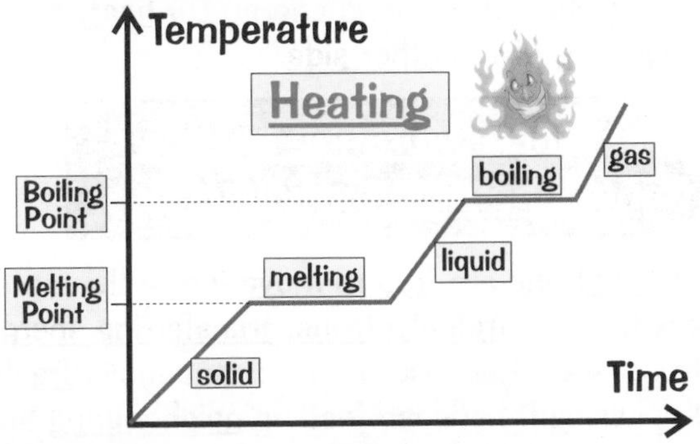

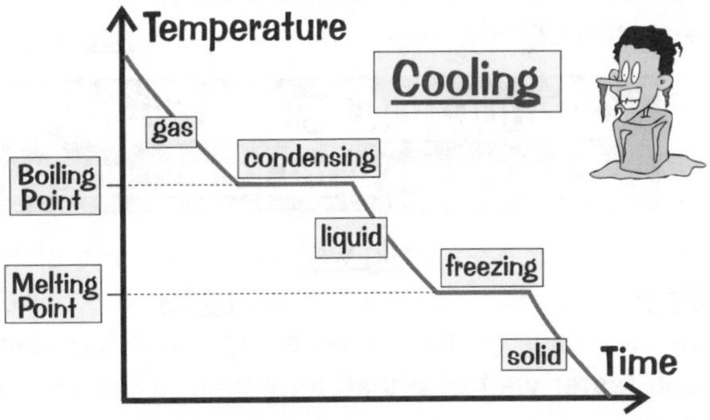

4) When a substance is condensing or freezing, bonds are forming between particles, which releases energy. This means the temperature doesn't go down until all the substance has turned into a liquid (condensing) or a solid (freezing).

Specific Latent Heat is the Energy Needed to Change State

1) The specific latent heat of melting is the amount of energy needed to melt 1 kg of material without changing its temperature (i.e. the material's got to be at its melting temperature already).
2) The specific latent heat of boiling is the energy needed to boil 1 kg of material without changing its temperature (i.e. the material's got to be at its boiling temperature already).
3) Specific latent heat is different for different materials, and it's different for boiling and melting. You don't have to remember what all the numbers are, though. Phew.
4) There's a formula to help you with all the calculations. And here it is:

Energy = Mass × Specific Latent Heat

EXAMPLE: The specific latent heat of water (for melting) is 334 000 J/kg. How much energy is needed to melt an ice cube of mass 7 g at 0 °C?

ANSWER: Energy = 0.007 × 334 000 J = 2338 J

If you're finding the mass or the specific latent heat you'll need to divide, not multiply — just to make your life a bit easier here's the formula triangle.

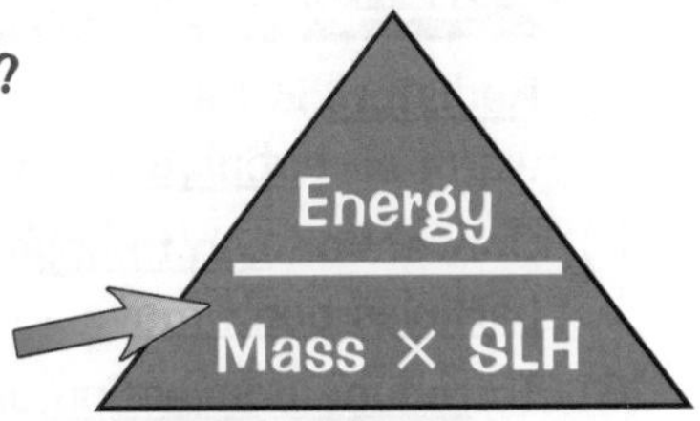

EXAMPLE: The specific latent heat of water (for boiling) is 2 260 000 J/kg. 2 825 000 J of energy is used to boil dry a pan of water at 100 °C. What was the mass of water in the pan?

ANSWER: Mass = Energy ÷ SLH = 2 825 000 ÷ 2 260 000 J = 1.25 kg

Breaking Bonds — Blofeld never quite manages it...

Melting a solid or boiling a liquid means you've got to break bonds between particles. That takes energy. Specific latent heat is just the amount of energy you need per kilogram of stuff. Incidentally, this is how sweating cools you down — your body heat's used to change liquid sweat into gas. Nice.

Conduction and Convection in the Home

If you build a house, there are regulations about doing it properly, mainly so that it doesn't fall down, but also so that it keeps the heat in. Easier said than done — there are several ways that heat is 'lost'.

Conduction Occurs Mainly in Solids

Houses lose a lot of heat through their windows even when they're shut. Heat flows from the warm inside face of the window to the cold outside face mostly by conduction.

1) In a solid, the particles are held tightly together. So when one particle vibrates, it bumps into other particles nearby and quickly passes the vibrations on.

2) Particles which vibrate faster than others pass on their extra kinetic energy to neighbouring particles. These particles then vibrate faster themselves.
3) This process continues throughout the solid and gradually the extra kinetic energy (or heat) is spread all the way through the solid. This causes a rise in temperature at the other side.

CONDUCTION OF HEAT is the process where vibrating particles pass on extra kinetic energy to neighbouring particles.

4) Metals conduct heat really well because some of their electrons are free to move inside the metal. Heating makes the electrons move faster and collide with other free electrons, transferring energy. These then pass on their extra energy to other electrons, etc. Because the electrons move freely, this is a much faster way of transferring energy than slowly passing it between jostling neighbouring atoms.
5) Most non-metals don't have free electrons, so warm up more slowly, making them good for insulating things — that's why metals are used for saucepans, but non-metals are used for saucepan handles.
6) Liquids and gases conduct heat more slowly than solids — the particles aren't held so tightly together, which prevents them bumping into each other so often. So air is a good insulator.

Convection Occurs in Liquids and Gases

1) When you heat up a liquid or gas, the particles move faster, and the fluid (liquid or gas) expands, becoming less dense.
2) The warmer, less dense fluid rises above its colder, denser surroundings, like a hot air balloon does.
3) As the warm fluid rises, cooler fluid takes its place. As this process continues, you actually end up with a circulation of fluid (convection currents). This is how immersion heaters work.

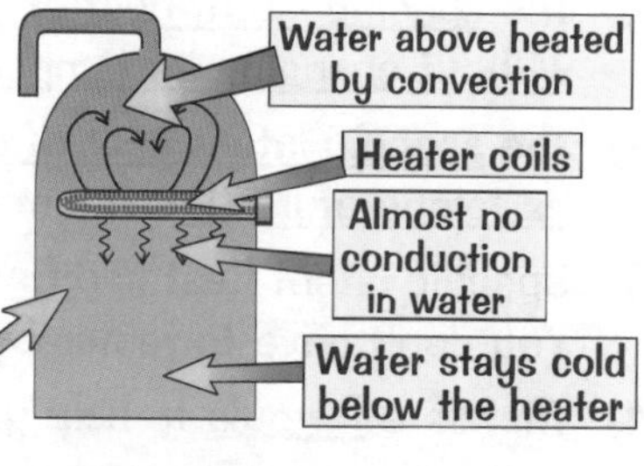

CONVECTION occurs when the more energetic particles move from the hotter region to the cooler region — and take their heat energy with them.

4) Radiators in the home rely on convection to make the warm air circulate round the room.
5) Convection can't happen in solids because the particles can't move — they just vibrate on the spot.
6) To reduce convection, you need to stop the fluid moving. Clothes, blankets and cavity wall foam insulation all work by trapping pockets of air. The air can't move so the heat has to conduct very slowly through the pockets of air, as well as the material in between.

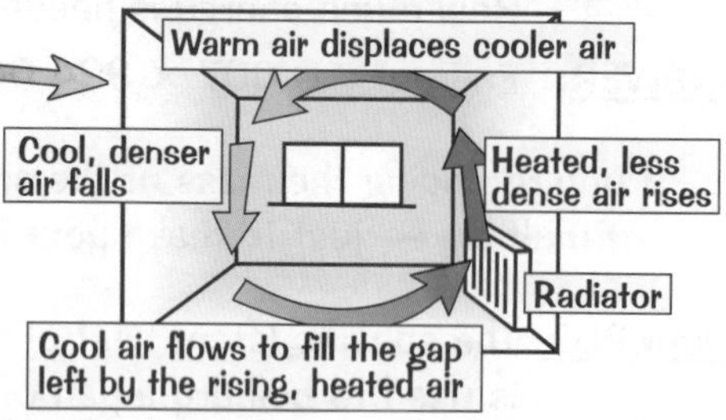

And the good old garden spade is a great example...

If a garden spade is left outside in cold weather, the metal bit will always feel colder than the wooden handle. But it isn't colder — it just conducts heat away from your hand quicker. The opposite is true if the spade is left out in the sunshine — it'll feel hotter because it conducts heat into your hand quicker.

Heat Radiation

Houses in Mediterranean countries are often painted white, to reflect heat from the Sun. In cold, cloudy Britain, we tend to leave our houses slate grey or brick red to absorb the heat. (Saves on paint, too.)

Radiation is How We Get Heat from the Sun

As well as by conduction and convection, heat can be transferred by radiation. Heat is radiated as infrared waves — these are electromagnetic waves that travel in straight lines at the speed of light (see p. 62).

Radiation is different from conduction and convection in several ways:

1) It doesn't need a medium (material) to travel through, so it can occur in a vacuum, like space. This is the only way that heat reaches us from the Sun.
2) It can only occur through transparent substances, like air, glass and water.
3) The amount of radiation emitted or absorbed by an object depends to a large extent on its surface colour and texture. This definitely isn't true for conduction and convection.

All Objects Emit and Absorb Heat Radiation

1) All objects are continually emitting and absorbing heat radiation.
2) The hotter an object gets, the more heat radiation it emits.
3) Cooler objects will absorb the heat radiation emitted by hotter things, so their temperature increases. You can feel heat radiation, for example if you're indoors and the Sun shines on you through a window.
4) Matt black surfaces are very good absorbers and emitters of radiation. You should really paint your radiators black to help emit heat radiation, but leave your fridge a nice shiny white to help reflect it.
5) Light-coloured, smooth and shiny objects are very poor absorbers and emitters of radiation. They effectively reflect heat radiation — e.g. some people put shiny foil behind their radiators to reflect radiation back into the room rather than heat up the walls.

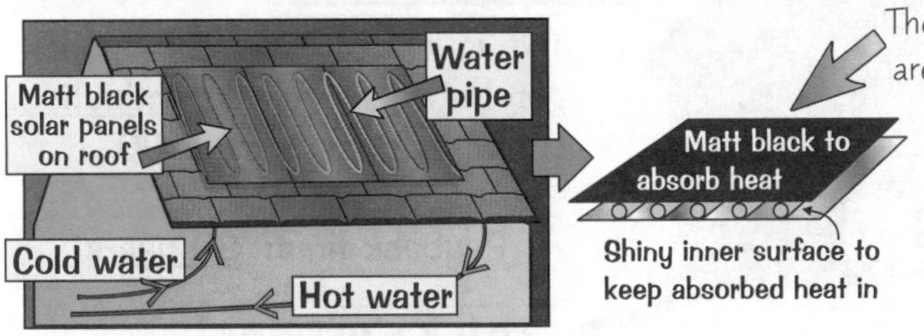

The panels for solar water heating are painted matt black to absorb as much heat as possible.

The shiny surface on a patio heater reflects heat downwards — onto the patio.

Heat Radiation is Important in Cooking

1) Grills and toasters heat food by infrared (heat) radiation. The heat radiated by a grill is absorbed by the surface particles of the food, increasing their kinetic energy. The heat energy is then conducted or convected to more central parts.
2) People often line their grill pan with shiny foil. This reflects the heat radiation back onto the bottom of the food being grilled, so the food is cooked more evenly. (It also stops the grill pan getting dirty, of course.)
3) Microwave ovens also use radiation to cook food — microwaves are electromagnetic waves that have a different wavelength to infrared (see p. 62).
4) Microwaves penetrate about 1 cm into the outer layer of food where they're absorbed by water or fat molecules, increasing their kinetic energy. The energy is then conducted or convected to other parts.
5) You don't cover food with foil in a microwave oven though — the microwaves will be reflected away so they won't cook the food, AND it can cause dangerous sparks inside the oven. It's okay to cover the food with glass or plastic though as microwaves can pass right through.

Radiate happiness — stand by the fire and smile...

The most confusing thing about radiation is that those white things on your walls called 'radiators' actually transfer most of their heat by convection, as rising warm air. They do radiate some heat too, of course, but whoever chose the name 'radiator' obviously hadn't swotted up their physics first.

Saving Energy

It's daft to keep paying for energy to heat your house only to let the heat escape straight out again.

Insulating Your House Saves Energy and Money

'Sources' can also waste energy if they're not very efficient.

1) Energy in the home is emitted and transferred (or wasted) in different areas.
2) Things that emit energy are called sources, e.g. radiators. Things that transfer and waste or lose energy are called sinks, e.g. windows and computers.
3) To save energy, you can insulate your house so the sinks 'drain' less energy, e.g. use curtains to reduce energy loss. You can also make sources and sinks more efficient, so they waste less energy, e.g. use energy-saving light bulbs instead of normal ones.
4) It costs money to buy and install insulation, or buy more efficient appliances, but it also saves you money, because your energy bills are lower.
5) Eventually, the money you've saved on energy bills will equal the initial cost — the time this takes is called the payback time.
6) If you subtract the annual saving from the initial cost repeatedly then eventually the one with the biggest annual saving must always come out as the winner, if you think about it.
7) But you might sell the house (or die) before that happens. If you look at it over, say, a five-year period then a cheap and cheerful hot water tank jacket wins over expensive double glazing.

$$\text{payback time} = \frac{\text{initial cost}}{\text{annual saving}}$$

Loft Insulation

Fibreglass 'wool' laid across the loft floor reduces conduction through the ceiling into the roof space.

Initial Cost: £200
Annual Saving: £100
Payback time: 2 years

Hot Water Tank Jacket

Reduces conduction.

Initial Cost: £60
Annual Saving: £15
Payback time: 4 years

These figures are rough. It'll vary from house to house.

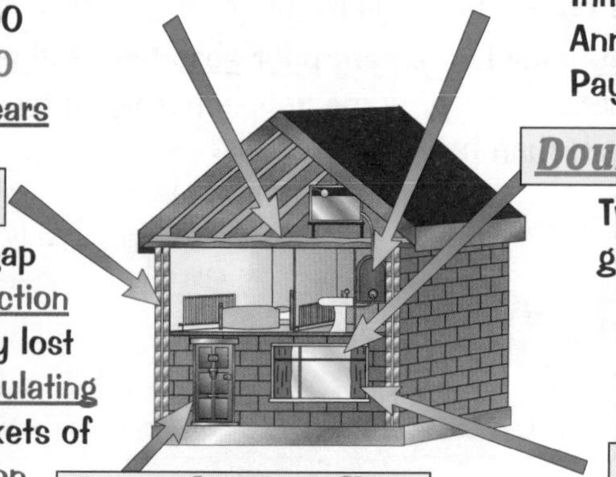

Cavity Walls & Insulation

Two layers of bricks with a gap between them reduce conduction but you still get some energy lost by convection. Squirting insulating foam into the gap traps pockets of air to minimise this convection.

Initial Cost: £150
Annual Saving: £100
Payback time: 18 months

(Heat is still lost through the walls by radiation though. Also, if there are any spaces where air is not trapped there'll still be some convection too.)

Double Glazing

Two layers of glass with an air gap between reduce conduction.

Initial Cost: £2400
Annual Saving: £80
Payback time: 30 years

Draught-proofing

Strips of foam and plastic around doors and windows stop hot air going out — reducing convection.

Initial Cost: £100
Annual Saving: £15
Payback time: 7 years

Thick Curtains

Reduce conduction and radiation through the windows.

Initial Cost: £180
Annual Saving: £20
Payback time: 9 years

Thermograms Show Where Your House is Leaking Heat

1) A thermogram is a picture taken with a thermal imaging camera.
2) Objects at different temperatures emit infrared rays of different wavelengths. The thermogram displays these temperatures as different colours. The hotter parts show up as white, yellow and red, whilst the colder parts are black, dark blue and purple. If a house looks 'hot', it's losing heat to the outside.
3) In this thermogram, the houses on the left and right are losing bucket-loads of heat out of their roofs (shown as red/yellow), but the one in the middle must have loft insulation as it's not losing half as much.

It looks like this house doesn't have any double glazing either... tut, tut.

I went to a physicist's stag night — the best man had booked a thermogram...

Insulating your house well is a really good way to save energy. Drawing the curtains is like putting on a jumper.

Efficiency

An open fire looks cosy, but a lot of its heat energy goes straight up the chimney, by convection, instead of heating up your living room. All this energy is 'wasted', so open fires aren't very efficient.

Machines Always Waste Some Energy

1) Useful machines are only useful because they convert energy from one form to another. Take cars for instance — you put in chemical energy (petrol or diesel) and the engine converts it into kinetic (movement) energy.

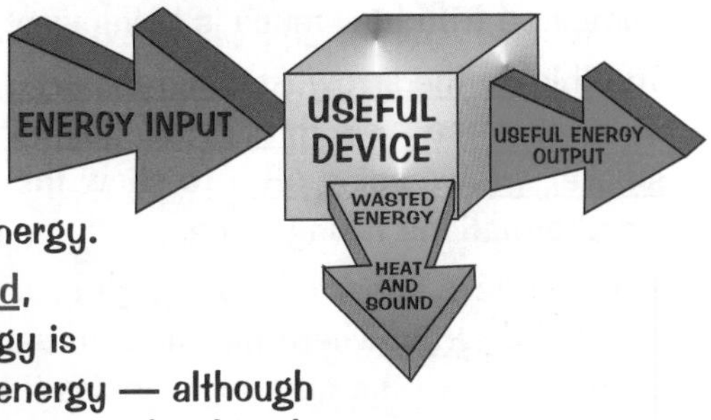

2) The total energy output is always the same as the energy input, but only some of the output energy is useful. So for every joule of chemical energy you put into your car you'll only get a fraction of it converted into useful kinetic energy.
3) This is because some of the input energy is always lost or wasted, often as heat. In the car example, the rest of the chemical energy is converted (mostly) into heat and sound energy. This is wasted energy — although you could always stick your dinner under the bonnet and warm it up on the drive home.
4) The less energy that is wasted, the more efficient the device is said to be.

More Efficient Machines Waste Less Energy

The efficiency of a machine is defined as:

$$\text{Efficiency} = \frac{\text{USEFUL Energy OUTPUT}}{\text{TOTAL Energy INPUT}} \ (\times 100\%)$$

1) To work out the efficiency of a machine, first find out the Total Energy INPUT. This is the energy supplied to the machine.
2) Then find how much useful energy the machine delivers — the Useful Energy OUTPUT. The question might tell you this directly, or it might tell you how much energy is wasted as heat/sound.
3) Then just divide the smaller number by the bigger one to get a value for efficiency somewhere between 0 and 1. Easy. If your number is bigger than 1, you've done the division upside down.

Electric kettle

180 000 J of electrical energy supplied

9000 J of heat given out to the room

Think about it!

$$\text{Efficiency} = \frac{\text{Useful En. Out}}{\text{Total En. In}} = \frac{171\,000}{180\,000} = 0.95$$

4) You can convert the efficiency to a percentage, by multiplying it by 100. E.g. 0.6 = 60%.
5) In the exam you might be told the efficiency and asked to work out the total energy input, the useful energy output or the energy wasted. So you need to be able to rearrange the formula.

EXAMPLE: An ordinary light bulb is 5% efficient. If 1000 J of light energy is given out, how much energy is wasted?

ANSWER: $\text{Total Input} = \frac{\text{Useful Output}}{\text{Efficiency}} = \frac{1000\text{ J}}{0.05} = 20\,000\text{ J}$,

so Energy Wasted = 20 000 − 1000 = 19 000 J

Shockingly inefficient, those ordinary light bulbs. Low-energy light bulbs are roughly 4 times more efficient, and last about 8 times as long. They're more expensive though.

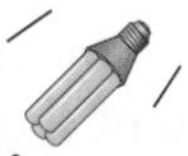
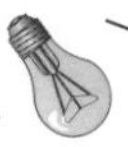

6) You can use information like this to draw a Sankey diagram, or use the equation to work out the efficiency of something from a Sankey diagram — coming up on the next page.

Efficiency = pages learned ÷ cups of tea made...

Some new appliances (like washing machines and fridges) come with a sticker with a letter from A to H on, to show how energy-efficient they are. A really well-insulated fridge might have an 'A' rating. But if you put it right next to the oven, or never defrost it, it will run much less efficiently than it should.

Sankey Diagrams

This is another opportunity for a MATHS question. Fantastic.
So best prepare yourself — here's what those Sankey diagrams are all about...

The Thickness of the Arrow Represents the Amount of Energy

Sankey diagrams are just energy transformation diagrams — they make it easy to see at a glance how much of the input energy is being usefully employed compared with how much is being wasted.

The thicker the arrow, the more energy it represents — so you see a big thick arrow going in, then several smaller arrows going off it to show the different energy transformations taking place.

You can have either a little sketch or a properly detailed diagram where the width of each arrow is proportional to the number of joules it represents.

Example —TV:

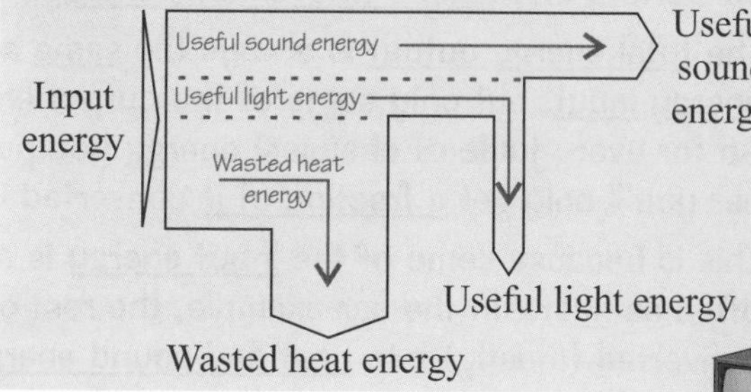

EXAMPLE — SANKEY DIAGRAM FOR A SIMPLE MOTOR:

HERE'S THE SKETCH VERSION:

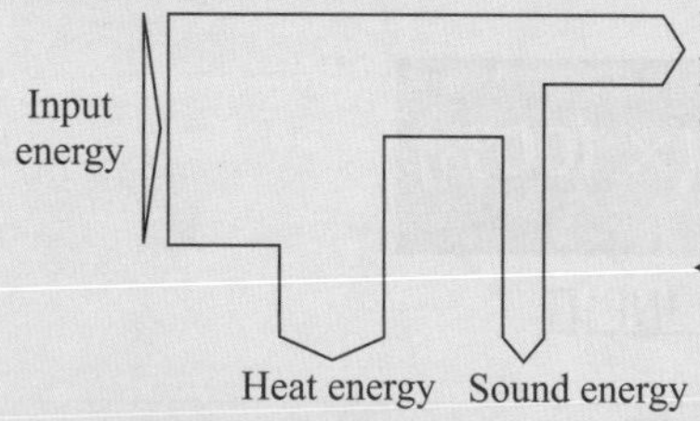

You don't know the actual amounts, but you can see that most of the energy is being wasted, and that it's mostly wasted as heat.

EXAM QUESTIONS:
With sketches, they're likely to ask you to compare two different devices and say which is more efficient. You generally want to be looking for the one with the thickest useful energy arrow(s).

AND HERE'S THE DETAILED ONE:

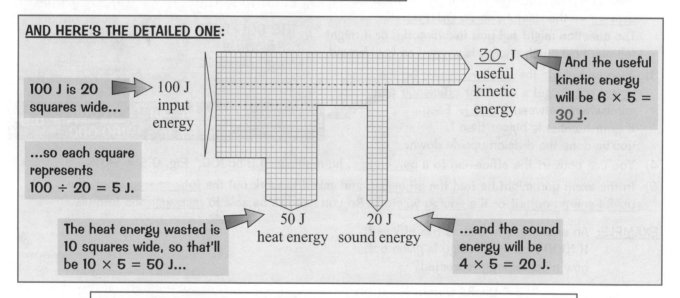

100 J is 20 squares wide...

...so each square represents 100 ÷ 20 = 5 J.

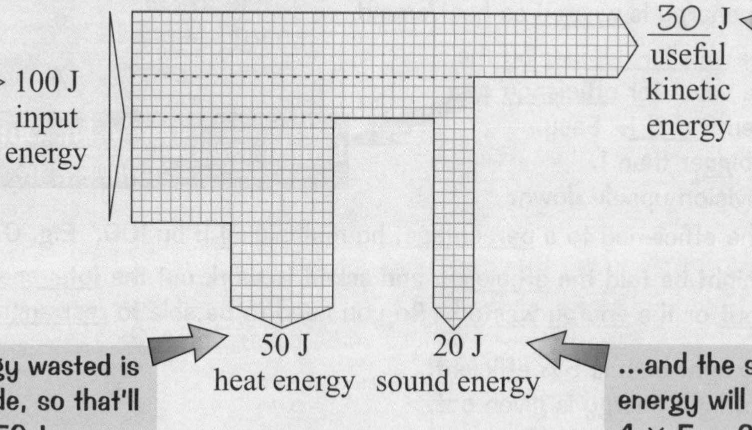

And the useful kinetic energy will be 6 × 5 = 30 J.

The heat energy wasted is 10 squares wide, so that'll be 10 × 5 = 50 J...

...and the sound energy will be 4 × 5 = 20 J.

EXAM QUESTIONS:
In an exam, the most likely question you'll get about detailed Sankey diagrams is filling in one of the numbers or calculating the efficiency. The efficiency is straightforward enough if you can work out the numbers (see p. 57).

Skankey diagrams — to represent the smelliness of your socks...

If they ask you to draw your own Sankey diagram in the exam, and don't give you the figures, a sketch is all they'll expect. Just give a rough idea of where the energy goes. E.g. a filament lamp turns most of the input energy into heat, and only a tiny proportion goes to useful light energy.

Wave Basics

Think about a toaster that glows when it heats up. It emits infrared radiation (heat) and a reddish light. You could conclude that heat and light must be similar forms of radiation — you'd be right. They're both electromagnetic waves, but before we move on to them, let's start with some wave basics.

Waves Have Amplitude, Wavelength and Frequency

Waves have certain features:

1) The amplitude is the displacement from the rest position to the crest. (NOT from a trough to a crest)
2) The wavelength is the length of a full cycle of the wave, e.g. from crest to crest.
3) Frequency is the number of complete cycles or oscillations passing a certain point per second. Frequency is measured in hertz (Hz). 1 Hz is 1 wave per second.

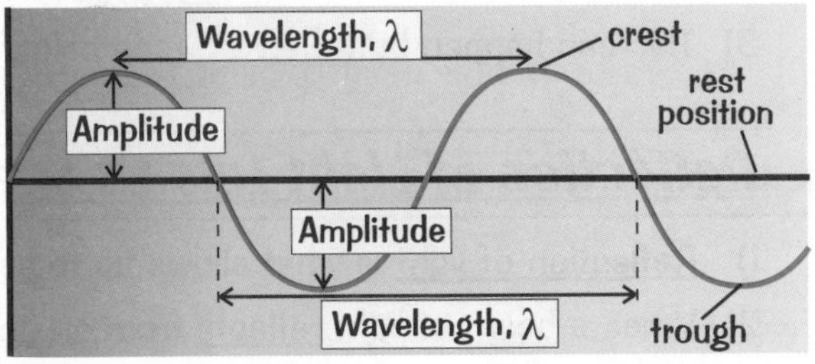

Wave Speed = Frequency × Wavelength

You need to learn how to use his equation:

Speed (m/s) = Frequency (Hz) × Wavelength (m)   OR $v = f\lambda$

Speed (v is for velocity)
Wavelength (that's the Greek letter 'lambda')
Frequency

EXAMPLE Eva is building a sandcastle. She estimates that 1 wave passes her sandcastle every 2 seconds, and that the crests of the waves are 90 cm apart. Calculate the speed, in metres per second, of the waves passing Eva's sandcastle.

In one second, half a wave passes, so the frequency is 0.5 Hz (hertz).

ANSWER: Speed = 0.5 × 0.90 = 0.45 m/s (Remember to change the 90 cm into metres first.)

You might be asked to calculate the frequency or wavelength instead of the speed though, so you need the good old triangle too...

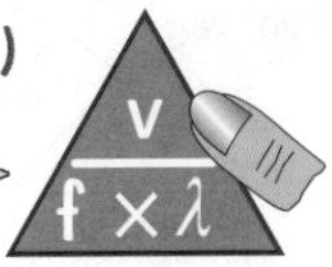

You Need to Convert Your Units First

1) The standard (SI) units involved in wave equations are: metres, seconds, m/s and hertz (Hz). Always CONVERT INTO SI UNITS (m, s, m/s, Hz) before you work anything out.
2) The trouble is waves often have high frequencies given in kHz or MHz, so make sure you learn this too:

1 kHz (kilohertz) = 1000 Hz   1 MHz (1 megahertz) = 1 000 000 Hz

3) Wavelengths can also be given in other units, e.g. km for long-wave radio.
4) There's worse still: The speed of light is 3×10^8 m/s = 300 000 000 m/s. This, along with numbers like 900 MHz = 900 000 000 Hz won't fit into some calculators. That leaves you three choices:
   1) Enter the numbers as standard form. For example, to enter 3×10^8, press [3] [EXP] [8].
   (Your calculator might have a different button for standard form — if you don't know what it is, find out...)
   2) Cancel three or six noughts off both numbers (so long as you're dividing them!) or...
   3) Do it entirely without a calculator (no really, I've seen it done).

EXAMPLE: A radio wave has a frequency of 92.2 MHz. Find its wavelength. (The speed of all EM waves is 3×10^8 m/s.)

ANSWER: You're trying to find λ using f and v, so you've got to rearrange the equation.
You need to convert the frequency into the SI unit, Hz: 92.2 MHz = 92 200 000 Hz
So $\lambda = v \div f = 3 \times 10^8 \div 92\ 200\ 000 = 3 \times 10^8 \div 9.22 \times 10^7 = 3.25$ m

It's probably easiest to use standard form here.

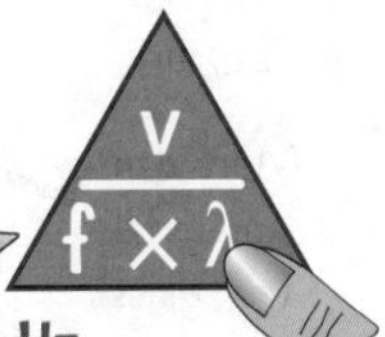

This stuff on formulas is really painful — I mean it MHz...

Yep, there's a helluva lot of maths on this page. Make sure you get your head around all the definitions too.

Wave Properties

Now you know the basics, let's have a look at some wave properties...

All Waves Can be Reflected, Refracted and Diffracted

1) Waves travel in a straight line through whatever substance they're travelling in.
2) When waves arrive at an obstacle (or meet a new material), their direction of travel can be changed.
3) This can happen by reflection (see below) or by refraction or diffraction (see next page).

Reflection of Light Lets Us See Things

1) Reflection of light is what allows us to see objects. Light bounces off them into our eyes.
2) When a beam of light reflects from an uneven surface such as a piece of paper, the light reflects off at different angles.
3) When it reflects from an even surface (smooth and shiny like a plane mirror) then it's all reflected at the same angle and you get a clear reflection.
4) The LAW OF REFLECTION applies to every reflected ray:

The normal is an imaginary line that's perpendicular (at right angles) to the surface at the point of incidence (where the light hits the surface).

Angle of INCIDENCE = Angle of REFLECTION

Note that these two angles are ALWAYS defined between the ray itself and the NORMAL, dotted below. Don't ever label them as the angle between the ray and the surface. Definitely uncool.

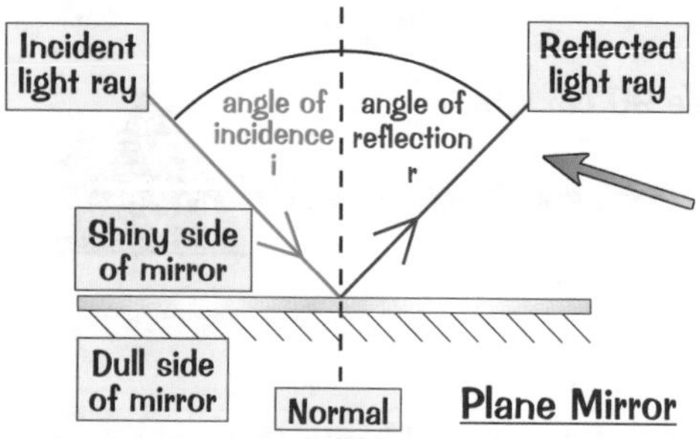

Plane Mirror

You have to know how to use ray diagrams like these two to show reflection. Just remember to draw in the normal first, then the incident and reflected rays at the same angle either side of this. Use a ruler.

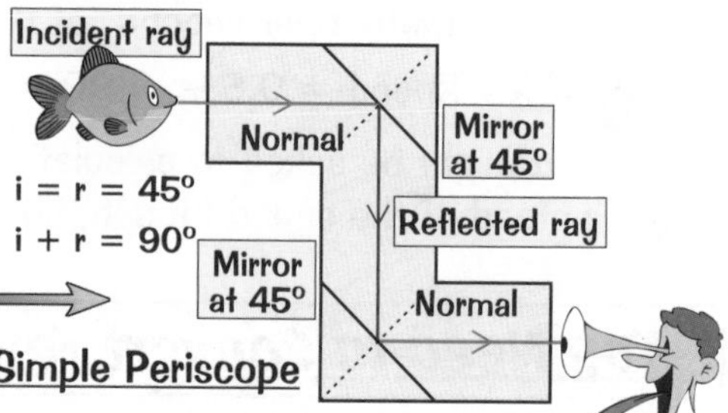

Simple Periscope

Total Internal Reflection Depends on the Critical Angle

1) A wave hitting a surface can experience total internal reflection. This can only happen when the light ray travels through a dense material like glass, water or Perspex® towards a less dense substance like air.
2) If the angle of incidence is big enough, the ray doesn't come out at all, but reflects back into the material.
3) Big enough means bigger than the critical angle for that particular material — every material has its own, different critical angle.

If the angle of incidence is...

...LESS than the Critical Angle:

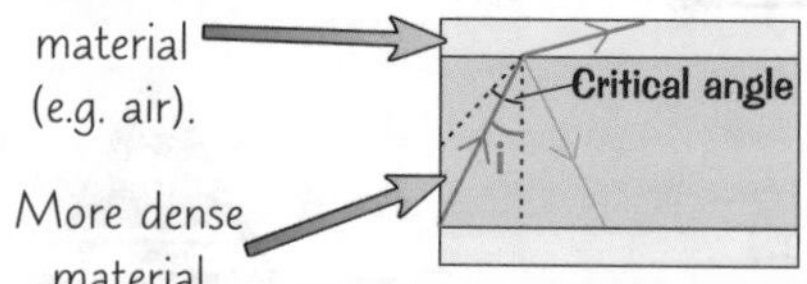

Most of the light is refracted into the outer layer, but some of it is internally reflected.

...EQUAL to the Critical Angle:

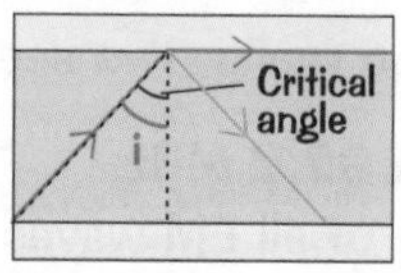

The ray would go along the surface (with quite a bit of internal reflection as well).

...GREATER than the Critical Angle:

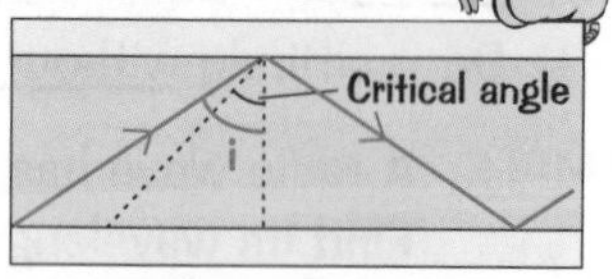

No light comes out. It's all internally reflected, i.e. total internal reflection.

Plane mirrors — what pilots use to look behind them...

This stuff on reflection ain't too complicated — and it's easy marks in the exam. Make sure you can scribble down some nice, clear ray diagrams and you should be well on your way to a great mark. Don't forget your ruler.

Diffraction and Refraction

If you thought reflection was good, you'll just love diffraction and refraction — it's awesome. If you didn't find reflection interesting then I'm afraid it's tough luck — you need to know about all three of them. Sorry.

Diffraction — Waves Spreading Out

1) All waves spread out ('diffract') at the edges when they pass through a gap or pass an object.
2) The amount of diffraction depends on the size of the gap relative to the wavelength of the wave. The narrower the gap, or the longer the wavelength, the more the wave spreads out.
3) A narrow gap is one about the same size as the wavelength of the wave. So whether a gap counts as narrow or not depends on the wave.
4) Light has a very small wavelength (about 0.0005 mm), so it can be diffracted but it needs a really small gap.
5) This means you can hear someone through an open door even if you can't see them, because the size of the gap and the wavelength of sound are roughly equal, causing the sound wave to diffract and fill the room...
6) ...But you can't see them unless you're directly facing the door because the gap is about a million times bigger than the wavelength of light, so it won't diffract enough.
7) If a gap is about the same size as the wavelength of a light, you can get a diffraction pattern of light and dark fringes, as shown here.

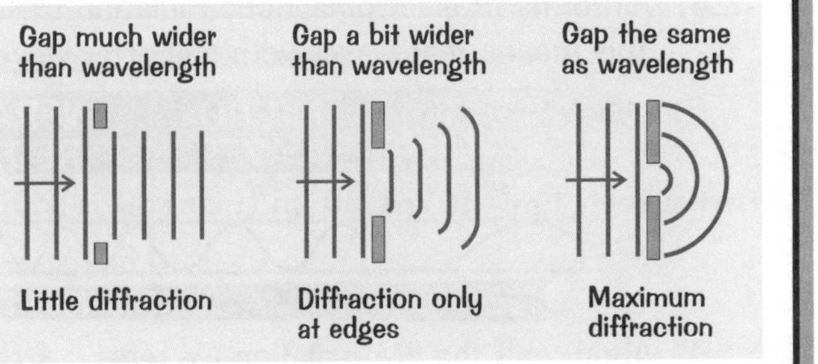

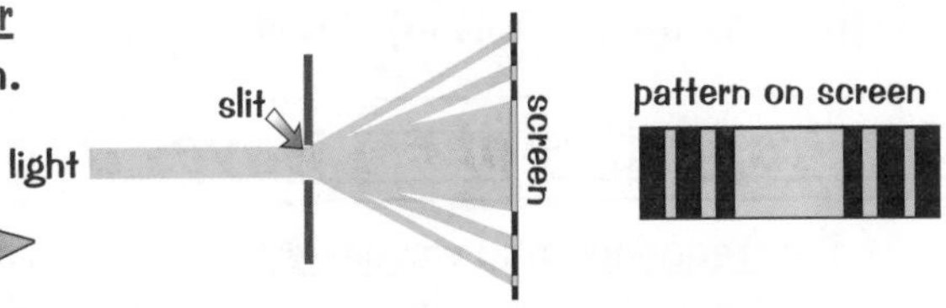

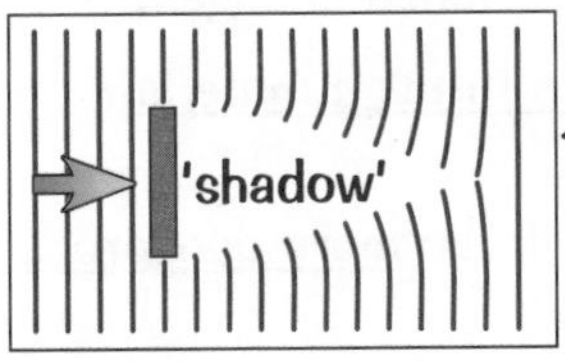

8) You get diffraction around the edges of obstacles too. The shadow is where the wave is blocked. The wider the obstacle compared to the wavelength, the less diffraction it causes, so the longer the shadow.

Refraction — Changing the Speed of a Wave Can Change its Direction

1) Waves travel at different speeds in substances which have different densities. So when a wave crosses a boundary between two substances (from glass to air, say) it changes speed:

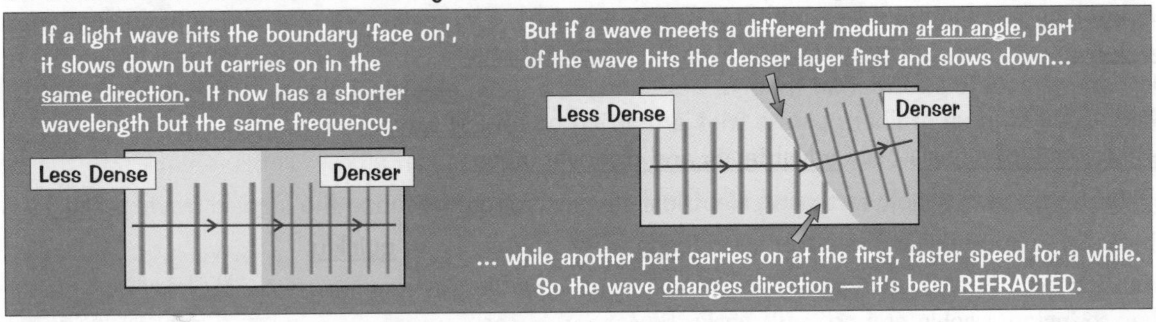

If a light wave hits the boundary 'face on', it slows down but carries on in the same direction. It now has a shorter wavelength but the same frequency.
Less Dense
Denser
But if a wave meets a different medium at an angle, part of the wave hits the denser layer first and slows down...
Less Dense
Denser
... while another part carries on at the first, faster speed for a while. So the wave changes direction — it's been REFRACTED.

2) E.g. when light passes from air into the glass of a window pane (a denser medium), it slows down — causing the light to refract towards the normal. When the light reaches the 'glass to air' boundary on the other side of the window, it speeds up and refracts away from the normal.
3) Waves are only refracted if they meet a new medium at an angle. If they're travelling along the normal (i.e. the angle of incidence is zero) they will change speed, but are NOT refracted — they don't change direction.

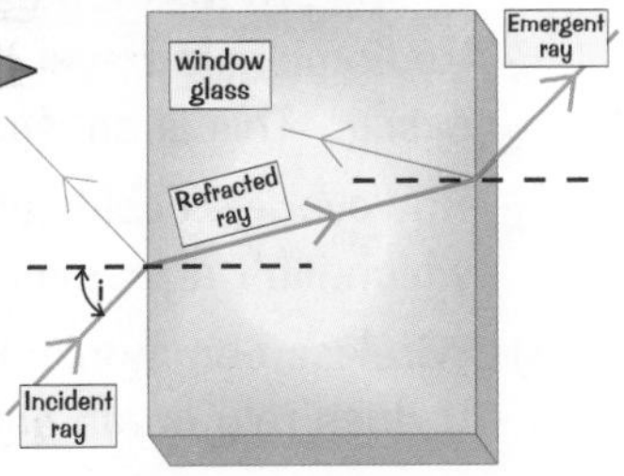

Lights, camera, refraction...

Remember that all waves can be diffracted. It doesn't matter what type of wave it is — sound, light, water... The key point to remember about refraction is that the wave has to meet a boundary at an angle.

EM Waves and Communication

Waves are brilliant. There is no end to the things you can do with a wave.
So let's have a closer look at those electromagnetic waves and marvel at their awesomeness...

There are Seven Types of Electromagnetic (EM) Waves

1) Electromagnetic radiation can occur at many different wavelengths.
2) In fact, there is a continuous spectrum of different wavelengths, but waves with similar wavelengths tend to have similar properties.
3) Electromagnetic radiation is conventionally split into seven types of waves — see below.
4) All forms of electromagnetic radiation travel at the same speed through a vacuum. This means that waves with a shorter wavelength have a higher frequency.

	RADIO WAVES	MICRO WAVES	INFRA RED	VISIBLE LIGHT	ULTRA VIOLET	X-RAYS	GAMMA RAYS
Wavelength →	1 m – 10^4 m	10^{-2} m (1 cm)	10^{-5} m (0.01 mm)	10^{-7} m	10^{-8} m	10^{-10} m	10^{-12} m

INCREASING FREQUENCY AND DECREASING WAVELENGTH →

5) About half the EM radiation we receive from the Sun is visible light. Most of the rest is infrared (heat), with some UV (ultraviolet) thrown in. UV is what gives us a suntan (see page 71).

The Properties of EM Waves Depend on Frequency and Wavelength

1) As the frequency and wavelength of EM radiation changes, its interaction with matter changes — i.e. the way a wave is absorbed, reflected or transmitted by any given substance changes.
2) As a rule, the EM waves at each end of the spectrum tend to be able to pass through material, whilst those nearer the middle are absorbed.
3) Also, the ones with higher frequency (shorter wavelength), like X-rays, tend to be more dangerous to living cells. That's because they have more energy.
4) When any EM radiation is absorbed it can cause heating and ionisation (if the frequency is high enough). Ionisation is where an atom or molecule either loses or gains electrons and it can be dangerous.

Different Sorts of Signals have Different Advantages

As well as cooking our food and keeping us warm (see p. 55), EM waves are used for communication. E.g. radio waves are used for radio, microwaves for mobile phones etc. — see the next few pages for more. Before you communicate information though, it's changed into an electrical signal, which is then sent off on its own (like you get in an ordinary phone line) or carried on an EM wave (see p. 70).
The different types of signals have advantages and disadvantages:

1) Using light (see next page), radio and electrical signals is great because the signals travel really fast.
2) Electrical wires and optical fibres can carry loads of information very quickly.
3) Information sent through optical fibres and electrical wires is pretty secure — they're inside a cable and so can't easily be tapped in to. Radio signals travel through the air, so they can be intercepted more easily. This is an issue for people using wireless internet networks.
4) However — cables can be difficult to repair if they get broken, which isn't a problem for wireless methods.
5) Wireless communication also has the advantage that it is portable (e.g. mobile phones, laptop wi-fi etc.). It does rely on an aerial to pick up a signal though, and signal strength often depends on location.

Wireless just means without wires — usually using radio and microwaves but infrared and light can be used too. TV, radio, mobile phones and computers all use wireless technology.

Where would Chris Moyles be without EM waves — I ask you...

In 1588, beacons were used on the south coast of England to relay the information that the Spanish Armada was approaching. As we know, light travels as electromagnetic waves, so this is an early example of transferring information using electromagnetic radiation — or wireless communication.

Communicating with Light

Light's a very useful wave for communicating — you can only read this book because it's reflecting light rays. But this page is really about using light to communicate over longer distances or in awkward places.

Communicating with Light Can Require a Code

1) Historically, light was used to speed up communication over long distances.
2) By creating a code of 'on-off' signals, a message could be relayed between stations far away, by flashing a light on and off in a way that could be decoded.
3) This is the principle behind the Morse code.
4) Each letter of the alphabet (and each number 0-9) is represented by a sequence of 'dots' and 'dashes' — which are pulses of light (or sound) that last for a certain length of time.
5) E.g. in the International Morse Code, the distress signal 'SOS' would be transmitted as · · · — — — · · · which is three short pulses of light, followed by three long pulses and then another three short.
6) The Morse code is a type of digital signal (see p. 70) because the light pulse is only either 'on' or 'off'.

Some letters from the International Morse Code are shown here:

A · — M — —
E · S · · ·
O — — — W · — —

E.g. the word 'awesome' is:
· — · — — · · · · — — — — — ·

Light Signals Can Travel Through Optical Fibres

Optical fibres can also be called fibre optics.

1) A more modern use of light for communication is the use of optical fibres, which can carry data over long distances as pulses of light or infrared radiation (see p. 65).
2) They work by bouncing waves off the sides of a very narrow core which is protected by outer layers.
3) The ray of light enters the fibre so that it hits the boundary between the core and the outer cladding at an angle greater than the critical angle for the material. This causes total internal reflection of the ray within the core (see page 60).
4) The pulse of light enters at one end and is reflected again and again until it emerges at the other end.
5) Optical fibres are increasingly being used for telephone and broadband internet cables, replacing the old electrical ones. They're also used for medical purposes — to 'see inside' the body without having to operate. You'll probably know them best though as the things that give us twinkly lights at the ends of the branches of artificial Christmas trees... yey, Christmas.

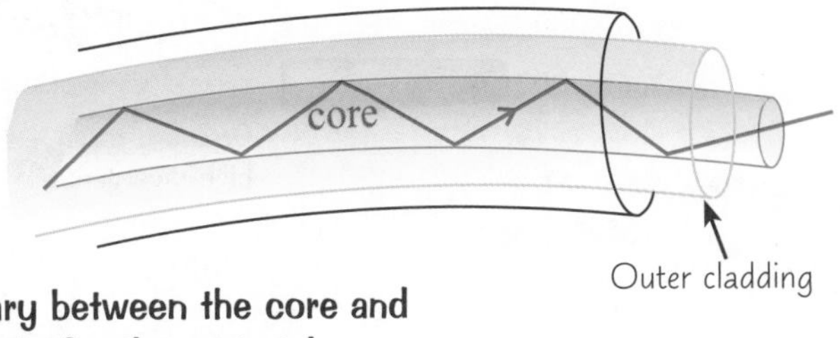

Using Light has lots of Advantages

1) Using light is a very quick way to communicate. In a vacuum, light travels at 300 000 000 m/s — it can't travel that fast through optical fibres (it's slowed down by about 30%) but it's still pretty quick.
2) Multiplexing means that lots of different signals can be transmitted down a single optical fibre at the same time, so you don't need as many cables.
3) As it's a 'digital' signal, there's little interference.

See page 70 for more on interference and multiplexing.

If you're not sure what life's about, try total internal reflection...

Here's something to make you go 'wow' (or '· — — — — — · — —') in amazement — an optical fibre, which is thinner than a human hair, can have over one million telephone calls going down it at the same time.

Lasers

Lasers are useful in lots of areas — manufacturing, surgery, dentistry, weaponry...
They're even used in CD players.

Lasers Produce Narrow, Intense Beams of Monochromatic Light

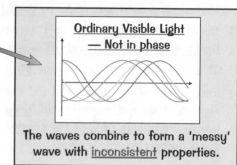

Ordinary visible light (e.g. daylight) is a combination of waves of different frequency and wavelength (and so colour) that are 'out of phase' with each other (i.e. the crests and troughs don't match).

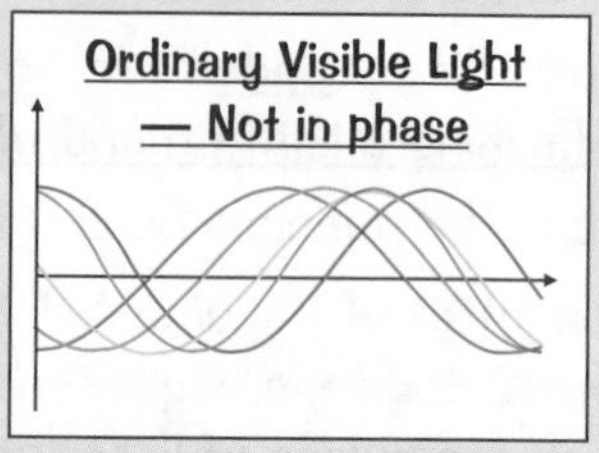

The waves combine to form a 'messy' wave with inconsistent properties.

A laser beam is just a special ray of visible light that has a few extra properties which make it special:

1) All the waves in a laser beam are at the same frequency (and wavelength). This makes the light monochromatic — which is just a fancy way of saying that it's all one single, pure colour.
2) The light waves are all in phase with each other — the troughs and crests line up, increasing the amplitude, so producing an intense beam. The waves in a laser beam are said to be coherent because they have a fixed phase difference (in this case a difference of zero, i.e. the waves are 'in phase').
3) Lasers have low divergence — the beam is narrow, and it stays narrow, even at a long distance from the light source (it doesn't diverge):

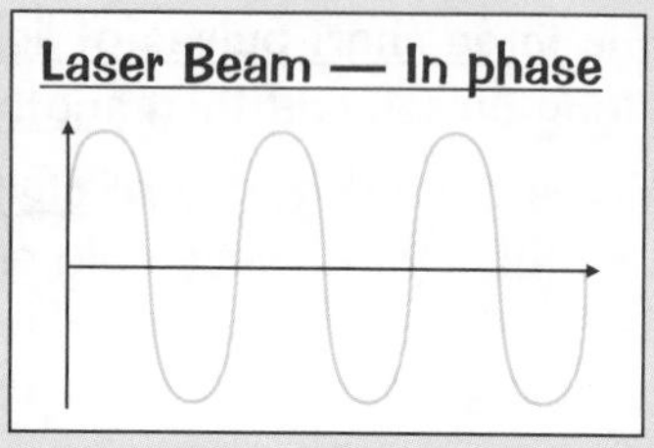

The combined wave has the same wavelength as the individual waves but an increased amplitude.

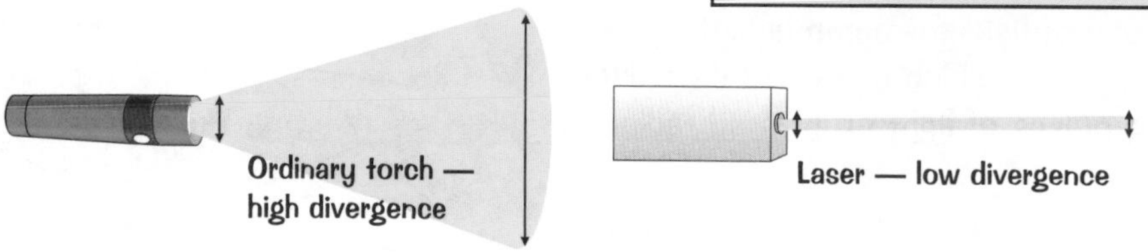

CD Players Use Lasers to Read Digital Information

1) The surface of a CD has a pattern of billions of shallow pits cut into it. The areas between the pits are called lands.
2) A laser shone onto the CD is reflected from the shiny bottom surface as it spins around in the player.
3) The beam is reflected from a land and a pit slightly differently — and this difference can be picked up by a light sensor. These differences in reflected signals can then be changed into an electrical signal.
4) The pits and lands themselves don't represent the digital ons and offs. It's actually a change in the reflected beam which represents on, while no change represents off.
5) An amplifier and a loudspeaker then convert the electrical signal into sound of the right pitch (frequency) and loudness.

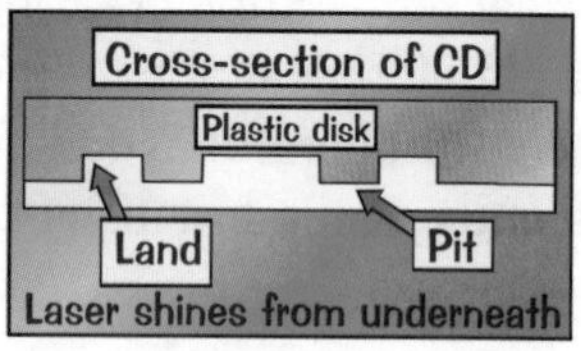

They seem like pits when you look from the top, anyway. But the laser shines from underneath, so it sees the pits as slightly raised areas.

Dynamite with a laser beam — guaranteed to blow your mind...

If you ever wondered where the name 'laser' came from, wonder no more — it stands for 'Light Amplification by Stimulated Emission of Radiation'. That won't be on the exam, but it may come up in a quiz sometime and your mates will (possibly) be impressed that you know it. The rest of the stuff IS on the exam, so go and learn it.

Infrared

Infrared radiation (or IR) may sound space-age but it's actually as common as beans on toast. You've probably used it several times today already without even knowing it.

Infrared Has Many Uses Around the Home...

1) Infrared radiation can be used in cooking, e.g. in grills and toasters (see p. 55).
2) Remote controls transfer information to TVs and DVD players using IR.
3) It can be used to transmit information between mobile phones or computers — but only over short distances.
4) Infrared sensors are used in security systems, e.g. burglar alarms and security lights. These sensors detect heat from an intruder's body.
5) Infrared can also be used instead of visible light to carry information through optical fibres (see page 63).

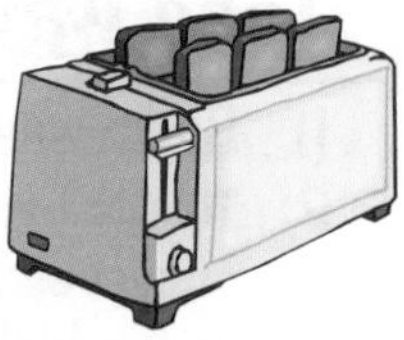

IR Can be Used to Monitor Temperature

1) Infrared radiation is also known as heat radiation. It's given out by hot objects — and the hotter the object, the more IR radiation it gives out.
2) This means infrared can be used to monitor temperatures. For example, heat loss through a house's uninsulated roof can be detected using infrared sensors (see page 56).

3) Infrared is also detected by night-vision equipment. The equipment turns it into an electrical signal, which is displayed on a screen as a picture. The hotter an object is, the brighter it appears. Police and the military use this to spot baddies running away, like you've seen on TV.

IR Signals Can Control Electrical Equipment

1) Remote controls emit pulses of IR to control electrical devices such as TVs or DVD players. If it was visible, you'd see it flickering when you pressed a button on the control.
2) The pulses act as a digital ('on/off') code (see p. 70) — similar to how Morse Code works.
3) The device will detect and decode the pattern of pulses coming from the remote control and follow the coded instruction.
4) E.g. a CD player might be programmed to know that a certain sequence of pulses at a particular speed means 'play', so when it receives this signal it will play the CD. A different sequence will tell it to 'pause', etc.
5) IR signals are used in the same way to transfer information between mobile phones and computers over short distances (so they're another form of wireless communication).
6) The main drawback is that you need to be close to the device you're operating, because the IR beam from a small, low-powered remote control is fairly weak.
7) You also need to point the beam straight at the detector on the device, because the IR waves only travel in a straight line.

Some remote controls, such as the ones on electronic car keys, use radio waves rather than IR. The radio waves can bend (diffract, see p. 61) — that's why you can open the car without pointing it at it.

Don't lose control of your sensors — this page isn't remotely hard...

Compared with all that stuff on lasers, infrared seems relatively low-tech. It's still amazingly useful though, and because infrared technology is relatively cheap and cheerful we can afford to use it to make our lives a bit easier (and safer) around the home. Bad news for criminals. Remember — crime doesn't pay, revision does.

Wireless Communication — Radio Waves

Wireless communication uses all sorts of EM waves, but for the next few pages we're just focusing on radio and microwaves — and how they're used for TV, radio, mobile phones etc.

Long Wavelengths Travel Well Through Earth's Atmosphere

1) Radio waves and microwaves (see p. 68) are good at transferring information over long distances.
2) This is because they don't get absorbed by the Earth's atmosphere as much as waves in the middle of the EM spectrum (like heat, for example), or those at the high-frequency end of the spectrum (e.g. gamma rays or X-rays).

You couldn't use high-frequency waves anyway — they'd be far too dangerous.

Radio Waves are Used Mainly for Communications

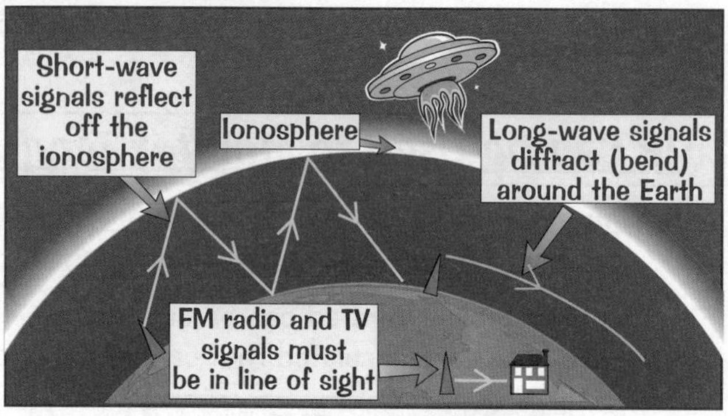
Short-wave signals reflect off the ionosphere
Ionosphere
Long-wave signals diffract (bend) around the Earth
FM radio and TV signals must be in line of sight

1) Radio waves are EM radiation with wavelengths longer than about 10 cm.
2) Different wavelengths of radio wave refract and diffract in different ways.
3) Long-wave radio (wavelengths of 1 – 10 km) can be transmitted from one place and received halfway round the world because they diffract (bend) around the curved surface of the Earth. This is explained in more detail below.
4) Radio waves used for TV and FM radio transmissions have very short wavelengths (10 cm – 10 m). To get reception, you must be in direct sight of the transmitter — the signal doesn't bend around hills or travel far through buildings.
5) Short-wave radio signals with wavelengths of about 10 m – 100 m can be received at long distances from the transmitter because of reflection in the ionosphere (see next page). Medium-wave signals (well, the shorter ones) can also reflect from the ionosphere, depending on atmospheric conditions and time of day.

Diffraction Makes a Difference to Signal Strength

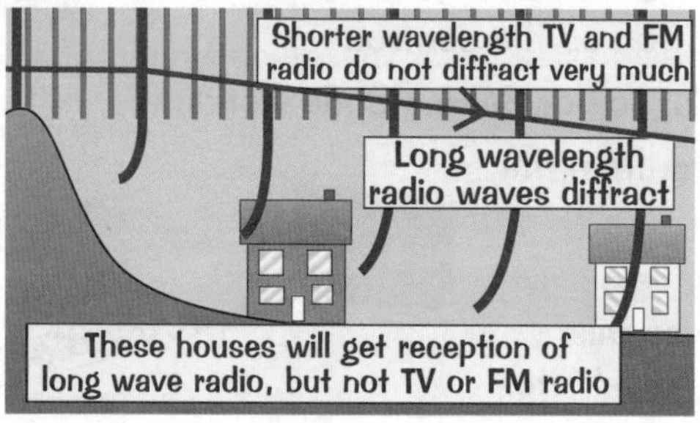
Shorter wavelength TV and FM radio do not diffract very much
Long wavelength radio waves diffract
These houses will get reception of long wave radio, but not TV or FM radio

1) Diffraction is when waves spread out at the edges when they pass through a gap or past an object (see p. 61).
2) The amount of diffraction depends on the wavelength of the wave, relative to the size of the gap or obstacle.
3) Longer wavelengths can encounter a lot of diffraction because they are large compared with the gap or obstacle.
4) This means that they are able to bend around corners and any obstacles — such as hills, tall buildings etc.
5) So longer wavelength radio waves can travel long distances between the transmitter and receiver without them having to be in the line of sight of each other. Shorter wavelength radio waves and microwaves (see p. 68) don't diffract very much, so the transmitters need to be located high up to avoid obstacles (and even then they can only cover short distances).
6) Some areas have trouble receiving shorter wavelength radio (and microwave) signals — e.g. if you live at the foot of a mountain you will probably have poor signal strength.
7) Diffraction can also occur at the edges of the dishes used to transmit signals. This results in signal loss — the wave is more spread out so the signal is weaker.

Concentrate — don't get diffracted...

So the key point on this page is that the longer the wavelength, the more it diffracts. This means that long waves bend round the Earth, while shorter waves need to be transmitted in the line of sight.

Wireless Communication — Radio Waves

It's not just diffraction that's affected by wavelength — refraction is too. And that's another property of waves which can either help or hinder communication signals.

Refraction Can Help Radio Waves Travel Further

When a wave comes up against something that has a different density, it changes speed.
If the wave hits the new substance at an angle, it changes direction. This is refraction (see p. 61).
When it happens high up in the atmosphere, it can help waves travel further for long distance communication.

1) UV radiation from the Sun creates layers of ionised atoms (atoms that have either gained or lost electrons) in the Earth's atmosphere. These electrically charged layers are called the ionosphere.
2) Radio waves travel faster through ionised parts of the atmosphere than non-ionised parts. This causes refraction.

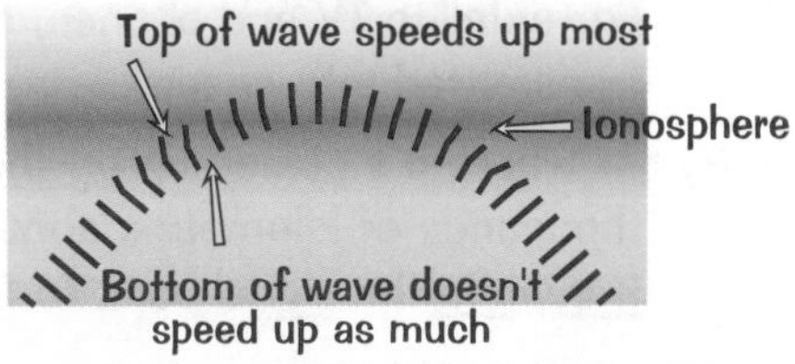

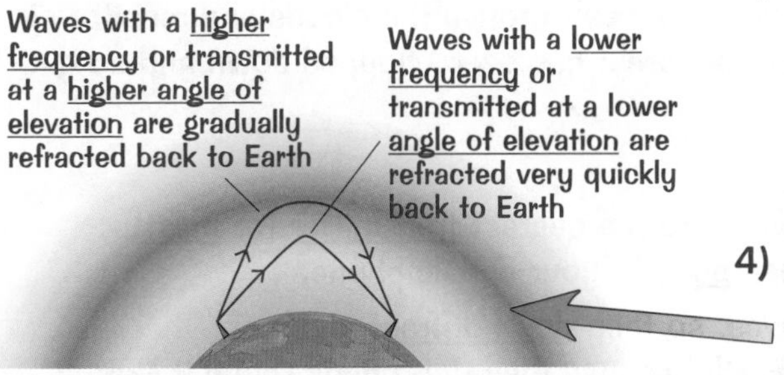

Waves with a higher frequency or transmitted at a higher angle of elevation are gradually refracted back to Earth
Waves with a lower frequency or transmitted at a lower angle of elevation are refracted very quickly back to Earth

3) Short-wave (with wavelengths of about 10 m – 100 m) and medium-wave (about 300 m) radio signals are refracted most in the ionosphere — they are effectively bounced back or reflected back to Earth. This means that short- and medium-wave radio signals can be received a long way from the transmitter.
4) The amount a wave is refracted in the ionosphere depends on its frequency and angle of elevation. High frequency / short wavelength signals such as short-wave radio don't refract as much as medium-wave.
5) Radio waves 'bounce' off the ionosphere in a similar way to how light waves totally internally reflect inside optical fibres (p. 63).
6) Refraction's not always good though. It can disrupt a signal by bending it away from the receiver dish.

Digital Radio Helps Reduce Interference

1) There's a limited number of radio wave frequencies that can be used to transmit a good analogue signal — so radio stations often broadcast using waves of very similar frequencies.
2) These analogue signals often suffer from interference because of this — similar waves covering a similar area can combine, which causes 'noise'. This is why radio stations near to each other use different frequencies — so they don't interfere as much.

Interference, noise and multiplexing are all covered on page 70.

3) Digital Audio Broadcasting (DAB) works in a different way to traditional radio broadcasts — it's digital to start with.
4) With DAB, many different signals are compressed, then transmitted as a single wave — this is known as multiplexing.
5) They are transmitted across a relatively small frequency bandwidth and separated out by the receivers at the other end. You need a DAB radio set to pick up and decode the signals.
6) DAB suffers less interference than traditional radio broadcasts, and since the signals from many stations can be broadcast at the same frequency (multiplexing), it means an increase in the potential number of radio stations available.
7) At the moment there are a limited number of DAB transmitters in the UK (and the world) so some areas can't receive digital radio signals at all.
8) Even if you can receive DAB, the sound quality is often not as good as a traditional FM radio broadcast, due to the compression of the signal.

Size matters — and my wave's longer than yours...

The various types of EM radiation have different uses because they have different wavelengths and frequencies, which gives them different properties. Make sure you understand why. And make sure you understand why DAB radio is better than traditional radio in some ways, but not in other ways. Hard cheese, isn't it.

Wireless Communication — Microwaves

Microwave communication involves microwaves — but of different wavelengths from those used in ovens.

Microwaves are Used for Satellite Communication...

1) Communication to and from satellites (including satellite TV signals and satellite phones) uses microwaves. But you need to use wavelengths which can pass easily through the Earth's watery atmosphere without too much absorption.
2) For satellite TV and phones, the signal from a transmitter is transmitted into space...
3) ... where it's picked up by the satellite's receiver dish orbiting thousands of kilometres above the Earth. The satellite transmits the signal back to Earth in a different direction...

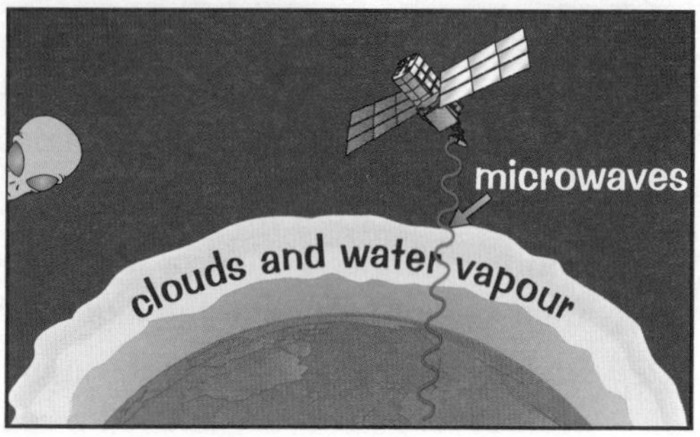

4) ... where it's received by a satellite dish on the ground.
5) Microwaves are also used by remote-sensing satellites — to 'see' through the clouds and monitor oil spills, track the movement of icebergs, see how much rainforest has been chopped down and so on.

...as well as Mobile Phones

1) Mobile phone calls travel as microwaves from your phone to the nearest transmitter (or mast). The transmitters pass signals between each other, then back to your mobile phone.
2) Microwaves have a shorter wavelength than radio waves, so they don't diffract much. This means they're affected by the curvature of the Earth because they don't bend round it like long-wave radio waves. It also means they're blocked more by large obstacles like hills because they can't bend round them.
3) This means that microwave transmitters need to be positioned in line of sight — they're usually high up on hilltops so they can 'see each other', and they're positioned fairly close together. If there's a hill or a man-made obstacle between your phone and the transmitter, you'll probably get a poor signal, or no signal at all.
4) The microwave frequencies used are partially absorbed by water, even though they can pass through the atmosphere. So in adverse weather (or if there's a lake nearby) there can be some signal loss through absorption or scattering. This is why you can lose satellite TV signal in a storm.
5) Sometimes there's interference between signals (see p. 70), which can also affect signal strength.

Mobile Masts May be Dangerous — but there's Conflicting Evidence

1) Microwaves used for communications need to pass through the Earth's watery atmosphere, but the microwaves used in microwave ovens have a different wavelength — they're actually absorbed by the water molecules in the food (see page 55).
2) It's the absorption that's harmful — if microwaves are absorbed by water molecules in living tissue, cells may be burned or killed.

3) Some people think that the microwaves emitted into your body from using a mobile phone or living near a mobile phone mast could damage your health.
4) There's no conclusive proof either way yet though. Lots of studies have been published, which has allowed the results to be checked, but so far they have given conflicting evidence.
5) Any potential dangers would be increased by prolonged exposure though — e.g. living close to a mast or using your phone all the time.
6) This means we have to carefully balance the potential risks and the benefits of this technology until we know more — in terms of where we locate masts and how much we choose to use our mobile phones.

Microwaves — used for TV AND for TV dinners...

Scientists publish the details of studies in scientific journals — this lets other scientists read and repeat the work to see if they agree. It's a good way to get results and conclusions repeated and checked.

EM Receivers

The air is chock-a-block full of EM waves, bounding around all over the shop. But most of them we can neither see nor hear. That's why we need receivers — to collect the information.

The Size of Receiver Depends on the Size of Wave

1) We use different receivers (sensors) to pick up the different types of EM waves used for communication — e.g. telescopes, satellite dishes, microscopes etc.
2) The minimum size of receiver needed is linked to the size of the wavelength of the wave — the longer the wavelength, the larger the receiver should be.
3) So radio waves need the biggest receivers, then microwaves, then infrared, then light waves...
4) This is because of diffraction (see p. 61) — when a wave enters a receiver it passes through a gap. If the wave is diffracted, it spreads out and you lose detail.
5) As you've already seen, the amount of diffraction is affected by the size of the gap compared to the wavelength — gaps about the same size as the wavelength cause lots of diffraction, but as the gap size increases there is less diffraction.
6) So the bigger the receiver compared with the wavelength of wave being received, the less diffraction it causes, so the clearer the information received is.

Telescopes Detect Different Types of EM Wave

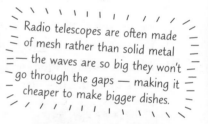

1) Telescopes help you to see distant objects clearer — e.g. astronomers look for very distant stars and galaxies using them.
2) Different telescopes are used to collect different EM waves — e.g. optical telescopes receive visible light, radio telescopes collect radio waves etc.
3) Bigger telescopes give us better resolution (i.e. lots of detail) because they cause less diffraction, so the information is clearer (see above).
4) Telescopes with small gaps compared to the wavelength they're looking for have limited resolving power — they are said to be diffraction-limited.
5) Light waves have a relatively small wavelength compared to radio waves.
6) Since radio waves can be more than 10 000 000 000 times bigger than light waves, this would mean having a ridiculously big receiver (about the size of the UK for a decent one). So we just make do with a lower resolution (although the dishes are still pretty huge).
7) To get round this, radio telescopes are often linked together and their signals combined to get more detailed information — acting like a single giant receiver.
8) A bigger receiver can also collect more EM waves, giving a more intense image — so a bigger telescope can observe fainter objects.

Radio telescopes are often made of mesh rather than solid metal — the waves are so big they won't go through the gaps — making it cheaper to make bigger dishes.

Optical Microscopes are Diffraction Limited

1) Optical microscopes have to be small, because you usually use them to look at small samples of tiny things in the lab — you want to collect light coming from a very small area only.
2) Their small size makes it hard to get a good resolution — the gap needs to be really small, so you still get some diffraction even though light has a small wavelength.

Mind the gap...

There's a lot more to telescopes than meets the eye (ho ho). Luckily, you don't have to know all the ins and outs of how they work for the exam, as long as you understand how diffraction limits them. Remember that telescopes can pick up invisible waves too, like microwaves and radio waves — but they have to be much much bigger. Microscopes are important too — make sure you know why their resolution is limited by size.

Analogue and Digital Signals

Sound and images can be sent as analogue signals, but digital technology is gradually taking over.

Information is Converted into Signals

1) To communicate any kind of information (e.g. sounds, pictures), it needs to be converted into electrical signals before it's transmitted.
2) These signals can then be sent long distances down telephone wires or carried on EM waves.
3) The signals can either be analogue or digital.

Analogue Signals Vary but Digital's Just On or Off

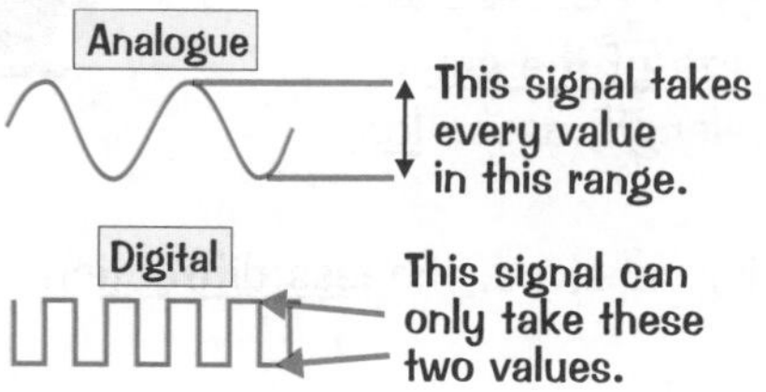
Analogue
This signal takes every value in this range.
Digital
This signal can only take these two values.

1) An analogue signal can take any value within a certain range. (Remember: analogue — any.) The amplitude and frequency of an analogue wave vary continuously.
2) A digital signal can only take two values. These values tend to be called on/off, or 1/0. For example, you can send data along optical fibres as short pulses of light.

Digital Signals Have Advantages Over Analogue

1) Digital and analogue signals weaken as they travel, so they might need to be amplified along their route.
2) They also pick up interference or noise from electrical disturbances or other signals (see box below).
3) When you amplify an analogue signal, the noise is amplified too — so every time it's amplified, the signal loses quality. The noise is easier to remove or ignore with digital, so the signal remains high quality.

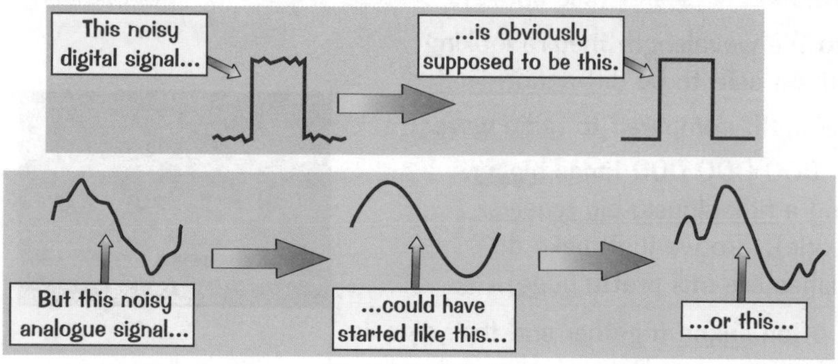
This noisy digital signal...
...is obviously supposed to be this.
But this noisy analogue signal...
...could have started like this...
...or this...

Interference

When two or more waves of a similar frequency meet, they can create one combined signal with a new amplitude.

This is called interference. You get it when two radio stations transmit on similar frequencies.

4) Another advantage of digital technology is that you can transmit several signals at the same time using just one cable or EM wave — this is called multiplexing.
5) Multiplexing happens in phone wires. When you're on the phone, your voice is converted into a digital signal and transmitted regularly at very small time intervals. In between your voice signals being transmitted, thousands of other people's voice signals can be slotted in or 'multiplexed'. The samples are separated out again at the other end so the person you called can hear you — and only you. This happens so quickly that you don't notice it.
6) The advantages of digital signals over analogue have played a big part in the 'switching over' from analogue to digital TV and radio broadcasts.

I've got loads of digital stuff — watch, radio, fingers...

Eeehh, I don't know about all this digital nonsense — ah reckon there were nowt wrong wi' carrier pigeons meself. Seriously though, digital signals are great — unless you live somewhere with poor reception of digital broadcasts, in which case you get no benefit at all. This is because if you don't get spot-on reception of digital signals in your area, you won't get a grainy signal (like with analogue TV and radio signals) — you'll get nothing at all.

Humans and the Environment

You've seen how useful EM waves can be for communication — but they can be pretty bad for us...

Ultraviolet Radiation Causes Skin Cancer

1) If you spend a lot of time in the sun, you can expect to get a tan and maybe sunburn.
2) But the more time you spend in the sun, the more chance you also have of getting skin cancer. This is because the Sun's rays include ultraviolet radiation (UV) which damages the DNA in your cells.
3) UV radiation can also cause you eye problems, such as cataracts, as well as premature skin aging (eek!).
4) Darker skin gives some protection against UV rays — it absorbs more UV radiation. This prevents some of the damaging radiation from reaching the more vulnerable tissues deeper in the body.
5) Everyone should protect themselves from the Sun, but if you're pale skinned, you need to take extra care, and use a sunscreen with a higher Sun Protection Factor (SPF).
6) An SPF of 15 means you can spend 15 times as long as you otherwise could in the sun without burning (as long as you keep reapplying the sunscreen).

EXAMPLE: Ruvani normally burns after 40 minutes in the sun. Before going to the beach, she applies sunscreen with SPF 8. For how long can she sunbathe before she will start to burn?

ANSWER: Time = 40 mins × 8 = 320 minutes = 5 hours and 20 minutes.

7) We're kept informed of the risks of exposure to UV — research into its damaging effects is made public through the media and advertising campaigns, and the government tells people how to keep safe to improve public health.
8) It's not just exposure to the Sun that's a problem — we are now being warned of the risks of prolonged use of sunbeds too. Tanning salons have time limits to make sure people are not over-exposed.

The Ozone Layer Protects Us from UV Radiation

1) Ozone is a molecule made of three oxygen atoms, O_3. There's a layer of ozone high up in the Earth's atmosphere.
2) The ozone layer absorbs some of the UV rays from the Sun — so it reduces the amount of UV radiation reaching the Earth's surface.
3) Recently, the ozone layer has got thinner because of pollution from CFCs — these are gases which react with ozone molecules and break them up. This depletion of the ozone layer allows more UV rays to reach us at the surface of the Earth (which, as you know, can be a danger to our health).

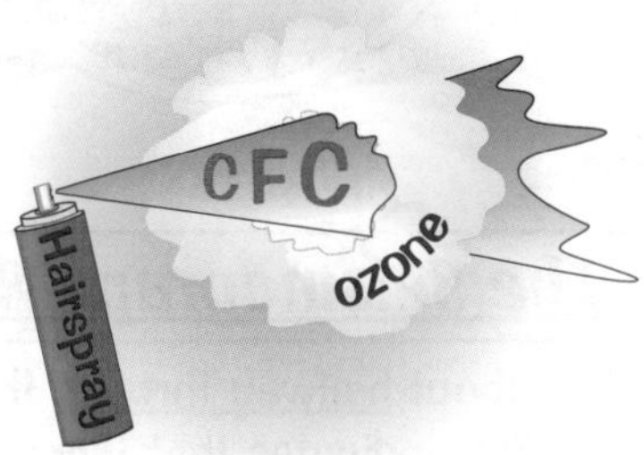

There's a Hole in the Ozone Layer over Antarctica

1) In winter, special weather effects cause the concentration of ozone over Antarctica to drop dramatically. It increases again in spring, but the winter concentration has been dropping. The low concentration looks like a 'hole' on satellite images.
2) Scientists now monitor the ozone concentration very closely to get a better understanding of why it's decreasing, and how to prevent further depletion.
3) Many different studies have been carried out internationally, using different equipment, to get accurate results — this helps scientists to be confident that their hypotheses and predictions are correct.
4) Studies led scientists to confirm that CFCs were causing the depletion of the ozone layer, so the international community banned them. We used to use CFCs all the time — e.g. in hairsprays and in the coolant for fridges — but now international bans and restrictions on CFC use have been put in place because of their environmental impact.

In 1987 lots of countries signed the Montreal Protocol, agreeing to reduce their use of CFCs.

Use protection — wear a hat...

Okay... time for a bit of risk balancing. Too much time in the sun can help cause skin cancer, but a bit of sun can be a good thing (it helps with your body's production of vitamin D). So don't avoid it altogether.

Seismic Waves

Waves don't just fly through the air — seismic waves travel inside the Earth. Scientists use seismic waves to investigate the Earth's inner structure (well it's a bit tricky to dig all the way down to have a look...).

Earthquakes Cause Different Types of Seismic Waves

1) When there's an earthquake somewhere, it produces shock waves which travel out through the Earth. We record these seismic waves all over the surface of the planet using seismographs.
2) Seismologists measure the time it takes for the shock waves to reach each seismograph.
3) They also note which parts of the Earth don't receive the shock waves at all.
4) There are two different types of seismic waves that travel through the Earth — P-waves and S-waves.

P-Waves are Longitudinal

Longitudinal waves

The vibrations are along the direction that the wave travels.

There's also a third type of wave — surface waves. But you don't need to know about those.

S-Waves are TranSverSe

Transverse waves

The vibrations are at right angles to the direction that the wave travels.

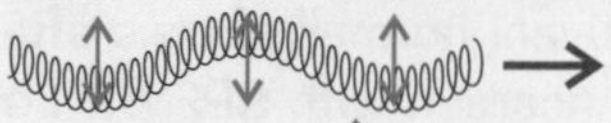

P-waves travel through solids and liquids. They travel faster than S-waves.

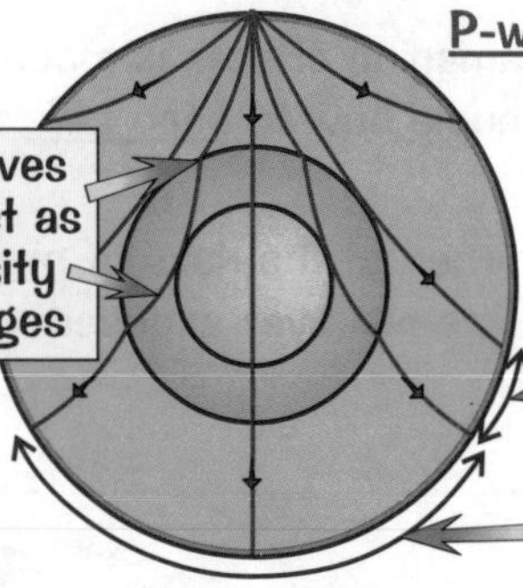

S-waves only travel through Solids. They are Slower than P-waves.

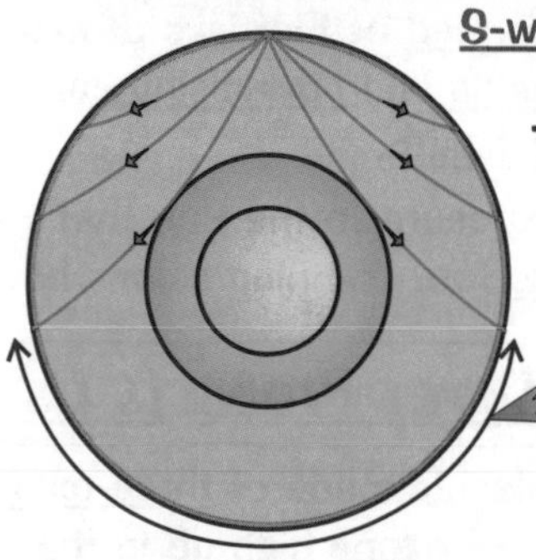

The Seismograph Results Tell Us What's Down There

1) About halfway through the Earth, P-waves change direction abruptly. This indicates that there's a sudden change in properties — as you go from the mantle to the core.
2) The fact that S-waves are not detected in the core's shadow tells us that the outer core is liquid — S-waves only pass through Solids.
3) P-waves seem to travel slightly faster through the middle of the core, which strongly suggests that there's a solid inner core.
4) Note that S-waves do travel through the mantle, which shows that it's solid. It only melts to form magma in small 'hot spots'.

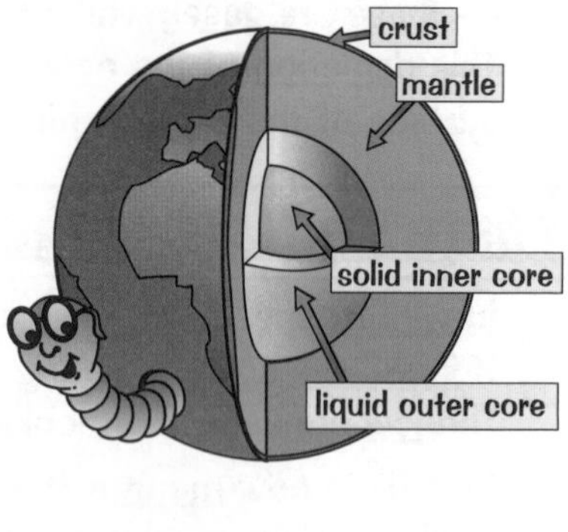

The Waves Curve with Increasing Depth

1) The waves change speed as the properties of the mantle and core change.
2) This change in speed causes the waves to change direction — which is refraction of course (see p. 61).
3) Most of the time the waves change speed gradually, resulting in a curved path.
4) But when the properties change suddenly, the wave speed changes abruptly, and the path has a kink.

Seismic waves — they reveal the terrible trembling truth...

Yet another way in which understanding about waves helps us know more about the world around us — or in this case, the world underneath us. Learning all this stuff about waves will definitely help you in your exam too, so that's a very big reason indeed to knuckle down and learn everything in this module.

Revision Summary for Module P1

Now a reward for ploughing through loads of pages of pretty intense science — a page of lovely questions. Okay, I know it seems a little daunting, but it's absolutely vital to check that you've learnt all the right stuff.

1) What is specific heat capacity?
2)* It takes 5000 J to heat 50 g of a substance by 40 °C. Calculate its specific heat capacity.
3) Explain why heating a pan of boiling water doesn't increase its temperature.
4)* How much energy is needed to boil dry a pan of 500 g of water at 100 °C?
(Specific latent heat of water for boiling = 2 260 000 J/kg.)
5) Briefly describe how heat is transferred through a) conduction, b) convection, and c) radiation.
6) Describe how heat radiation is used to cook food a) under a grill, and b) in a microwave oven.
7) Describe three ways of saving energy in the home and explain how each one works.
8)* How much energy is wasted if a hairdrier that's 20% efficient has a total energy input of 200 000 J?
9) Sketch a Sankey diagram to show the energy transformations in the hairdrier mentioned above.
10) Sketch a typical transverse wave and explain all its main features.
11) Sketch and label a diagram explaining reflection in a plane mirror.
12) Briefly describe what happens to a wave when it is a) diffracted, and b) refracted.
13) List the seven types of electromagnetic wave in order of wavelength (smallest to largest).
14) Explain why Morse code is a digital signal.
15) Describe how light signals can travel through optical fibres.
16) Explain the properties of laser beams which make them a) monochromatic, and b) coherent.
17) Describe how lasers are used in CD players.
18) Briefly explain how infrared radiation is used to control electrical equipment.
19) Explain why long-wave radio waves can bend around obstacles.
20) Briefly describe what happens to radio waves in the ionosphere.
21) Give two advantages and two disadvantages of using DAB.
22) Describe how satellites are used for communication.
23) Why are microwave transmitters located in high places and close together?
24) Explain why scientists are concerned about the dangers of:
a) mobile phone use, and b) the thinning of the ozone layer.
25) Explain how diffraction affects the size of receiver needed to pick up different wave signals.
26) Explain the difference between analogue and digital signals.
27) Why are CFCs so bad?
28) Name and describe two types of wave produced by an earthquake.
29) Name your top five cool bits of physics in this module.

* Answers on p. 132

Classification

It seems to be a basic human urge to want to classify things — that's the case in biology anyway...

Classification is Organising Living Organisms into Groups

1) Classification systems are important in science because they help us to understand how organisms are related (evolutionary relationships) and how they interact with each other (ecological relationships).
2) Classification systems can be natural or artificial:

   Natural classification systems are based on the evolutionary relationships and genetic similarities between organisms.

   Artificial classification systems are based on appearance rather than genes. They're used to identify organisms.

3) Living things are divided into kingdoms (e.g. the plant kingdom).
4) The kingdoms are then subdivided into smaller and smaller groups — phylum, class, order, family, genus, species.

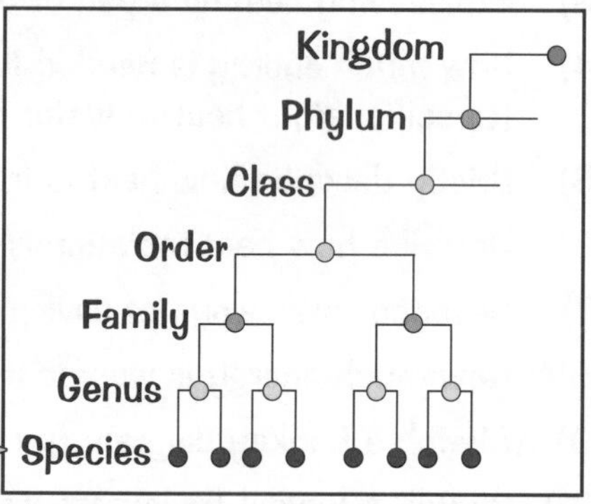

5) A genus is a group of closely-related species — and a species is a group of organisms that can interbreed to produce fertile offspring (see the next page).
6) It can be difficult to classify organisms into these distinct groups though because many organisms share characteristics of multiple groups.

Classification Systems Change Over Time

1) When a classification system is created it fits everything we know so far about different groups of organisms.
2) But as scientists discover new species (and learn more about the species that they've already discovered) they might have to adapt classification systems to fit their new findings:

- Newly discovered species might not really fit into any of the categories. These could be living species or newly discovered fossils, e.g. the archaeopteryx fossil has features of two different classes (birds and reptiles), so it's hard to know where to place it.
- DNA sequencing allows us to see genetic differences between different groups. As this data is collected, we might find out that two groups aren't actually as closely related as we'd thought — or two groups that we thought were very different might turn out to be close relatives.

Evolutionary Relationships can be Shown with Evolutionary Trees

1) You can draw evolutionary trees to show how closely related different species are to each other. It's just like drawing a family tree.
2) Evolutionary trees show common ancestors and relationships between species. The more recent the common ancestor, the more closely related the two species — and the more characteristics they're likely to share.
3) To find out about the evolutionary relationships between organisms, scientists analyse lots of different genes responsible for lots of different characteristics.
4) Studying lots of characteristics for a large group of organisms involves analysing huge amounts of DNA data and is only really possible thanks to advances in ICT.

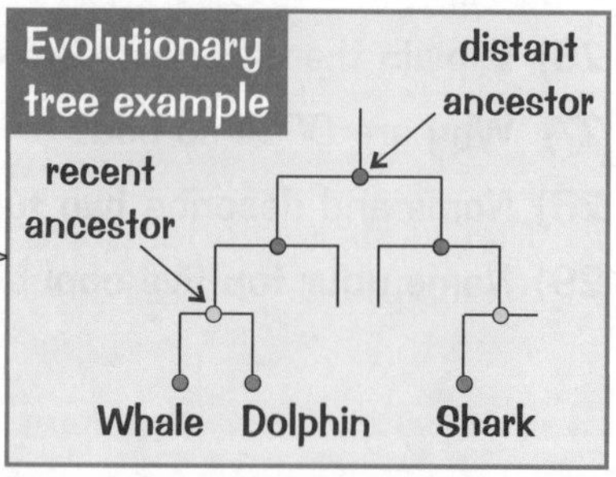

Whales and dolphins have a recent common ancestor so are closely related. They're both more distantly related to sharks.

Every evolutionary tree has a few bad apples...

There are loads of different types of organisms out there — so no wonder classification systems can get a bit unwieldy. This makes life no easier for you, I'm afraid — you've got to know about classification for your exam.

Species

There are millions of species. And you need to know them all for your exam. (Just kidding.) You do, however, need to know exactly what a species is — it's a little bit more complicated than you might have thought...

Sorting Organisms into Species Can Be Quite Tricky

1) The word 'species' crops up all the time in biology. You need to know exactly what it means:

A SPECIES is a group of organisms which can INTERBREED to produce FERTILE OFFSPRING.

2) Classifying organisms into species isn't always straightforward — there are a few problems:

Asexual Reproduction

Some organisms, such as bacteria, reproduce asexually. Asexual reproduction is where an organism reproduces by making a copy of itself. There is no interbreeding with another organism so they don't fit the definition of a species.

Hybrids

If you interbreed a male from one species with a female from a different species you'll get a hybrid (that's if you get anything at all). For example, a mule is a cross between a donkey and a horse. But hybrids are usually infertile so they aren't new species — this makes it difficult to classify them.

Evolution is a Continuous Process

Organisms change and evolve over time (see page 82), so the way they've been classified might also have to change. Sometimes a group of organisms will change so much it will form a new species — but it can be difficult to tell when this has happened.

The Binomial System Gives Everything a Two-part Name

1) In the binomial system, each species is given a two-part Latin name. The first part refers to the genus that the organism belongs to and the second part refers to the species.

E.g. Humans are known as *Homo sapiens*. '*Homo*' is the genus that they belong to and '*sapiens*' is the species.

E.g. Lions are known as *Panthera leo*. '*Panthera*' is the genus that they belong to and '*leo*' is the species.

The genus name is sometimes abbreviated to a capital letter with a full stop after it. E.g. *E. coli* is short for *Escherichia coli*.

2) The binomial system is pretty important — it's used by scientists all over the world.
3) It means that scientists in different countries or who speak different languages all refer to a particular species by the same name — avoiding potential confusion.

Closely Related Species Have Recent Common Ancestors

1) Similar species often share a recent common ancestor (see previous page), so they're closely related in evolutionary terms. They often look very alike and tend to live in similar types of habitat, e.g. whales and dolphins.
2) This isn't always the case though — closely related species may look very different if they have evolved to live in different habitats, e.g. llamas and camels.
3) So to explain the similarities and differences between species, you have to consider how they're related in evolutionary terms AND the type of environment they've adapted to survive in.

Binomial system — uh oh, sounds like maths...

It's possible to breed lions and tigers together — it's true — they produce hybrids called tigons and ligers. They look a bit like lions and a bit like tigers... as you'd expect. In the same way, a bat is (probably) just a hybrid of a bird and a cat. And a donkey is the result of breeding a dog and a monkey. Really, I swear.

Pyramids of Biomass and Numbers

A trophic level is a feeding level. It comes from the Greek word trophe meaning 'nourishment'. The amount of energy, biomass and usually the number of organisms all decrease as you move up a trophic level.

You Need to be able to Understand and Draw Pyramids of Biomass

Luckily it's pretty easy — they'll give you all the information you need to do it in the exam.
Here's an example of a food chain you might be given:

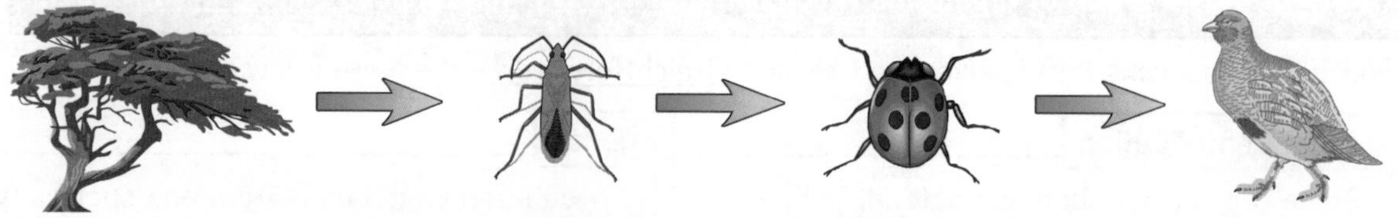

1000 kg of pear tree feeds... 5 kg of aphids which feeds... 1.5 kg of ladybirds which feeds... 0.5 kg of partridge.

These figures are the 'dry biomass' for each organism — see below.

1) Each bar on a pyramid of biomass shows the mass of living material at that stage of the food chain — basically how much all the organisms at each level would 'weigh' if you put them all together.
2) So the 'pear tree' bar on this pyramid would need to be longer than the 'aphids' bar, which in turn should be longer than the 'ladybirds' bar... and so on.
3) The pear tree goes at the bottom because it's at the bottom of the food chain.
4) Biomass pyramids are almost always pyramid-shaped because biomass is lost at each stage in the food chain (see next page).

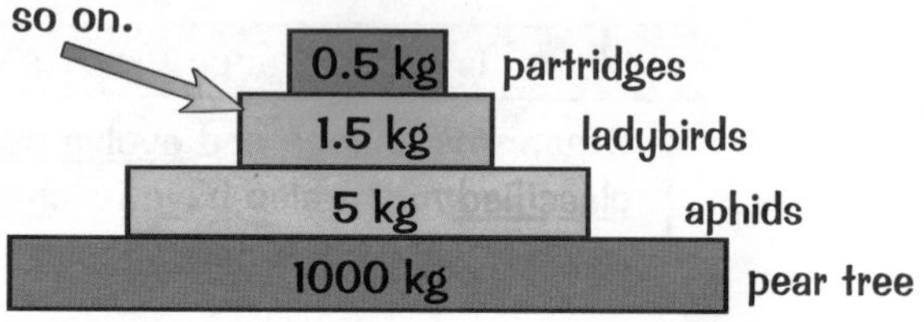

5) To construct a pyramid of biomass you use the 'dry biomass' of the organisms, i.e. you'd dry out all the water from the organisms before weighing them.
6) Measuring dry biomass can be difficult though because you have to kill the organisms to work it out. This might be okay for an area of grass but it would be unethical to kill lots of animals every time you wanted to make a pyramid of biomass.
7) It can sometimes be difficult to construct an accurate pyramid of biomass because some organisms feed at more than one trophic level. For example, partridges might feed on both ladybirds and aphids so the pyramid above would be wrong.

Pyramids of Biomass and Pyramids of Numbers can be Different Shapes

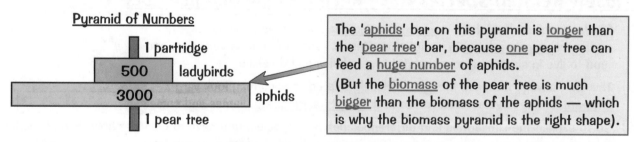

1) Pyramids of numbers are similar to pyramids of biomass, but each bar on a pyramid of numbers shows the number of organisms at that stage of the food chain — not their mass.
2) Pyramids of biomass are nearly always pyramid-shaped, but pyramids of numbers can be other shapes:

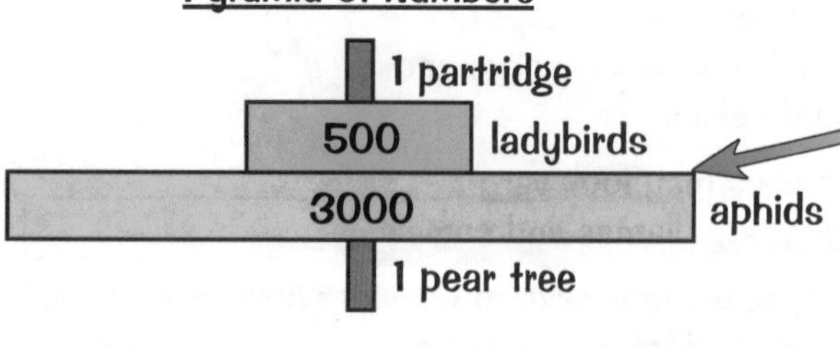

The 'aphids' bar on this pyramid is longer than the 'pear tree' bar, because one pear tree can feed a huge number of aphids.
(But the biomass of the pear tree is much bigger than the biomass of the aphids — which is why the biomass pyramid is the right shape).

Constructing pyramids is a breeze — just ask the Egyptians...

If you're drawing a pyramid to scale, make sure you know exactly how much room you're going to need before you start. Trust me — there's nothing worse than drawing a lovely bar representing 1000 kg of apple tree, then realising you haven't got enough space to fit the earwigs in. Just thinking about it's making me feel uneasy...

Energy Transfer and Energy Flow

Organisms need to get their energy from somewhere. Producers can capture their own (by photosynthesis) but everything else has to eat to get it. You need to know about how it's passed on.

All That Energy Just Disappears Somehow...

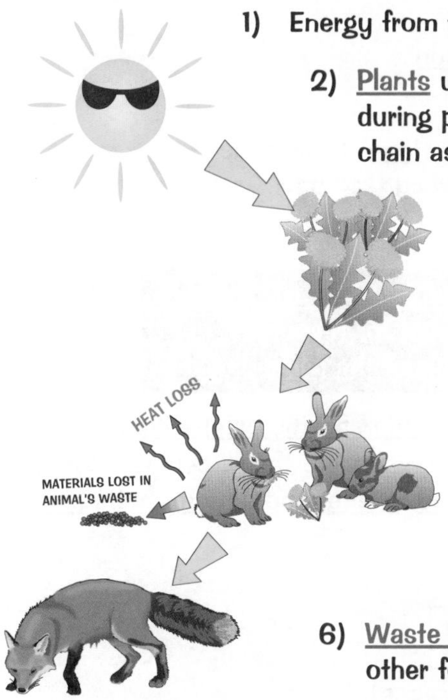

1) Energy from the Sun is the source of energy for nearly all life on Earth.
2) Plants use a small percentage of the light energy from the Sun to make food during photosynthesis. This energy then works its way through the food chain as animals eat the plants and each other.
3) The energy lost at each stage is used for staying alive, i.e. in respiration, which powers all life processes.
4) Most of this energy is eventually lost to the surroundings as heat. This is especially true for mammals and birds, whose bodies must be kept at a constant temperature which is normally higher than their surroundings.
5) Material and energy are also lost from the food chain as waste products. Egestion is when food that can't be digested passes out as faeces. Excretion is when the waste products of bodily processes are released e.g. urine.
6) Waste products and uneaten parts (e.g. bones) can become starting points for other food chains. For example, houseflies just love to eat faeces. Yum.

Material and energy are both lost at each stage of the food chain. This explains why you get biomass pyramids. Most of the biomass is lost and so does not become biomass in the next level up. It also explains why you hardly ever get food chains with more than about five trophic levels. So much energy is lost at each stage that there's not enough left to support more organisms after four or five stages.

You Need to be Able to Interpret Data on Energy Flow

rosebush: 80 000 kJ greenfly: 10 000 kJ ladybird: 900 kJ bird: 40 kJ

1) The numbers show the amount of energy available to the next level. So 80 000 kJ is the amount of energy available to the greenfly, and 10 000 kJ is the amount available to the ladybird.
2) You can work out how much energy has been lost at each level by taking away the energy that is available to the next level from the energy that was available from the previous level. Like this:

   Energy lost at 1st trophic level as heat and waste products = 80 000 kJ – 10 000 kJ = 70 000 kJ.
3) You can also calculate the efficiency of energy transfer — this just means how good it is at passing on energy from one level to the next.

$$\text{efficiency} = \frac{\text{energy available to the next level}}{\text{energy that was available to the previous level}} \times 100$$

So at the 1st trophic level, efficiency of energy transfer = 10 000 kJ ÷ 80 000 kJ × 100 = 12.5% efficient.

Ah ah ah ah stayin' alive, stayin' alive...

The Bee Gees were definitely on to something — staying alive is important, but it does require a lot of energy. Remember — hardly any of this energy makes it to the next level in the food chain and most of it's lost as heat.

Interactions Between Organisms

Organisms interact in tons of different ways...

Organisms Compete to Survive

1) In order to survive and reproduce, organisms must COMPETE against each other for the resources that they need to live (e.g. food and shelter).
2) Similar organisms in the same habitat will be in the closest competition because they'll be competing for similar ecological niches.

> A species' ecological 'niche' is how it fits in to its ecosystem. It depends on things like where the individuals live and what they feed on.

3) There are two types of competition between organisms:

> INTERSPECIFIC COMPETITION is where organisms compete for resources against individuals of another species.

> INTRASPECIFIC COMPETITION is where organisms compete for resources against individuals of the same species.

4) Intraspecific competition often has a bigger impact on organisms than interspecific competition.
5) This is because individuals of the same species have exactly the same needs, so they'll compete for lots of resources. E.g. a blue tit might compete with another blue tit for food, shelter and a mate, but a blue tit and a great tit might only compete for the same food source.

Populations of Prey and Predators Go in Cycles

In a community containing prey and predators (as most of them do of course):

1) The population of any species is usually limited by the amount of food available.
2) If the population of the prey increases, then so will the population of the predators.
3) However as the population of predators increases, the number of prey will decrease.

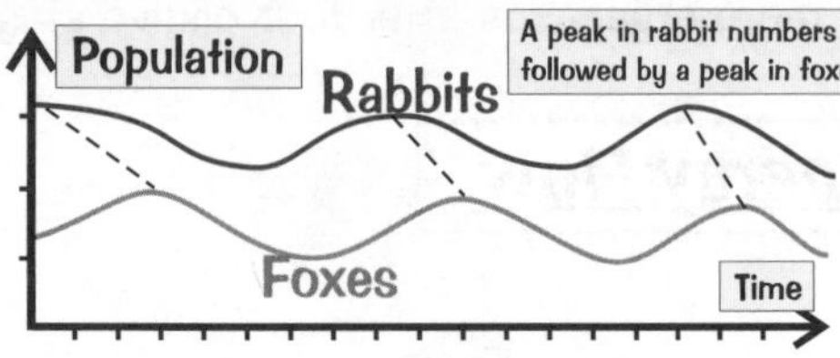

E.g. More grass means more rabbits.
More rabbits means more foxes.
But more foxes means less rabbits.
Eventually less rabbits will mean less foxes again.
This up and down pattern continues...

4) Predator-prey cycles are always out of phase with each other. This is because it takes a while for one population to respond to changes in the other population. E.g. when the number of rabbits goes up, the number of foxes doesn't increase immediately because it takes time for them to reproduce.

Parasitic and Mutualistic Relationships are Other Types of Interactions

Some organisms depend entirely on other species to survive. So where an organism lives and its abundance (population size) is often influenced by the distribution and abundance of these species.

1) PARASITES live off a host. They take what they need to survive, without giving anything back. This often harms the host — which makes it a win-lose situation.
   - Tapeworms absorb lots of nutrients from the host, causing them to suffer from malnutrition.
   - Fleas are parasites. Dogs gain nothing from having fleas (unless you count hundreds of bites).

2) MUTUALISM is a relationship where both organisms benefit — so it's a win-win relationship.
   - 'Cleaner species' e.g. oxpeckers live on the backs of buffalo. Not only do they eat pests on the buffalo, like ticks, flies and maggots (providing the oxpeckers with a source of food), but they also alert the animal to any predators that are near, by hissing.
   - Lots of plants are pollinated by insects, allowing them to reproduce. In return, the insects get a sip of sweet, sugary nectar.

Adaptations

If that stuff about parasites and fleas left you scratching your head (groan), then you'll be pleased to read about something a bit different. The next few pages are about adaptation. Oh boy...

Adaptations Help Organisms to Survive

1) Adaptations are the features that organisms have that make them better suited to their environment.
2) Organisms that are adapted to their environment are better able to compete for resources.
3) This means that they're more likely to survive, reproduce and pass on their adaptations to their offspring.

Organisms can be Specialists or Generalists

SPECIALISTS are organisms which are highly-adapted to survive in a SPECIFIC HABITAT. For example giant pandas are adapted to eat just bamboo.

GENERALISTS are organisms that are adapted to survive in a RANGE OF DIFFERENT HABITATS. For example black rats are able to survive in forests, cities and in areas of farmland.

1) In a habitat where the conditions are stable (i.e. they're not changing), specialists will out-compete generalists as they're better adapted to the specific conditions.
2) But if the conditions in the habitat change (e.g. a species of prey becomes extinct), specialists will be out-competed by generalists. Specialists won't be adapted to the new conditions, but generalists are adapted to a range of conditions so will be more likely to survive.

Some Organisms Have Biochemical Adaptations to Extreme Conditions

1) Some organisms can tolerate extreme conditions, e.g. a very high or low pH or temperature.
2) Organisms that are adapted to live in seriously extreme conditions (like super hot volcanic vents or at high pressure on the sea bed) are called extremophiles.
3) In order to survive these sorts of harsh conditions, organisms have some pretty nifty adaptations:

Example 1

- Extremophile bacteria that live in very hot environments have enzymes that work best at a much higher optimum temperature than enzymes from other organisms.
- These enzymes are able to function normally at temperatures that would denature (destroy) enzymes from other organisms. For example, the bacteria *Thermus thermophilus* grows best in environments where the temperature is about 65°C.

Example 2

- Organisms that live in very cold environments sometimes have special antifreeze proteins.
- These proteins interfere with the formation and growth of ice crystals in the cells, stopping the cells from being damaged by ice.

Doctor doctor, I only eat bamboo... *I think you need to talk to a specialist about that...*

The wolf in Little Red Riding Hood had some great adaptations for eating children — big eyes for seeing, big ears for hearing and big sharp teeth for biting. The one adaptation it was missing was an axe-proof exoskeleton.

Adaptations to Cold Environments

Different organisms are adapted to cope with different temperatures. They need to make sure they're not too hot or too cold, otherwise the enzymes controlling the reactions in their cells will go haywire.

Some Organisms Have Adapted to Living in Cold Environments

1) Organisms that live in cold environments have a whole host of adaptations to help them survive.
2) Most adaptations to cold environments are based on reducing heat loss to the environment.

Anatomical Adaptations Can Reduce Heat Loss

Anatomical adaptations are features of an organism's anatomy (body structure) that help it to survive. Anatomical adaptations to the cold include:

1) Having a thick coat or a layer of blubber to insulate the body and trap heat in.
2) Having a large size and compact body shape to give a small surface area to volume ratio. This reduces heat loss as less body heat can be lost through the surface of the skin.

SURFACE AREA TO VOLUME RATIOS

- A surface area to volume ratio is just a way of comparing how much surface area something has compared to it's size.
- Small objects have larger surface area to volume ratios than large objects.
- In cold environments, large organisms lose less heat to their surroundings than small organisms — because of their smaller surface area to volume ratio.

1 cm cube

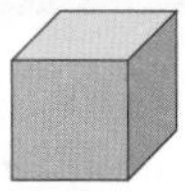

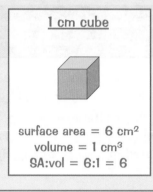

surface area = 6 cm^2
volume = 1 cm^3
SA:vol = 6:1 = 6

2 cm cube

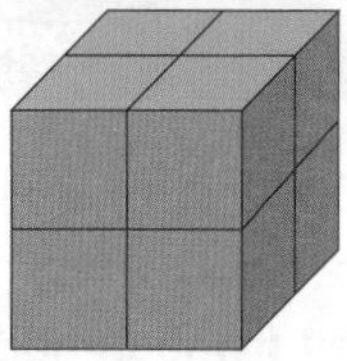

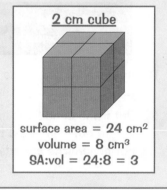

surface area = 24 cm^2
volume = 8 cm^3
SA:vol = 24:8 = 3

3) Having counter-current heat exchange systems:
   - Animals like penguins have to stand on cold ice all day.
   - Blood vessels going to and from the feet carry blood that flows in opposite directions.
   - The vessels pass close to each other, allowing heat to transfer between them.
   - Warm blood flowing in arteries to the feet heats cold blood returning to the heart in the veins.
   - This means that the feet stay cold, but it stops cold blood from cooling down the rest of the body.

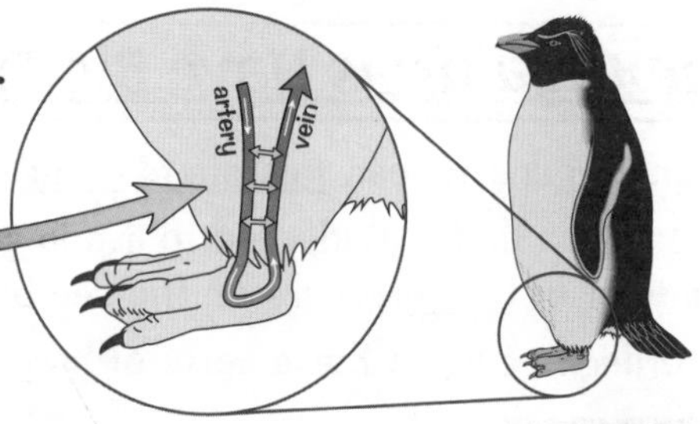

Some Organisms Also Have Behavioural Adaptations to the Cold

1) Many species migrate to warmer climates during the winter months to avoid having to cope with the cold conditions.
2) Other species hibernate during the winter months. This saves energy as the animal doesn't have to find food or keep itself as warm as if it was active.
3) Some species (like penguins) huddle together to keep warm.

Now I know why Dad refuses to put the heating on...

It's not his fault he's got a smaller surface area to volume ratio than me. He's just lucky to be so well adapted to the cold — what with his thick layer of blubber and hairy shoulders to keep him warm. It's just not fair. Make sure you've got surface area to volume ratios sussed — you'll need them on the next page too.

Adaptations to Hot and Dry Environments

Brrrrr. Trying to survive in freezing conditions isn't easy, but keeping your cool when it's hot and stuffy is no walk in the park either...

Some Organisms Have Adapted to Living in Hot Environments

Keeping cool in hot environments is all about increasing heat loss and reducing heat gain.

Behavioural Adaptations Can Increase Heat Loss and Reduce Heat Gain

1) Animals that live in very hot climates often spend the day in the shade or underground to minimise the amount of heat their bodies gain from their surroundings.
2) Animals can also reduce their heat gain by being active at night, when it is much cooler.
3) Animals can increase heat loss by bathing in water. As the water evaporates it transfers heat from the skin to the surroundings, cooling the animal down.

Anatomical Adaptations Can Also Increase Heat Loss

1) Animals that are adapted to survive in hot environments are often small. This gives them a large surface area to volume ratio (see previous page), which allows them to lose more body heat to their surroundings.
2) Other adaptations, like having large ears, can also increase an animal's surface area to volume ratio and help them to lose heat. Large thin ears allow more blood to flow near the surface of the skin — so more heat from the blood can be radiated to the surroundings.
3) Some animals (e.g. camels) store fat in just one part of the body (e.g. the camel's hump) — this stops the rest of the body from being too well insulated and allows heat to be lost more easily.

Some Organisms Have Adapted to Living in Dry Environments

Organisms that live in dry environments have to be adapted to minimise the amount of water that they lose to the environment.

Some desert plants...

1) ... have a rounded shape, giving them a small surface area to volume ratio to minimise water loss from the surface.
2) ... have a thick waxy layer (called a cuticle) and spines instead of leaves to further reduce water loss.
3) ... store water in their stems to allow them to survive in times of extreme drought.
4) ... have shallow, but very extensive, roots to ensure water is absorbed quickly over a large area.

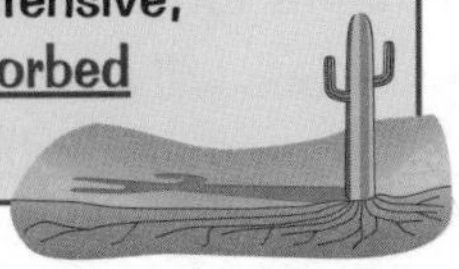

Some desert animals...

1) ... have specialised kidneys that allow them to produce very concentrated urine, with a very low water content.
2) ... have no sweat glands, preventing them from losing water through sweating.
3) ... spend lots of time in underground burrows, where the air contains more moisture than on the surface.

That's a lovely cravat — no it's not, it's a cacti...

Remember, a large surface area compared to volume increases heat loss — which is great for organisms living in hot environments. But it also means water is lost more easily — not so great in dry environments.

Evolution and Speciation

Evolution is where species change slowly over time. It's the genetic variation between the individuals of a species that makes evolution possible.

Only the Fittest Survive

Charles Darwin came up with a really important theory about evolution.
It's called the theory of natural selection:

Charles Darwin

1) Darwin knew that organisms in a species show wide variation. He also knew that organisms have to compete for limited resources in an ecosystem.
2) Darwin concluded that the organisms that are the best adapted (the fittest) would be more successful competitors and would be more likely to survive. This idea is called the 'survival of the fittest'.
3) The successful organisms that survive are more likely to reproduce and pass on the adaptations that made them successful to their offspring.
4) The organisms that are less well adapted would be less likely to survive and reproduce, so they are less likely to pass on their characteristics to the next generation.
5) Over time, successful adaptations become more common in the population and the species changes — it evolves.

New Discoveries Have Helped to Develop the Theory of Natural Selection

1) Darwin's theory wasn't perfect — he couldn't give a good explanation for why new characteristics appeared or exactly how individual organisms passed on beneficial adaptations to their offspring.
2) That's because DNA wasn't discovered until 50 years after his theory was published.
3) We now know that adaptations are controlled by genes. New adaptations arise because of mutations (changes in DNA). Successful adaptations are passed on to future generations in the genes that parents contribute to their offspring.

The Development of a New Species is Called Speciation

1) Over a long period of time, organisms may change so much because of natural selection that a completely new species is formed. This is called speciation.
2) Speciation happens when populations of the same species change enough to become reproductively isolated — this means that they can't interbreed to produce fertile offspring.
3) Reproductive isolation can be caused by geographic isolation. Here's how:

- A physical barrier divides a population of a species, e.g. a river changes its course. The two new populations are unable to mix.
- Different mutations create different new features in the two groups of organisms.
- Natural selection works on the new features so that, if they are of benefit, they spread through each of the populations.
- Since conditions on each side of the barrier will be slightly different, the features that are beneficial will be different for each population.
- Eventually, individuals from the two populations will have such different features that they won't be able to breed together to produce fertile offspring. They'll have become reproductively isolated and the two groups will be separate species.

"Natural selection" — sounds like vegan chocolates...

Natural selection's all about the organisms with the best characteristics surviving to pass on their genes so that the whole species ends up adapted to its environment. It doesn't happen overnight though.

Theories of Evolution

There's no doubt about it — Darwin was a very intelligent guy. Lots of people didn't agree with his theory though, in fact it made some people downright angry. It's a hard life being a scientist.

Not Everyone Agreed with Darwin...

Darwin's theory of evolution by natural selection was very controversial at the time — for various reasons...

1. The theory went against common religious beliefs about how life on Earth developed — it was the first plausible explanation for our own existence without the need for a "Creator" (God). This was very bad news for the religious authorities of the time, who ridiculed his ideas.

2. Darwin couldn't explain why new, useful characteristics appeared or how they were inherited (see previous page).

3. There wasn't enough evidence to convince many scientists, because not many other studies had been done into how organisms change over time.

Lamarck Had a Conflicting Theory of Evolution

Darwin's theory of evolution, which he published in a book called 'On the Origin of Species', wasn't the only one. A French chap called Lamarck had a different idea:

1) Lamarck argued that if a characteristic was used a lot by an animal then it would become more developed. Lamarck reckoned that these acquired characteristics could be passed on to the animal's offspring. For example, if a rabbit did a lot of running and developed big leg muscles, Lamarck believed that the rabbit's offspring would also have big leg muscles.

2) But people eventually concluded that acquired characteristics don't have a genetic basis — so they're unable to be passed on to the next generation. This is why Lamarck's theory was rejected.

Nowadays, Most People Accept Darwin's Theory

The theory of evolution by natural selection is now widely accepted.
Here are a couple of reasons why:

1) The theory has been debated and tested independently by a wide range of scientists, and no-one has managed to conclusively prove that the theory is wrong.

2) The theory offers a plausible explanation for so many observations of plants and animals, e.g. their physical characteristics and behavioural patterns.

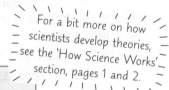

For a bit more on how scientists develop theories, see the 'How Science Works' section, pages 1 and 2.

This stuff's not too tricky — you should find it a walk in Lamarck...

Because his theory turned out to be flawed, it's all too easy to poke fun at Lamarck. Remember though that he was a very smart guy and just happened to get the wrong end of the stick. When he first published it, his work was praised by many other successful scientists. Poor old Lamarck — it wasn't that bad a theory.

The Carbon Cycle and Decomposition

Carbon is constantly moving between the atmosphere, the soil and living things in the carbon cycle.

The Carbon Cycle Shows How Carbon is Recycled

Carbon is an important element in the materials that living things are made from.
It's constantly being recycled in nature:

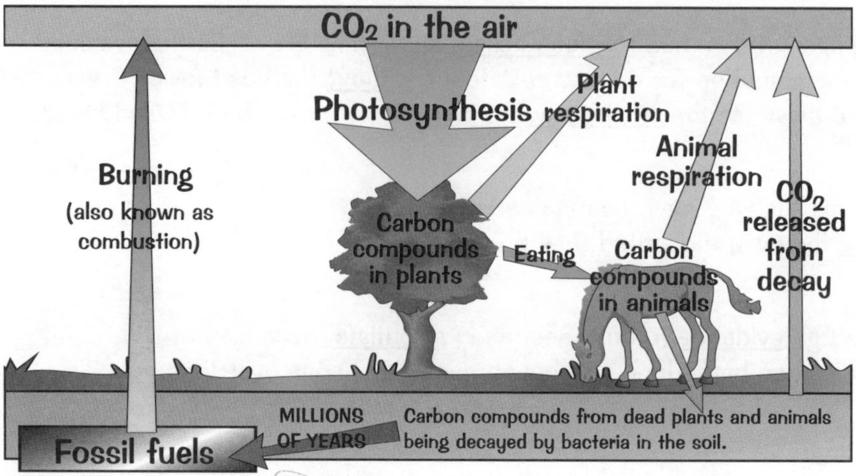

This diagram isn't half as bad as it looks. Learn these important points:

1) There's only one arrow going down. The whole thing is 'powered' by photosynthesis.
2) In photosynthesis plants convert the carbon from CO_2 in the air into sugars. Plants can then incorporate this carbon into other carbohydrates, as well as fats and proteins.
3) Eating passes the carbon compounds in the plant along to animals in a food chain or web.
4) Both plant and animal respiration while the organisms are alive releases CO_2 back into the air.
5) Plants and animals eventually die and decay. They're then broken down by bacteria and fungi in the soil. These decomposers release CO_2 back into the air by respiration as they break down the material.
6) Over millions of years, material from dead plants and animals can also form fossil fuels like coal and oil. When these fossil fuels are burned CO_2 is released back into the air.

Decomposition is Slower in Waterlogged and Acidic Soils

1) Recycling of carbon and other nutrients takes longer in waterlogged soils than in well-drained soils.
2) This is because the bacteria and fungi that decompose organic material usually need oxygen to respire and produce energy. Waterlogged soils don't have much oxygen — so the decomposers have less energy and work more slowly.
3) Nutrient recycling also takes longer in highly acidic soils than in neutral soils. This is because extremes of pH slow down the reproduction of decomposers or kill them outright.

Carbon is Also Recycled in The Sea

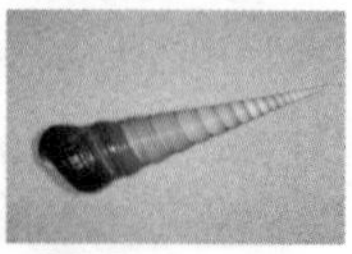

CO_2 in waiting.

1) There's another major recycling pathway for carbon in the sea.
2) Millions of species of marine organisms make shells made of carbonates.
3) When these organisms die the shells fall to the ocean floor and eventually form limestone rocks.
4) The carbon in these rocks returns to the atmosphere as CO_2 during volcanic eruptions or when the rocks are weathered down.
5) The oceans can also absorb large amounts of CO_2, acting as huge stores of carbon called 'carbon sinks'.

Come on out, it's only a little carbon cycle, it can't hurt you...

Much. But if you revise this page you'll be able to beat the carbon questions into submission in the exam. Yay.

The Nitrogen Cycle

Nitrogen, just like carbon, is constantly being recycled. So the nitrogen in your proteins might once have been in the air. And before that it might have been in a plant. Or even in some horse wee. Nice.

Nitrogen is Recycled in the Nitrogen Cycle

1) The atmosphere contains 78% nitrogen gas, N_2. This is very unreactive and so it can't be used directly by plants or animals.
2) Nitrogen is needed for making proteins for growth, so living organisms have to get it somehow.
3) Plants get their nitrogen from the soil, so nitrogen in the air has to be turned into nitrates before plants can use it. Nitrogen compounds are then passed along food chains and webs as animals eat plants (and each other).
4) Decomposers (bacteria and fungi in the soil) break down proteins in rotting plants and animals, and urea in animal waste, into ammonia. This returns the nitrogen compounds to the soil — so the nitrogen in these organisms is recycled.

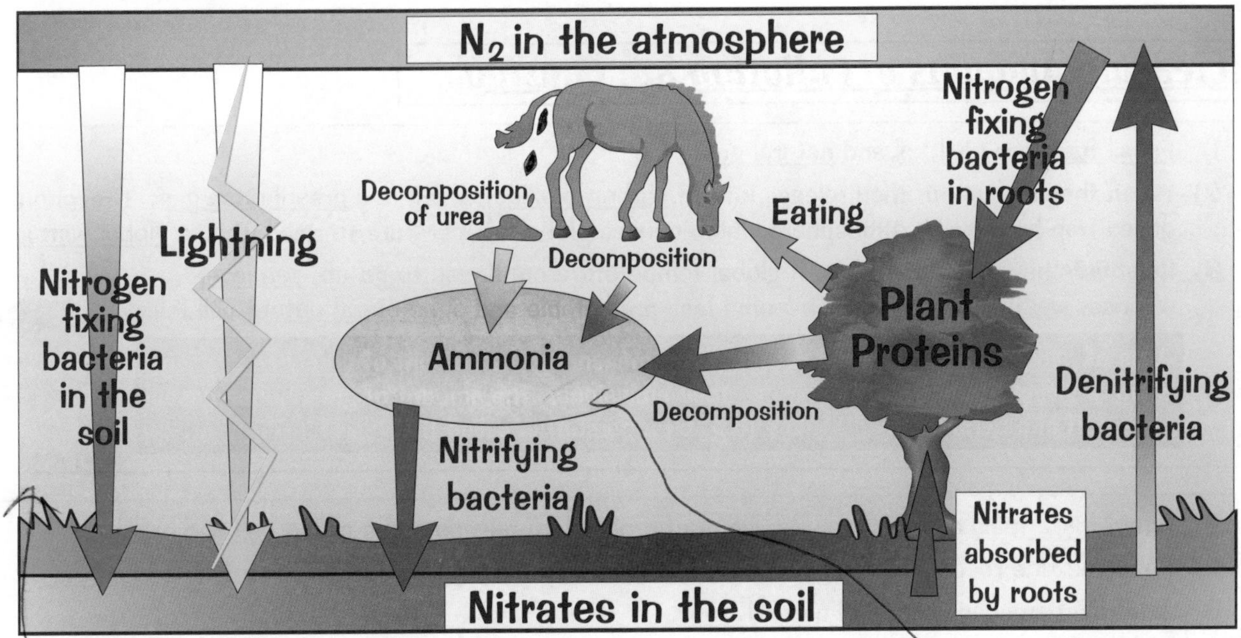

5) Nitrogen fixation isn't an obsession with nitrogen — it's the process of turning N_2 from the air into nitrogen compounds in the soil which plants can use. There are two main ways that this happens:
   a) Lightning — there's so much energy in a bolt of lightning that it's enough to make nitrogen react with oxygen in the air to give nitrates.
   b) Nitrogen-fixing bacteria in roots and soil (see below).
6) There are four different types of bacteria involved in the nitrogen cycle:
   a) DECOMPOSERS — decompose proteins and urea and turn them into ammonia.
   b) NITRIFYING BACTERIA — turn ammonia in decaying matter into nitrates.
   c) NITROGEN-FIXING BACTERIA — turn atmospheric N_2 into nitrogen compounds that plants can use.
   d) DENITRIFYING BACTERIA — turn nitrates back into N_2 gas. This is of no benefit to living organisms.
7) Some nitrogen-fixing bacteria live in the soil. Others live in nodules on the roots of legume plants (e.g. peas and beans). This is why legume plants are so good at putting nitrogen back into the soil. The plants have a mutualistic relationship (see page 78) with the bacteria — the bacteria get food (sugars) from the plant, and the plant gets nitrogen compounds from the bacteria to make into proteins. So the relationship benefits both of them.

It's the cyyyycle of liiiiife...

People sometimes forget that when we breathe in, we're breathing in mainly nitrogen. It's a pretty boring gas, colourless and with no taste or smell. But nitrogen is vital to living things, because the amino acids that join together to make proteins (like enzymes) all contain nitrogen.

Human Impact on the Environment

Pollution is one of the hot topics in the news at the moment (literally, if you're talking global warming).

Human Population is Increasing

1) The world's human population is rising exponentially — which means it's increasing very quickly.
2) Populations increase when the birth rate (the number of people who are born each year) is higher than the death rate (the number of people who die each year).
3) The rapidly increasing population is putting pressure on the environment — more resources are being used up and more pollution's being produced.
4) The higher standard of living amongst more developed countries demands even more resources, and although these developed countries have only a small proportion of the world's population, they cause a large proportion of the pollution.

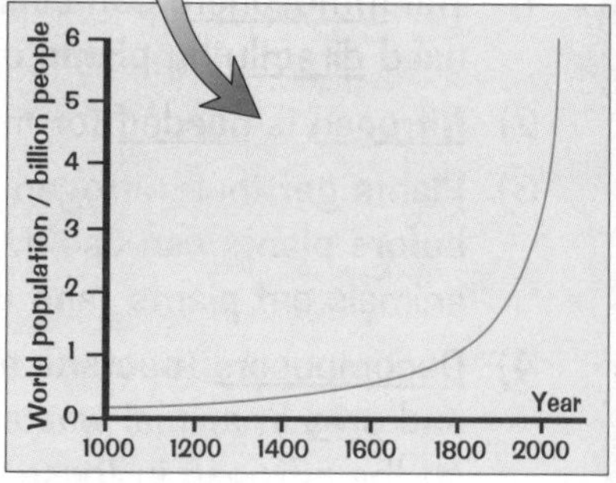

Increasing Amounts of Pollution are Causing...

1) GLOBAL WARMING

1) Fossil fuels are coal, oil and natural gas.
2) When they're burned, they release lots of carbon dioxide, which is a greenhouse gas. Greenhouse gases trap heat in the atmosphere which causes global temperature to rise. This is global warming.
3) Scientists have predicted that, if global temperature continues to go up, sea level will rise, weather systems will become less predictable and agricultural output will fall.

Lots of people, companies and countries are measuring the amount of greenhouse gases they're giving off, so they can reduce their emissions. The amount of greenhouse gases given off in a certain period of time (e.g. by a person) is called their carbon footprint.

2) ACID RAIN

1) When fossil fuels and waste materials are burned they release a gas called sulfur dioxide.
2) Sulfur dioxide reacts with water in the atmosphere to form sulfuric acid which falls as acid rain.
3) Acid rain damages soils, and can kill trees.
4) Acid rain can cause lakes to become more acidic. This has a severe effect on the lake's ecosystem. Many organisms are sensitive to changes in pH and can't survive in more acidic conditions. Many plants and animals die.
5) Acid rain damages limestone, ruining buildings and stone statues.

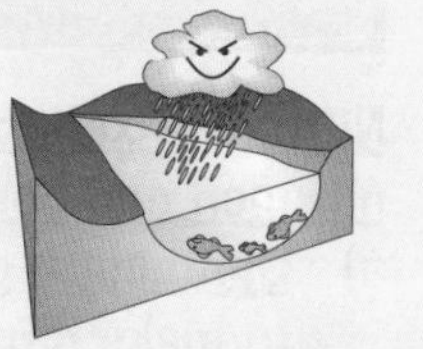

3) OZONE DEPLETION

1) CFCs (chlorofluorocarbons) used to be used in aerosols, fridges, air-conditioning units, and polystyrene foam.
2) They break down ozone in the upper atmosphere.
3) This allows more harmful UV rays to reach the Earth's surface.
4) Being exposed to more UV rays will increase the risk of skin cancer (although this can be reduced with suncream). Australia has high levels of skin cancer because it is under an ozone hole.
5) The increase in UV rays might also kill plankton in the sea — this could have a massive effect on the sea ecosystem because plankton are at the bottom of the food chain. Scientists predict that fish levels will drop (meaning, among other things, less food for us to eat).

Global warming — you might need to invest in a new pair of shorts...

More people means more demand for food, energy, land and raw materials — and more waste and pollution. The worst culprits are people like us in developed countries who want energy for their comfortable lifestyles.

Human Impact on the Environment

There are a few different ways to gauge just how badly we are polluting the planet — here are two of 'em.

Indicator Species Can Be Used to Show Pollution

By looking for indicator species, you can tell if an area is polluted or not.

1) Some species can only survive in unpolluted conditions, so if you find lots of them, you know it's a clean area.

   Lichens are used to monitor air quality — they're damaged by pollution. The cleaner the air, the greater the diversity of lichens that survive.

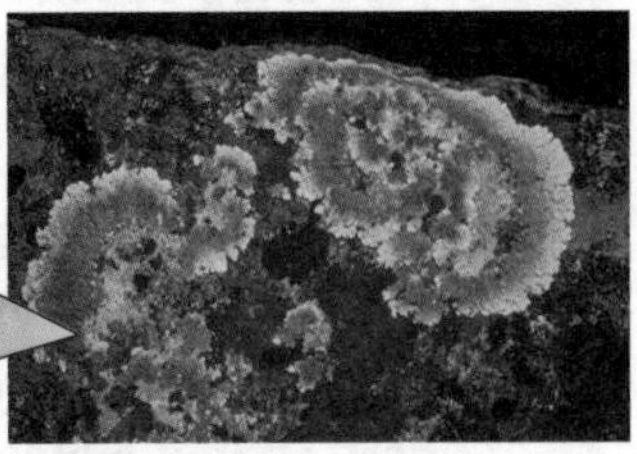

   Mayfly larvae are used to monitor water quality — they can't survive in polluted water. The cleaner the water, the more mayfly larvae survive.

2) Other species have adapted to live in polluted conditions — so if you see a lot of them you know there's a problem.

   Water lice, rat-tailed maggots and sludgeworms all indicate polluted water. But out of these, rat-tailed maggots and sludgeworms indicate a very high level of pollution.

Pollution Level Can Be Measured

There are a couple of ways of using indicator species to measure pollution:

1) You could do a simple survey to see if a species is present or absent from an area. This is a quick way of telling whether an area is polluted or not, but it's no good for telling how polluted an area is.
2) Counting the number of times an indicator species occurs in an area will give you a numerical value, allowing measurements from different areas to be compared so you can see how polluted an area is.

You can also measure pollution directly, for example:

1) Sensitive instruments can measure the concentrations of chemical pollutants, e.g. carbon dioxide or sulfur dioxide, in samples of air or water.
2) Satellite data can also be used to indicate pollutant level, e.g. satellites can show where the ozone layer is thin or absent, which is linked to the CFC level (see previous page).

Both Ways of Looking at Pollution Level Have Their Weaknesses

	Advantages	Disadvantages
Living methods (indicator species)	• Using living methods is a relatively quick, cheap and easy way of saying whether an area is polluted or not. No expensive equipment or highly trained workers are needed.	• Factors other than pollution (e.g. temperature) can influence the survival of indicator species so living methods aren't always reliable.
Non-living methods	• Directly measuring the pollutants gives reliable, numerical data that's easy to compare between different sites. • The exact pollutants can be identified too.	• Non-living methods often require more expensive equipment and trained workers than methods that use indicator species.

These are just a few examples — you may be able to think of other advantages and disadvantages of the two methods.

Sludgeworms and rat-tailed maggots — harbingers of doom...

I don't envy the person that has to trudge through the polluted water looking for rat-tailed maggots. Monitoring pollution is important though — it can have some pretty big impacts — so someone's gotta do it.

Endangered Species

Loads of species are endangered these days. But we can do things to help...

Many Factors Can Cause a Species to Become Extinct

1) ENDANGERED species, like tigers, have very low numbers left in the wild. They're in danger of becoming EXTINCT, where there's none of them at all — like the dodo and woolly mammoth.
2) Species are at risk of extinction if the following factors fall below a critical level:
   - The number of habitats — it's hard for organisms to find resources like food and shelter if there aren't enough suitable habitats to support them.
   - The number of individuals — if there are only a few individual members of a species left, it'll be hard to find mates. It also means there won't be much genetic variation in the population.
   - Genetic variation — this is the number of different alleles (forms of a gene) in a population. If genetic variation is low, then a species is less likely to be able to adapt to changes in the environment or survive the appearance of a new disease.

You Need to be Able to Evaluate Conservation Programmes

Conservation programmes are designed to help save endangered plants and animals. They involve things like protecting habitats, creating artificial environments and captive breeding.
You can EVALUATE how successful a conservation programme is likely to be by looking at:

1) GENETIC VARIATION — the species being conserved should have enough genetic variation to survive the appearance of new diseases and to cope with environmental change (see above).
2) VIABILITY OF POPULATIONS — populations should be able to reproduce — so they must contain both males and females of reproductive age. They should also be large enough to prevent related individuals having to breed together — this is called inbreeding and it reduces genetic variation.
3) AVAILABLE HABITATS — there should be plenty of suitable habitats to live in. The right type of habitat is especially important if the organisms being conserved are specialists (see page 79).
4) INTERACTION BETWEEN SPECIES — it's important that species interact with each other as they would in their natural environment, e.g. predator species should be allowed to hunt prey.

Conservation Programmes Benefit Wildlife and Humans

Conservation programmes do more than just benefit endangered species — they often help humans too:

1) PROTECTING THE HUMAN FOOD SUPPLY — over-fishing has greatly reduced fish stocks in the world's oceans. Conservation programmes can ensure that future generations will have fish to eat.
2) ENSURING MINIMAL DAMAGE TO FOOD CHAINS — if one species becomes extinct it will affect all the organisms that feed on and are eaten by that species, so the whole food chain is affected. This means conserving one species may help others to survive.
3) PROVIDING FUTURE MEDICINES — many of the medicines we use today come from plants. Undiscovered plant species may contain new medicinal chemicals. If these plants are allowed to become extinct, perhaps through rainforest destruction, we could miss out on valuable medicines.
4) CULTURAL ASPECTS — individual species may be important in a nation's or an area's cultural heritage, e.g. the bald eagle is being conserved in the USA as it is regarded as a national symbol.

It's a shame exams aren't an endangered species...

Even if you're someone who hates all plants and animals and much prefers concrete, remember that there are human benefits to protecting wildlife — and you need to know what they are.

Sustainable Development

It's not all doom and gloom... if we do things sustainably we'll be OK.

Development Has to be Sustainable

As the human population gets bigger...

1) We need to produce more food — so we'll need more land for farming.
2) We use up more energy. At the moment the vast majority of energy comes from burning fossil fuels. But these are rapidly running out — we need to find an alternative energy source.
3) We're producing more waste — it all needs to be put somewhere and a lot of it's polluting the Earth.

We need to find a way to exist where we don't damage the environment. This is 'sustainable development':

SUSTAINABLE DEVELOPMENT means providing for the needs of today's increasing population without harming the environment.

Sustainable development needs to be carefully planned and it needs to be carried out all over the Earth. This means there needs to be cooperation locally, nationally and internationally.

EXAMPLES OF WHAT'S BEING DONE TO PROMOTE SUSTAINABLE DEVELOPMENT:

1) Fishing quotas have been introduced to prevent some types of fish, such as cod, from becoming extinct in certain areas. This means they'll still be around in years to come.
2) To make the production of wood and paper sustainable there are laws insisting that logging companies plant new trees to replace those that they've felled.

Education is important. If people are aware of the problems, they may be more likely to help — e.g. by not buying certain types of fish and only buying wood products from sustainably managed forests. Sustainable development also helps endangered species by considering the impacts on their habitats.

Case Study: Whales — Some Species are Endangered

1) Whales have commercial value (they can be used to make money) when they're alive and dead.
2) They're a tourist attraction — people go to some areas especially to see the whales.
3) Whale meat and oil can be used, and cosmetics can be made from a waxy substance in their intestines. However, this has led to some species of whale becoming endangered.
4) The International Whaling Commission (IWC) has struggled to get nations to agree to restrict whaling. In 1982 the member nations declared a stop to whaling, the only exception being Norway, which still catches whales. Taking a small number of whales ('culling') for scientific research is allowed and is carried out by Japan, Iceland and the Faroe Islands.
5) But it's hard to check that countries are sticking to the agreement, and even when anyone is caught, the IWC doesn't have the authority to enforce any kind of punishment. So a lot of illegal whaling goes on.
6) Some whales are kept in captivity — there are different views about this:
   - Whales don't have much space in captivity and they are sometimes used for entertaining people. Some people think it's wrong that the whales lose their freedom and that they would be much happier in the wild, but captive whales do increase awareness of the animals and their problems.
   - Captive breeding programmes allow whales to be bred in numbers and released back into the wild.
   - Research on captive whales can help us understand their needs better to help conservation. There is still a lot we don't fully understand about whales, e.g. whale communication, their migration patterns and how they survive in very deep water.

Fishermen are just too effishent...

(groan...)

Whales are amazing animals — it'd be a huge pity if they were wiped out and weren't around for future generations. It's not just deliberate hunting that's a problem for them — they often get tangled up in fishing nets or collide with ships. And pollution doesn't do them much good either. It's a tough life.

Revision Summary for Module B2

Believe it or not, it's already time for another round of questions. Do as many as you can and if there are some that you're finding really fiddly, don't panic. Have a quick flick over the relevant topics and give the questions another go once you've had another chance to read the pages. Good luck — not that you need it.

1) What group comes between 'family' and 'species' when classifying organisms?
2) Give two reasons why classification systems change over time.
3) What is a species?
4) What is the binomial system? Explain why it is important.
5) Why might two unrelated species look very similar?
6) What does each bar on a pyramid of biomass represent?
7) Below are two pyramid diagrams. One is a pyramid of biomass and one is a pyramid of numbers. Which diagram is which? Explain your answer.

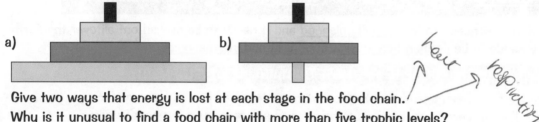

a)
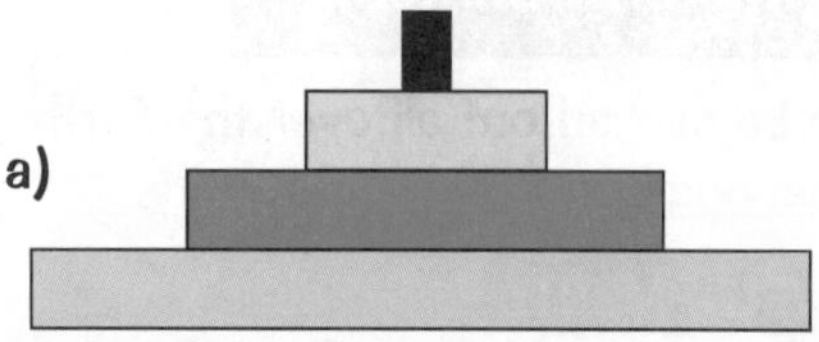
b)
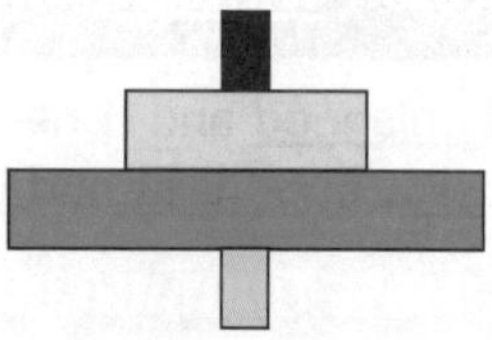

8) Give two ways that energy is lost at each stage in the food chain.
9) Why is it unusual to find a food chain with more than five trophic levels?
10) What is intraspecific competition?
11) Sketch a graph of prey and predator populations and explain the pattern shown.
12) What is the difference between a parasitic and a mutualistic relationship? Give an example of each.
13) 'In a habitat with stable conditions, specialists will out-compete generalists.' True or false?
14) Describe how extremophile bacteria are able to survive very high temperatures.
15) What are antifreeze proteins?
16) How does having a small surface area to volume ratio help organisms to keep warm in cold climates?
17) Explain how counter-current heat exchange systems keep penguins from getting too cold.
18) Describe one anatomical adaptation that increases heat loss for an animal that lives in a hot environment.
19) Describe two ways that desert plants are adapted to survive in dry conditions.
20) Describe Darwin's theory of evolution by natural selection.
21) Describe how speciation can happen through geographical isolation.
22) How did Lamarck's theory of evolution contrast with Darwin's?
23) Give two reasons why the theory of evolution by natural selection is now widely accepted.
24) Explain how carbon is removed from the air in the carbon cycle.
25) Describe two processes that release carbon dioxide into the atmosphere.
26) Explain the role that decomposers play in the nitrogen cycle.
27) What role do nitrogen-fixing bacteria play in the nitrogen cycle?
28) What does the term 'carbon footprint' mean?
29) Name a gas that causes acid rain. Where does this gas come from?
30) Give one effect of ozone depletion from pollution by CFCs.
31) What are indicator species? Give examples.
32) Give one disadvantage of using indicator species to measure pollution.
33) Give four factors you'd look at to evaluate a conservation programme.
34) Give four ways in which conservation programmes benefit humans.
35) What are the commercial values of whales?
36) Name two aspects of whale biology that we don't fully understand.

The Earth's Structure

This page is all about the structure of the Earth — what the planet's like inside, and how scientists study it...

The Earth has a Crust, a Mantle and a Core

1) The crust is Earth's thin outer layer of solid rock (its average depth is 20 km).
2) The lithosphere includes the crust and upper part of the mantle, and is made up of a jigsaw of 'tectonic plates'. The lithosphere is relatively cold and rigid, and is over 100 km thick in places.
3) The mantle is the solid section between the crust and the core. Near the crust it's very rigid. As you go deeper into the mantle the temperature increases — here it becomes less rigid and can flow very slowly (it behaves like it's semi-liquid).
4) The core is just over half the Earth's radius. The inner core is solid, while the outer core is liquid.
5) Radioactive decay creates a lot of the heat inside the Earth. This heat creates convection currents in the mantle, which causes the plates of the lithosphere to move.

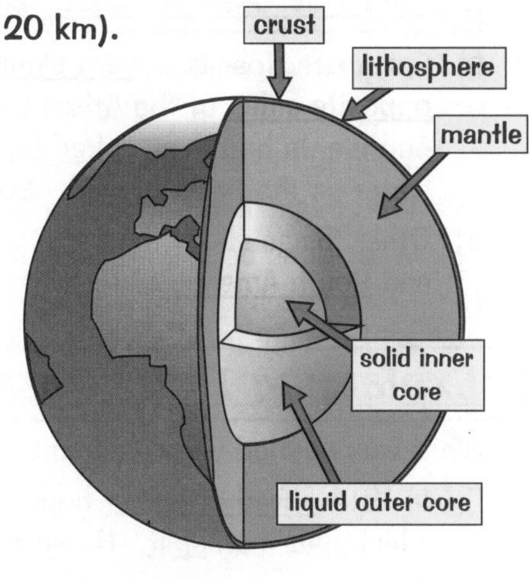

The Earth's Surface is Made Up of Large Plates of Rock

1) Tectonic plates are like big rocky rafts that float on the mantle (they're less dense than the mantle).
2) This map shows where the edges of the plates are. As they move, the continents move too.
3) The plates move very slowly — at a speed of about 2.5 cm per year.
4) Volcanoes and earthquakes often occur where the plates meet. It's the movement of the plates against each other that causes them.

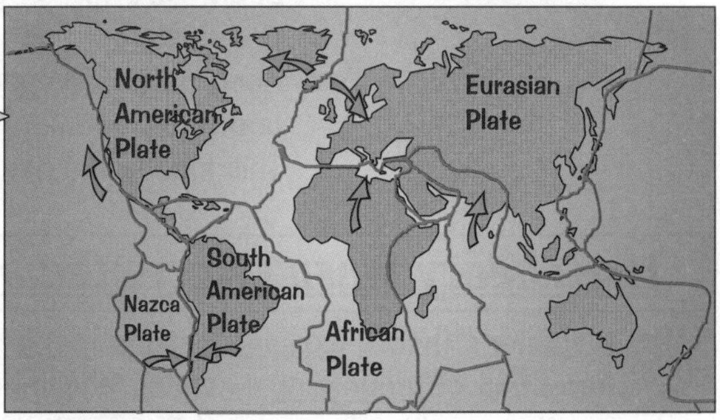

Seismic Waves Can Tell Us What's Below The Crust

1) It's difficult to study the inner structure of the Earth — you can't get at it directly, because the crust is too thick to drill through.
2) Scientists use seismic waves (shock waves) to study the Earth's structure. These are produced by earthquakes. Seismic waves can also be produced by setting off a big man-made explosion at the Earth's surface.
3) By measuring the time that it takes for these waves to travel through the Earth, and where they are detected, scientists can draw conclusions about the structure of the Earth.

There are two types of seismic wave that can travel through the Earth — P-waves and S-waves. P-waves travel through solids and liquids. S-waves can only travel through solids.

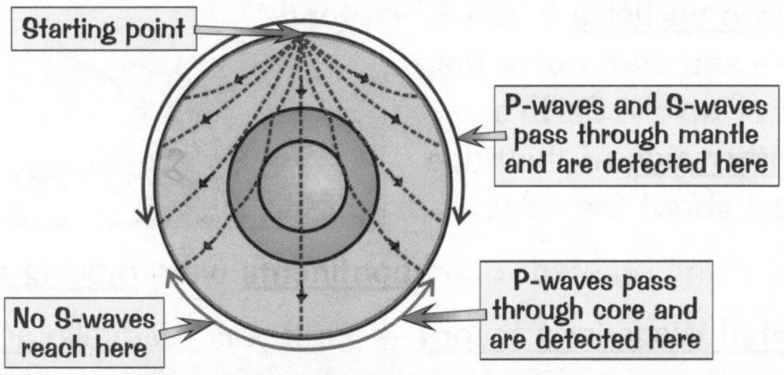

1) S-waves can travel through the mantle, which shows that it's solid.
2) But S-waves are not detected in the core's shadow, so the outer core must be liquid.
3) P-waves travel faster through the middle of the core, which suggests that the inner core is solid.

2.5 cm a year — that's as fast as your fingernails grow...

So everyone standing on the surface of our little blue-green planet is actually floating round very slowly on a sea of semi-liquid rock. Make sure you understand the stuff about tectonic plates — there's more coming up...

Plate Tectonics

The idea that the Earth's surface is made up of moving plates of rock has been around since the early twentieth century. But it took a while to catch on.

Observations About the Earth Hadn't Been Explained

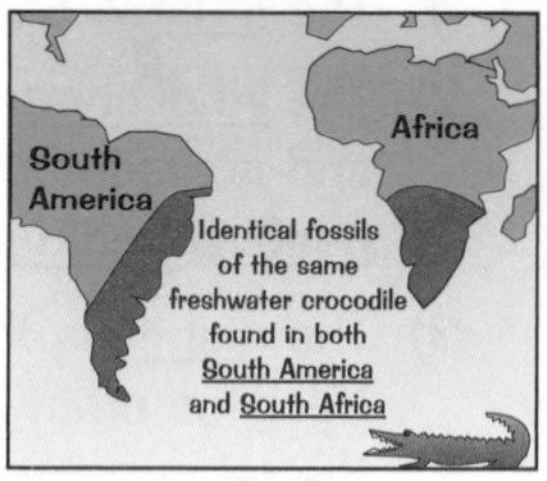

1) For years, fossils of very similar plants and animals had been found on opposite sides of the Atlantic Ocean. Most people thought this was because the continents had been linked by 'land bridges', which had sunk or been covered by water as the Earth cooled. But not everyone was convinced, even back then.
2) Other things about the Earth puzzled people too — like why the coastlines of Africa and South America fit together and why there are fossils of sea creatures in the Alps.

Explaining These Observations Needed a Leap of Imagination

What was needed was a scientist with a bit of insight... a smidgeon of creativity... a touch of genius...

1) In 1914 Alfred Wegener hypothesised that Africa and South America had previously been one continent which had then split. He started to look for more evidence to back up his hypothesis. He found it...
2) E.g. there were matching layers in the rocks on different continents, and similar earthworms living in both South America and South Africa.

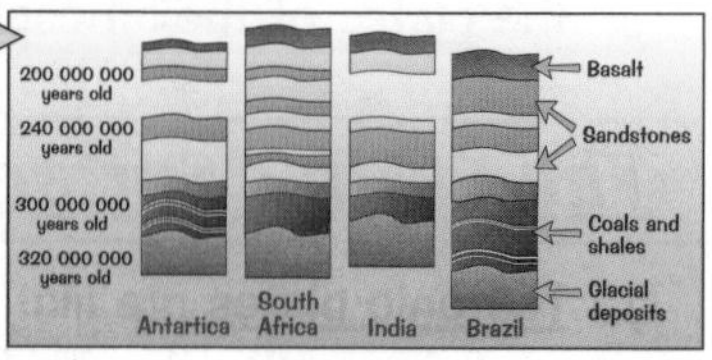

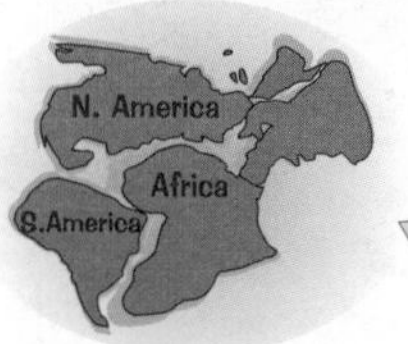

3) Wegener's theory of 'continental drift' supposed that about 300 million years ago there had been just one 'supercontinent' — which he called Pangaea. According to Wegener, Pangaea broke into smaller chunks, and these chunks (our modern-day continents) are still slowly 'drifting' apart. This idea is the basis behind the modern theory of plate tectonics.

The Theory Wasn't Accepted at First — for a Variety of Reasons

1) Wegener's theory explained things that couldn't be explained by the 'land bridge' theory (e.g. the formation of mountains — which Wegener said happened as continents smashed into each other). But it was a big change, and the reaction from other scientists was hostile.
2) The main problem was that Wegener's explanation of how the 'drifting' happened wasn't convincing (and the movement wasn't detectable). Wegener claimed the continents' movement could be caused by tidal forces and the Earth's rotation — but other geologists showed that this was impossible.

Eventually, the Evidence Became Overwhelming

1) In the 1960s, scientists investigated the Mid-Atlantic ridge, which runs the whole length of the Atlantic.
2) They found evidence that magma (molten rock) rises up through the sea floor, solidifies and forms underwater mountains that are roughly symmetrical either side of the ridge. The evidence suggested that the sea floor was spreading — at about 10 cm per year.
3) Even better evidence that the continents are moving apart came from the magnetic orientation of the rocks. As the liquid magma erupts out of the gap, iron particles in the rocks tend to align themselves with the Earth's magnetic field — and as it cools they set in position. Now then... every half million years or so the Earth's magnetic field swaps direction — and the rock on either side of the ridge has bands of alternate magnetic polarity, symmetrical about the ridge.

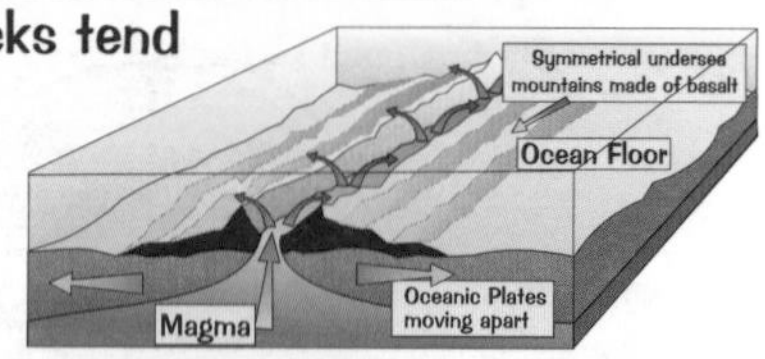

4) This was convincing evidence that new sea floor was being created... and continents were moving apart.
5) All the evidence collected by other scientists supported Wegener's theory — so it was gradually accepted.

I told you so — but no one ever believes me...

Wegener wasn't right about everything, but his main idea was correct. The scientific community was a bit slow to accept it, but once there was more evidence to support it, they got on board. That's science for you...

Volcanic Eruptions

The theory of plate tectonics not only explains why the continents move, it also makes sense of natural hazards such as volcanoes and earthquakes.

Volcanoes are Formed by Molten Rock

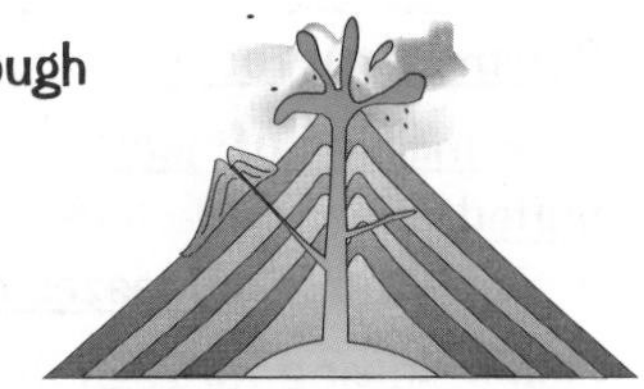

1) Volcanoes occur when molten rock (magma) from the mantle emerges through the Earth's crust.
2) Magma rises up (through the crust) and 'boils over' where it can — sometimes quite violently if the pressure is released suddenly. (When the molten rock is below the surface of the Earth it's called magma — but when it erupts from a volcano it's called lava.)

Oceanic and Continental Crust Colliding Causes Volcanoes

1) The crust at the ocean floor is denser than the crust below the continents.
2) When two tectonic plates collide, a dense oceanic plate will be forced underneath a less dense continental plate. This is called subduction.
3) Oceanic crust also tends to be cooler at the edges of a tectonic plate — so the edges sink easily, pulling the oceanic plate down.
4) As the oceanic crust is forced down it melts and starts to rise. If this molten rock finds its way to the surface, volcanoes form.

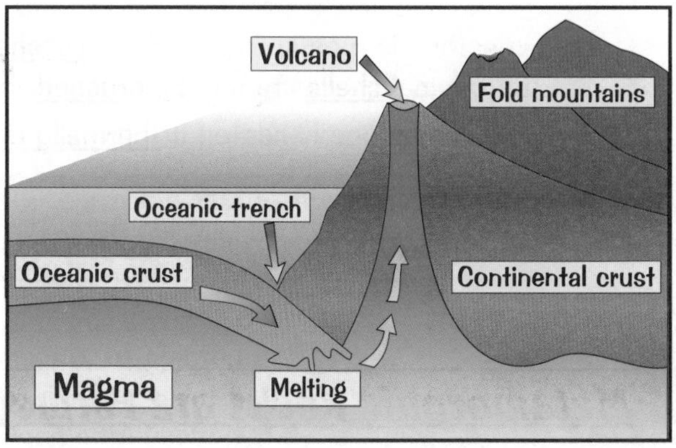

Volcanic Activity Forms Igneous Rock

1) Igneous rock is made when any sort of molten rock cools down and solidifies. Lots of rocks on the surface of the Earth were formed this way.
2) The type of igneous rock (and the behaviour of the volcano) depends on how quickly the magma cools and the composition of the magma.
3) Some volcanoes produce magma that forms iron-rich basalt. The lava from the eruption is runny, and the eruption is fairly safe. (As safe as you can be with molten rock at 1200 °C, I suppose.)
4) But if the magma is silica-rich rhyolite, the eruption is explosive. It produces thick lava which can be violently blown out of the top of the volcano. Crikey.

Geologists Try to Predict Volcanic Eruptions

1) Geologists study volcanoes to try to find out if there are signs that a volcanic eruption might happen soon — things like magma movement below the ground near to a volcano.

2) Being able to spot these kinds of clues means that scientists can predict eruptions with much greater accuracy than they could in the past.
3) It's tricky though — volcanoes are very unpredictable. Most likely, scientists will only be able to say that an eruption's more likely than normal — not that it's certain. But even just knowing that can save lives.

Make the Earth move for you — stand next to a volcano...

Volcanoes can erupt with huge force, so it might seem odd to choose to live near one. But there are benefits — volcanic ash creates very fertile soil that's great for farming. It would be much safer if eruptions could be predicted accurately — geologists aren't there yet, but their predictions are getting better all the time.

The Three Different Types of Rock

Scientists classify rocks according to how they're formed. The three different types are: sedimentary, metamorphic and igneous. Sedimentary rocks are generally pretty soft, while igneous rocks are well hard.

There are Three Steps in the Formation of Sedimentary Rock

1) Sedimentary rocks are formed from layers of sediment laid down in lakes or seas.
2) Over millions of years the layers get buried under more layers and the weight pressing down squeezes out the water.
3) Fluids flowing through the pores deposit natural mineral cement.

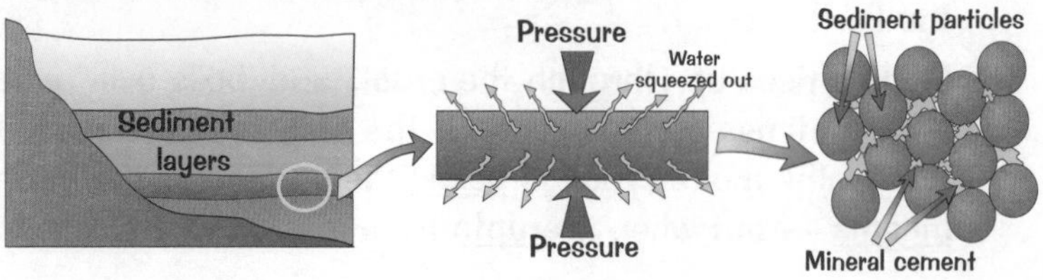

Limestone is a Sedimentary Rock Formed from Seashells

1) Limestone is mostly formed from seashells. It's mostly calcium carbonate and grey/white in colour. The original shells are mostly crushed, but there can still be quite a few fossilised shells remaining.
2) When limestone is heated it thermally decomposes to make calcium oxide and carbon dioxide:

calcium carbonate → calcium oxide + carbon dioxide

$$CaCO_3(s) \rightarrow CaO(s) + CO_2(g)$$

Thermal decomposition is when one substance chemically breaks down into at least two new substances when it's heated.

Metamorphic Rocks are Formed from Other Rocks

1) Metamorphic rocks are formed by the action of heat and pressure on sedimentary (or even igneous) rocks over long periods of time.
2) The mineral structure and texture may be different, but the chemical composition is often the same.
3) So long as the rocks don't actually melt they're classed as metamorphic. If they melt and turn to magma, they're gone (though they may eventually resurface as igneous rocks).

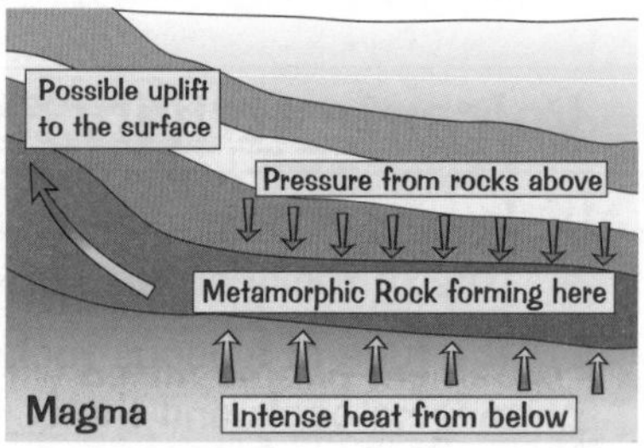

Marble is a Metamorphic Rock Formed from Limestone

1) Marble is another form of calcium carbonate.
2) Very high temperatures and pressures break down the limestone and it reforms as small crystals.
3) This gives marble a more even texture and makes it much harder.

Igneous Rocks are Formed from Fresh Magma

1) Igneous rocks are formed when magma cools (see previous page).
2) They contain various different minerals in randomly arranged interlocking crystals — this makes them very hard.
3) Granite is a very hard igneous rock (even harder than marble). It's ideal for steps and buildings.

Igneous rocks are real cool — or they're magma...

There are a few scientific terms on this page that you need to learn, but there's nothing too tricky to get your head round. Just remember that limestone is a sedimentary rock, marble is a metamorphic rock and granite is an igneous rock. And that's why granite is harder than marble, which is harder than limestone. Job's a good 'un.

Construction Materials

Loads of different construction materials are made from stuff found in the Earth's crust.
For example, there are metals like aluminium and iron, rocks such as granite, limestone and marble, and then there are man-made materials like bricks, cement, concrete and glass.

Aluminium and Iron are Extracted from Ores in Rocks

Rocks are usually a mixture of minerals. Ores are minerals we can get useful materials from. Aluminium and iron are construction materials that can be extracted from their ores.

Glass is Made by Melting Limestone, Sand and Soda

1) Just heat up limestone (calcium carbonate) with sand (silicon dioxide) and soda (sodium carbonate) until it melts.
2) When the mixture cools it comes out as glass. It's as easy as that. Eat your heart out Mr Pilkington.

Bricks are Made from Clay

1) Clay is a mineral formed from weathered and decomposed rock. It's soft when it's dug up out of the ground, which makes it easy to mould into bricks.
2) But it can be hardened by firing at very high temperatures. This makes it ideal as a building material — bricks can withstand the weight of lots more bricks on top of them.

Limestone and Clay are Heated to Make Cement

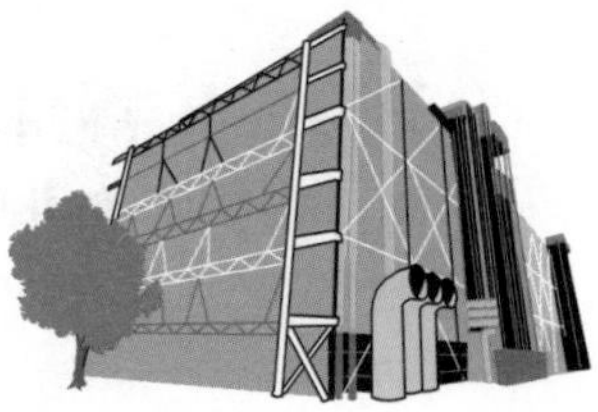

1) Clay contains aluminium and silicates.
2) Powdered clay and powdered limestone are roasted in a rotating kiln to make a complex mixture of calcium and aluminium silicates, called cement.
3) When cement is mixed with water a slow chemical reaction takes place. This causes the cement to gradually set hard.
4) Cement can be mixed with sand, aggregate (gravelly stuff) and water to make concrete.
5) Concrete is a very quick and cheap way of constructing buildings — and it shows... — concrete has got to be the most hideously unattractive building material ever known.
6) Reinforced concrete is a 'composite material' — it's a combination of concrete and a solid steel support (like steel rods). It's a better construction material than ordinary concrete because it combines the hardness of concrete with the flexibility and the strength of steel. (It isn't any prettier than plain old concrete though...)

Extracting Rocks Can Cause Environmental Damage

1) Quarrying uses up land and destroys habitats. It costs money to make quarry sites look pretty again.
2) Transporting rock can cause noise and pollution.
3) The quarrying process itself produces dust and makes a lot of noise — they often use dynamite to blast the rock out of the ground.
4) Disused sites can be dangerous. Every year people drown in former quarries that have been turned into (very very deep) lakes. Disused mines have been known to collapse — this can cause subsidence (including huge holes appearing and buildings cracking, railway lines twisting etc.).

Bricks are like eggs — they both have to be laid...

If red houses are made of red bricks and blue houses are made of blue bricks, then what colour bricks are greenhouses made of? If you said green, then you're not properly awake and most likely you need to go back and read the page again. If you correctly identified that a greenhouse is made of glass rather than green bricks, then continue to the next page. Once you've learnt all the above, obviously.

Extracting Pure Copper

Copper is dug out of the ground as a copper ore (like chalcopyrite or malachite). Then the metal is extracted from it by mixing the ore with carbon and heating. The copper you get this way isn't pure enough to use in electrical conductors (the purer it is, the better it conducts). But it can be purified using another method...

Electrolysis is Used to Obtain Very Pure Copper

1) Electrolysis means "splitting up with electricity" — in this case passing a current through a piece of impure copper splits the pure copper off from the nasty impurities.
2) The copper is immersed in a liquid (called the electrolyte) which conducts electricity. Electrolytes are usually free ions dissolved in water. Copper(II) sulfate solution is the electrolyte used in purifying copper — it contains Cu^{2+} ions.
3) The electrical supply acts like an electron pump. This is what happens:

> 1) It pulls electrons off copper atoms at the anode, causing them to go into solution as Cu^{2+} ions.
> 2) It then offers electrons at the cathode to nearby Cu^{2+} ions to turn them back into copper atoms.
> 3) The impurities are dropped at the anode as a sludge, whilst pure copper atoms bond to the cathode.

Here's a diagram of the apparatus you need for the job — you could be asked to label it in the exam, so make sure you learn it.

The cathode is the negative electrode. It starts as a thin piece of pure copper and more pure copper adds to it.

Pure copper is deposited on the pure cathode (–ve)

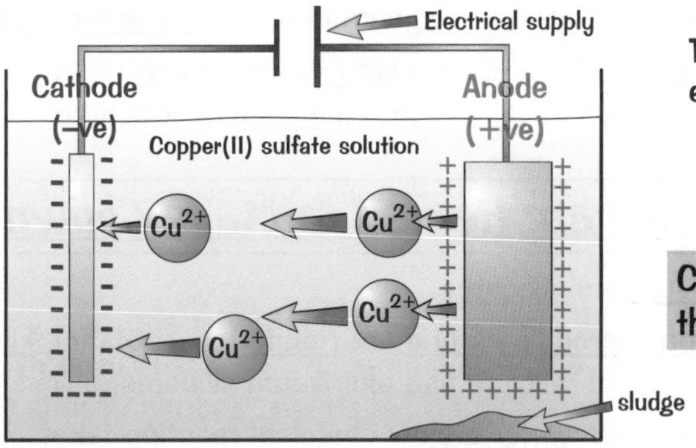

The anode is the positive electrode. It's just a big lump of impure copper, which will dissolve.

Copper dissolves from the impure anode (+ve)

The reaction at the cathode is:

$$Cu^{2+}_{(aq)} + 2e^- \rightarrow Cu_{(s)}$$

REDUCTION is the gain of electrons (OR the removal of oxygen) — so this is an example of a reduction reaction.

The reaction at the anode is:

$$Cu_{(s)} \rightarrow Cu^{2+}_{(aq)} + 2e^-$$

OXIDATION is the loss of electrons (OR the addition of oxygen) — so this is an example of an oxidation reaction.

During electrolysis, copper dissolves away from the anode and is deposited at the cathode. So the anode loses mass and the cathode gains mass. (The electrolysis process is often allowed to go on for weeks and the cathode can be twenty times bigger at the end of it.)

Recycling Copper Saves Money and Resources

1) It's cheaper to recycle copper than it is to mine and extract new copper from its ore.
2) And recycling copper uses only 15% of the energy that'd be used to mine and extract the same amount.
3) But it can be hard to convince people that it's worth the effort to sort and recycle their metal waste. Even then you have to sort out the copper from all the other waste metal — which takes time and energy.

Revision and electrolysis — they can both go on for weeks...

Don't get tripped up by the two definitions of oxidation/reduction on this page. You need to know both of them — but it's important to remember that in this case you aren't adding or removing any oxygen, just electrons. Make sure you've got a handle on how electrolysis works — it's a really useful way to purify metals...

Alloys

Different metals have different properties, but by combining them with other elements you can create a new material that keeps some of the properties of the original materials, and has some extra properties too.

An Alloy is a Mixture of a Metal and Other Elements

1) Alloys can be a mixture of two or more different metals (like brass or bronze).
2) They can also be a mixture of a metal and a non-metal (like steel).
3) Alloys often have properties that are different from the metals they are made from — and these new properties often make the alloy more useful than the pure metal.

Steel is an Alloy of Iron and Carbon

1) Steel is harder than iron.
2) Steel is also stronger than iron, as long as the amount of carbon does not get larger than about 1%.
3) Iron on its own will rust (corrode) fairly quickly, but steel is much less likely to rust. A small amount of carbon makes a big difference.
4) A lot of things are made from steel — girders, bridges, engine parts, cutlery, washing machines, saucepans, ships, drill bits, cars etc. There's more about steel in car manufacture on the next page.

Brass, Bronze, Solder and Amalgam are also Alloys

1) Brass is an alloy of copper and zinc. Most of the properties of brass are just a mixture of those of the copper and zinc, although brass is harder than either of them. Brass is used for making brass musical instruments (trumpets, trombones, French horns etc.). It's also used for fixtures and fittings such as screws, springs, doorknobs etc.
2) Bronze is an alloy of copper and tin. It's much harder and stronger than tin, and it's more resistant to corrosion than either copper or tin. Bronze is used to make springs and motor bearings. It's also used to make bells, and it's used in sculpture.
3) Solder is usually an alloy of lead and tin. Unlike pure materials it doesn't have a definite melting point, but gradually solidifies as it cools down. This is pretty useful if you want to solder things together.
4) An amalgam is an alloy containing mercury. A large-scale use of one kind of amalgam is in dentistry, for filling teeth.

Modern fillings tend to be made from tooth-coloured resin instead. This is partly because amalgam fillings are dark silvery in colour, and therefore rather obvious in your mouth, and partly because some people worry that the mercury in the amalgam could cause health problems (although there's not much evidence for this).

Some Alloys are Smart

1) Nitinol is the name given to a family of alloys of nickel and titanium that have shape memory.
2) This means they "remember" their original shape, and go back to it even after being bent and twisted.
3) This has increased the number of uses for alloys. You can get specs with Nitinol frames — these can be bent and even sat on and they still go back into their original shape.

I eat bits of metal all day — it's my staple diet...

You need metals or alloys with different properties for different uses. For example, to make an engine part that's going to get very hot, you need to use something with a high melting point. And if you're building an aircraft you're going to need something that's strong and light. If you get a question in the exam about what alloy is best for a particular job, just use a bit of common sense and you'll be fine.

Building Cars

There are loads of different materials in your average car — different materials have different properties and so have different uses. Makes sense.

Iron and Steel Corrode Much More than Aluminium

Iron corrodes easily. In other words, it rusts. ← The word "rust" is only used for the corrosion of iron, not other metals.

Rusting only happens when the iron's in contact with both oxygen (from the air) and water.

The chemical reaction that takes place when iron corrodes is an oxidation reaction. The iron gains oxygen to form iron(III) oxide. Water then becomes loosely bonded to the iron(III) oxide and the result is hydrated iron(III) oxide — which we call rust.

Learn the word equation for the reaction: **iron + oxygen + water → hydrated iron(III) oxide**

Unfortunately, rust is a soft crumbly solid that soon flakes off to leave more iron available to rust again. And if the water's salty or acidic, rusting will take place a lot quicker. Cars in coastal places rust a lot because they get covered in salty sea-spray. Cars in dry deserty places hardly rust at all.

Aluminium doesn't corrode when it's wet. This is a bit odd because aluminium is more reactive than iron. What happens is that the aluminium reacts very quickly with oxygen in the air to form aluminium oxide. A nice protective layer of aluminium oxide sticks firmly to the aluminium below and stops any further reaction taking place (the oxide isn't crumbly and flaky like rust, so it won't fall off).

Car Bodies: Aluminium or Steel?

Aluminium has two big advantages over steel:

1) It has a much lower density, so the car body of an aluminium car will be lighter than the same car made of steel. This gives the aluminium car much better fuel economy, which saves fuel resources.
2) A car body made with aluminium corrodes less and so it'll have a longer lifetime.

But aluminium has a massive disadvantage. It costs a lot more than iron or steel. That's why car manufacturers tend to build cars out of steel instead.

You Need Various Materials to Build Different Bits of a Car

1) Steel is strong and it can be hammered into sheets and welded together — good for the bodywork.
2) Aluminium is strong and has a low density — it's used for parts of the engine, to reduce weight.
3) Glass is transparent — cars need windscreens and windows.
4) Plastics are light and hardwearing, so they're used as internal coverings for doors, dashboards etc. They're also electrical insulators, used for covering electrical wires.
5) Fibres (natural and synthetic) are hard-wearing, so they're used to cover the seats and floor.

Unless you can afford leather seats, that is.

Recycling Cars is Important

1) As with all recycling, the idea is to save natural resources, save money and reduce landfill use.
2) At the moment a lot of the metal from a scrap car is recycled, though most of the other materials (e.g. plastics, rubber etc.) go into landfill. But European laws are now in place saying that 85% of the materials in a car (rising to 95% of a car by 2015) must be recyclable.
3) The biggest problem with recycling all the non-metal bits of a car is that they have to be separated before they can be recycled. Sorting out different types of plastic is a pain in the neck.

CGP jokes — 85% recycled since 1996...

When manufacturers choose materials for cars, they have to weigh up alternatives — they balance safety, environmental impact, and cost. In the exam, you could be asked to do the same. Sounds fun.

Acids and Bases

You'll find acids and bases at home, in industry and in the lab — they're an important set of chemicals.

The pH Scale and Universal Indicator

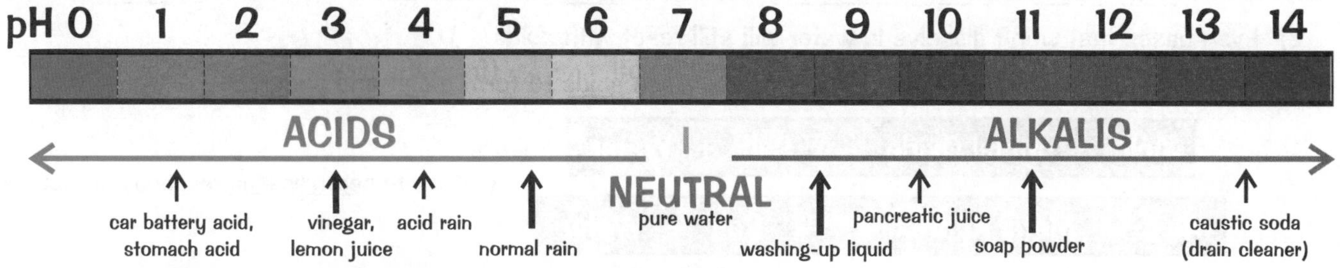

An Indicator is a Dye That Changes Colour

1) The dye in an indicator changes colour depending on the pH of a substance.
2) Universal indicator is a combination of dyes. It changes colour gradually as the pH changes.
3) It's very useful for estimating the pH of a solution. You just add a drop of the indicator to your solution, then compare the colour it turns to a colour chart (like the one above) to work out the pH.
4) Some indicators change colour suddenly at a particular pH.
   E.g. phenolphthalein changes suddenly from colourless to pink as the pH rises above 8.

The pH Scale Goes from 0 to 14

1) A very strong acid has pH 0. A very strong alkali has pH 14.
2) A neutral substance has pH 7 (e.g. pure water).

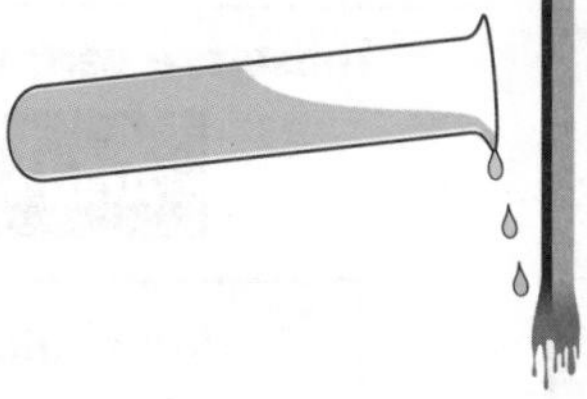

Acids and Bases Neutralise Each Other

An ACID is a substance with a pH of less than 7. Acids form H^+ ions in water.
The pH of an acid is determined by the concentration of the H^+ ions.

A BASE is a substance with a pH of greater than 7.
An ALKALI is a base that is soluble in water. Alkalis form OH^- ions in water.

The reaction between acids and bases is called neutralisation. Make sure you learn it:

$$\text{acid} + \text{base} \rightarrow \text{salt} + \text{water}$$

Neutralisation can also be seen in terms of H^+ and OH^- ions like this, so learn it too:

$$H^+ + OH^- \rightleftharpoons H_2O$$

This symbol ($\rightleftharpoons$) means the reaction is reversible. There's more on this on page 103.

When an acid neutralises a base (or vice versa), the products are neutral, i.e. they have a pH of 7.

This'll give you a firm base for Chemistry...

There's no getting away from acids and bases in Chemistry, or even in real life. They are everywhere — acids are found in loads of foods, like vinegar and fruit, and as food flavourings and preservatives, whilst alkalis (particularly sodium hydroxide) are used to help make all sorts of things from soaps to ceramics.

Reactions of Acids

When you mix an acid and a base, exactly what you end up with depends on which acid and base you use...

Metal Oxides and Metal Hydroxides are Bases

1) Some metal oxides and metal hydroxides dissolve in water. These soluble compounds are alkalis.
2) Even bases that won't dissolve in water will still react with acids.
3) So, all metal oxides and metal hydroxides react with acids to form a salt and water.

Acid + Metal Oxide → Salt + Water

Acid + Metal Hydroxide → Salt + Water

(These are neutralisation reactions, of course.)

hydrochloric acid	+	copper oxide	→	copper chloride	+	water
$2HCl$	+	CuO	→	$CuCl_2$	+	H_2O
sulfuric acid	+	potassium hydroxide	→	potassium sulfate	+	water
H_2SO_4	+	$2KOH$	→	K_2SO_4	+	$2H_2O$
nitric acid	+	sodium hydroxide	→	sodium nitrate	+	water
HNO_3	+	$NaOH$	→	$NaNO_3$	+	H_2O
phosphoric acid	+	sodium hydroxide	→	sodium phosphate	+	water
H_3PO_4	+	$3NaOH$	→	Na_3PO_4	+	$3H_2O$

Acids and Carbonates Produce Carbon Dioxide

These are very like the ones above — they just produce carbon dioxide as well.

Acid + Carbonate → Salt + Water + Carbon dioxide

hydrochloric acid	+	sodium carbonate	→	sodium chloride	+	water	+	carbon dioxide
$2HCl$	+	Na_2CO_3	→	$2NaCl$	+	H_2O	+	CO_2
sulfuric acid	+	calcium carbonate	→	calcium sulfate	+	water	+	carbon dioxide
H_2SO_4	+	$CaCO_3$	→	$CaSO_4$	+	H_2O	+	CO_2
phosphoric acid	+	sodium carbonate	→	sodium phosphate	+	water	+	carbon dioxide
$2H_3PO_4$	+	$3Na_2CO_3$	→	$2Na_3PO_4$	+	$3H_2O$	+	$3CO_2$

Acids and Ammonia Produce Ammonium Salts

And lastly...

Acid + Ammonia → Ammonium salt

hydrochloric acid	+	ammonia	→	ammonium chloride
HCl	+	NH_3	→	NH_4Cl
sulfuric acid	+	ammonia	→	ammonium sulfate
H_2SO_4	+	$2NH_3$	→	$(NH_4)_2SO_4$
nitric acid	+	ammonia	→	ammonium nitrate
HNO_3	+	NH_3	→	NH_4NO_3

If you're not sure how molecular formulas or balanced equations work, have a look back at pages 30-31. It's really important to know it for this module too.

The last reaction with nitric acid produces the famous ammonium nitrate fertiliser (see pages 101-102).

Acid + Revision → Insomnia Cure...

In the exam you could be asked to give the name of the salt formed when any of the four acids mentioned on this page is added to a metal oxide, hydroxide or carbonate, or ammonia. They might ask you to write a word or symbol equation for the reaction too. Try out lots of different combinations until you understand how all of them work.

Fertilisers

There's a lot more to using fertilisers than making your garden look nice and pretty...

Fertilisers Provide Plants with the Essential Elements for Growth

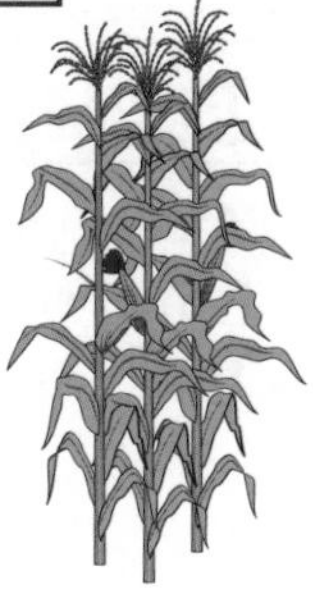

1) The three main essential elements in fertilisers are nitrogen, phosphorus and potassium. If plants don't get enough of these elements, their growth and life processes are affected.
2) These elements may be missing from the soil if they've been used up by a previous crop.
3) Fertilisers replace these missing elements or provide more of them. This helps to increase the crop yield, as the crops can grow faster and bigger. For example, fertilisers add more nitrogen to plant proteins, which makes the plants grow faster.
4) The fertiliser must first dissolve in water before it can be taken in by the crop roots.

Ammonia Can be Neutralised with Acids to Produce Fertilisers

As you saw on page 100, ammonia is a base and can be neutralised by acids to make ammonium salts. Ammonia is really important to world food production, because it's a key ingredient of many fertilisers.

1) If you neutralise nitric acid with ammonia you get ammonium nitrate. It's an especially good fertiliser because it has nitrogen from two sources, the ammonia and the nitric acid — kind of a double dose.
2) Ammonium sulfate can also be used as a fertiliser. You make it by neutralising sulfuric acid with ammonia.
3) Ammonium phosphate is a fertiliser made by neutralising phosphoric acid with ammonia.
4) Potassium nitrate is also a fertiliser — it can be made by neutralising nitric acid with potassium hydroxide.

Fertilisers are Really Useful — But They Can Cause Big Problems

The population of the world is rising rapidly. Fertilisers increase crop yield, so the more fertiliser we make, the more crops we can grow, and the more people we can feed. But if we use too many fertilisers we risk polluting our water supplies and causing eutrophication.

Fertilisers Damage Lakes and Rivers — Eutrophication

1) When fertiliser is put on fields some of it inevitably runs off and finds its way into rivers and streams.
2) The level of nitrates and phosphates in the river water increases.
3) Algae living in the river water use the nutrients to multiply rapidly, creating an algal bloom (a carpet of algae near the surface of the river). This blocks off the light to the river plants below. The plants cannot photosynthesise, so they have no food and they die.
4) Aerobic bacteria feed on the dead plants and start to multiply. As the bacteria multiply they use up all the oxygen in the water. As a result pretty much everything in the river dies (including fish and insects).

   Aerobic just means that they need oxygen to live.
5) This process is called EUTROPHICATION, which basically means 'too much of a good thing'.

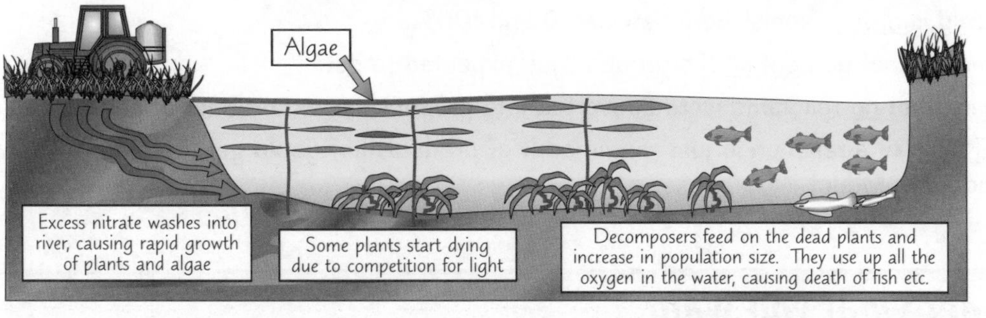
Algae
Excess nitrate washes into river, causing rapid growth of plants and algae
Some plants start dying due to competition for light
Decomposers feed on the dead plants and increase in population size. They use up all the oxygen in the water, causing death of fish etc.

As the picture shows, too many nitrates in the water cause a sequence of 'mega-growth', 'mega-death' and 'mega-decay' involving most of the plant and animal life in the water.

There's nowt wrong wi' just spreadin' muck on it...

Unfortunately, no matter how good something is, there's nearly always a downside. It's a good idea to learn the eutrophication diagram really, really well, and make sure you understand it. Learn it mini-essay style.

Preparing Fertilisers

Ammonium nitrate is a commonly used fertiliser, and you can make it from a few simple chemicals in the lab. If you're going to do real live experiments (like this one) in a chemistry lab, you might want to know how much of the reactants have actually been converted to product, i.e. what the percentage yield of your reaction is.

Preparing Ammonium Nitrate in the Lab

You can make most fertilisers using this titration method — just choose the right acid (nitric, sulfuric or phosphoric) and alkali (ammonia or potassium hydroxide) to get the salt you want. You'll need ammonia and nitric acid to make ammonium nitrate.

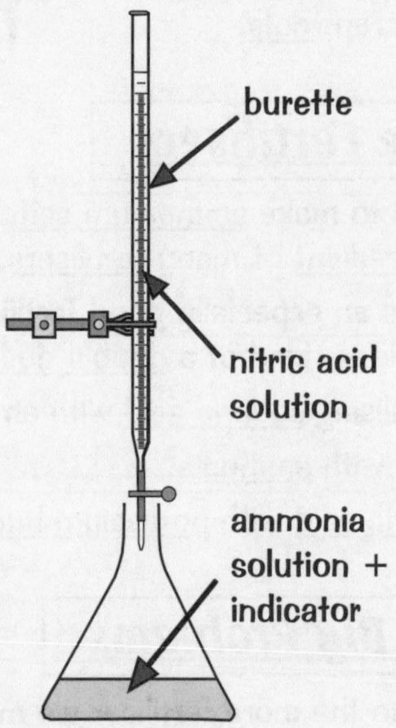

1) Set up your apparatus as in the diagram. Add a few drops of methyl orange indicator to the ammonia — it'll turn yellow.
2) Slowly add the nitric acid from the burette into the ammonia, until the yellow colour just changes to red. Gently swirl the flask as you add the acid. Go especially slowly when you think the alkali's almost neutralised.
   Methyl orange is yellow in alkalis, but red in acids, so this colour change means that all the ammonia has been neutralised and you've got ammonium nitrate solution.
3) To get solid ammonium nitrate crystals, gently evaporate the solution until only a little bit is left. Leave it to crystallise.
4) The ammonium nitrate crystals aren't pure — they've still got methyl orange in them. To get pure ammonium nitrate crystals, you need to note exactly how much nitric acid it took to neutralise the ammonia, and then repeat the titration using that volume of acid, but no indicator.

Percentage Yield Compares Actual with Predicted Yield

The mass of product that you end up with is called the YIELD of a reaction.

You should realise that in practice you never get a 100% yield, as not all of the reactant will be converted into product. This means that the amount of product will be slightly less than you would expect if it worked absolutely perfectly.

The more reactants you start with, the higher the actual yield will be — that's pretty obvious. But the percentage yield doesn't depend on the amount of reactants you started with — it's a percentage.

- Percentage yield is always somewhere between 0 and 100%.
- 100% yield means that you got all the product you expected to get.
- 0% yield means that no reactants were converted into product, i.e. no product at all was made.
- The predicted yield of a reaction is just the amount of product that you'd get if all the reactant was converted into product.

You can't always get what you want...

Unfortunately, no matter how careful you are, you won't get a 100% yield in any reaction. You'll always get a little loss of product. In industry, people work very hard to keep wastage as low as possible — so reactants that don't react first time are collected and recycled whenever possible. Make sure that you've got the hang of all this, because there's more about it coming up on the next page...

The Haber Process

The Haber process takes nitrogen and hydrogen gas and uses them to make ammonia (NH_3). It's named after Fritz Haber, the German chemist who developed it, and it's an important industrial process because the ammonia produced is needed for making fertilisers.

The Haber Process is a Reversible Reaction

$$N_2 + 3H_2 \rightleftharpoons 2NH_3$$

A reversible reaction is one that proceeds in both directions.

1) The nitrogen is obtained easily from the air, which is 78% nitrogen (and 21% oxygen).
2) The hydrogen comes from the cracking of oil fractions or natural gas.
3) Because the reaction is reversible not all the nitrogen and hydrogen will convert to ammonia.
4) The N_2 and H_2 which don't react are recycled and passed through again so none is wasted.

INDUSTRIAL CONDITIONS
PRESSURE: High (200 atmospheres); TEMPERATURE: 450 °C; CATALYST: Iron

Because the Reaction is Reversible, There's a Compromise to be Made

1) Higher pressures favour the forward reaction (producing ammonia from nitrogen and hydrogen), so the pressure is set at 200 atmospheres. This high pressure increases the percentage yield of ammonia.
2) High temperatures favour the reverse reaction (where ammonia is broken down to give N_2 and H_2) — so high temperature decreases the percentage yield of ammonia.
3) The trouble is, lower temperatures mean slow reaction rates. So manufacturers tend to use high temperatures anyway, to increase the reaction rate.
4) 450 °C is the optimum temperature — it gives a fast reaction rate and a reasonable percentage yield. In other words, it's a compromise — better to wait 20 seconds for a 10% yield than to have to wait 60 seconds for a 20% yield.
5) The unused H_2 and N_2 are recycled, so nothing is wasted.

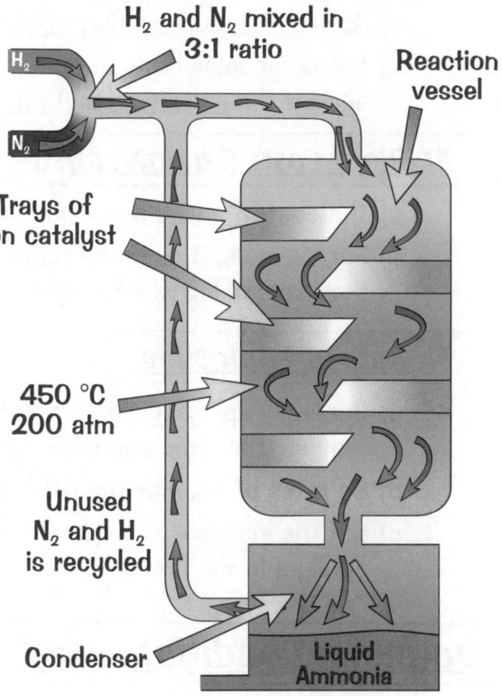

The Iron Catalyst Speeds Up the Reaction and Keeps Costs Down

1) The iron catalyst makes the reaction go faster, which gets it to the equilibrium proportions more quickly. But remember, the catalyst doesn't affect the position of equilibrium (i.e. the % yield).
2) Without the catalyst the temperature would have to be raised even further to get a quick enough reaction, and that would reduce the % yield even further. So the catalyst is very important.

200 atmospheres — that could give you a headache...

The Haber process makes ammonia, which is used to make fertilisers, which are great (although they can cause environmental problems too). Because it's a reversible reaction, certain factors need to be controlled to increase the percentage yield. Remember — the temperature is raised to increase speed not yield.

Minimising the Cost of Production

Things like fast reaction rates and high % yields are nice in industry — but in the end, the most important thing is keeping costs down. It all comes down to maximum efficiency...

Production Cost Depends on Several Different Factors

There are five main things that affect the cost of making a new substance. It's these five factors that companies have to consider when deciding if, and then how, to produce a chemical.

1) Price of Energy

a) Industry needs to keep its energy bills as low as possible.

b) If a reaction needs a high temperature, the running costs will be higher.

2) Cost of Raw Materials

a) This is kept to a minimum by recycling any materials that haven't reacted.

b) A good example of this is the Haber process. The % yield of the reaction is quite low (about 10%), but the unreacted N_2 and H_2 can be recycled to keep waste to a minimum.

3) Labour Costs (Wages)

a) Everyone who works for a company has got to be paid.

b) Labour-intensive processes (i.e. those that involve many people), can be very expensive.

c) Automation cuts running costs by reducing the number of people involved.

d) But companies have always got to weigh any savings they make on their wage bill against the initial cost and running costs of the machinery.

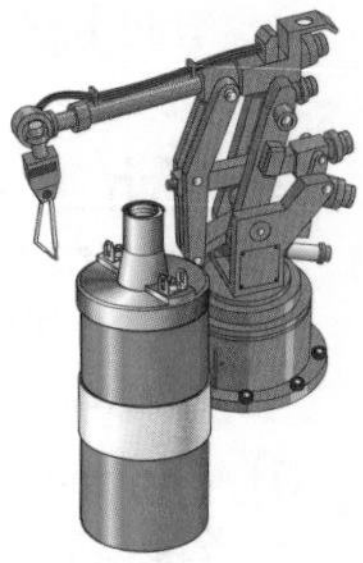

4) Plant Costs (Equipment)

a) The cost of equipment depends on the conditions it has to cope with.

b) For example, it costs far more to make something to withstand very high pressures than something which only needs to work at atmospheric pressure.

5) Rate of Production

a) Generally speaking, the faster the reaction goes, the better it is in terms of reducing the time and costs of production.

b) So rates of reaction are often increased by using catalysts.

c) But the increase in production rate has to balance the cost of buying the catalyst in the first place and replacing any that gets lost.

Optimum Conditions are Chosen to Give the Lowest Cost

1) Optimum conditions are those that give the lowest production cost per kg of product — even if this means compromising on the speed of reaction or % yield. Learn the definition:

OPTIMUM CONDITIONS are those that give the LOWEST PRODUCTION COST.

2) However, the rate of reaction and percentage yield must both be high enough to make a sufficient amount of product each day.

3) Don't forget, a low percentage yield is okay, as long as the starting materials can be recycled.

This will make it as cheap as chips...

In industry, compromises must be made, just like in life, and the Haber process is a prime example of this. You need to learn those five different factors affecting cost, and the definition of 'optimum conditions'. Cover the page and scribble it all down — keep doing it until you get it all right.

Salt

And now for a page all about sodium chloride (NaCl), or salt as it's known to its friends. In hot countries they get salt by pouring sea water into big flat open tanks and letting the Sun evaporate the water, leaving the salt behind. This is no good in a cold country like Britain though — there isn't enough sunshine.

Salt is Mined from Underneath Cheshire

1) In Britain salt is extracted from underground deposits left millions of years ago when ancient seas evaporated. There are huge deposits of this rock salt under Cheshire.
2) Rock salt is a mixture of salt and impurities. It's drilled, blasted and dug out and brought to the surface using machinery.
3) It can also be mined by pumping hot water underground. The salt dissolves and the salt solution is forced to the surface by the pressure of the water — this is called solution mining.
4) When the mining is finished, it's important to fill in the holes in the ground. If not, the land could collapse and slide into the holes — this is called subsidence.
5) Rock salt can be used in its raw state on roads to stop ice forming, or the salt can be separated out and used to preserve or enhance the flavour in food or for making chemicals. If salt's going to be used to make chemicals, usually the first thing they do is electrolyse it using the chlor-alkali process.

Electrolysis of Brine Gives Hydrogen, Chlorine and NaOH

Concentrated brine (sodium chloride solution) is electrolysed industrially using a set-up a bit like this one:

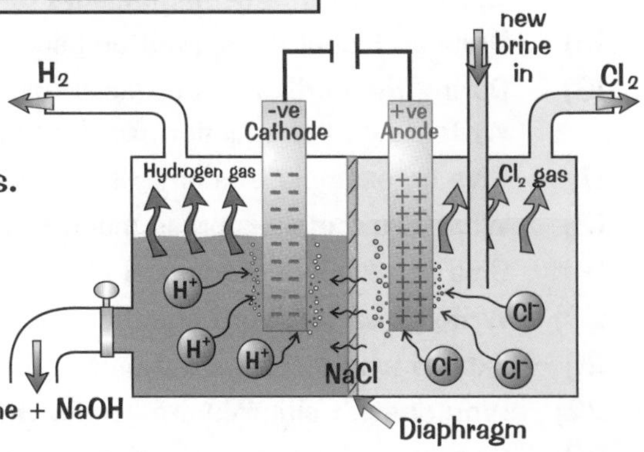

The electrodes are made of an inert material — this is so they won't react with the electrolyte or the products of the electrolysis.

There are three useful products:

a) Hydrogen gas is given off at the (–ve) cathode.
b) Chlorine gas is given off at the (+ve) anode.
c) Sodium hydroxide (NaOH) is formed from the ions left in solution.

These are collected and used to make all sorts of things (see below).

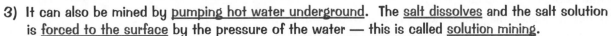

The Half-Equations — Make Sure the Electrons Balance

The sodium chloride solution contains four different ions: Na^+, OH^-, Cl^- and H^+.

1) At the cathode, two hydrogen ions accept one electron each to become one hydrogen molecule.

Cathode: $2H^+ + 2e^- \rightarrow H_2$

2) At the anode, two chloride (Cl^-) ions lose one electron each to become one chlorine molecule.

Anode: $2Cl^- - 2e^- \rightarrow Cl_2$

Oxidation is the loss of electrons, and reduction is the gain of electrons. So the reaction at the anode is an oxidation reaction, and the reaction at the cathode is a reduction reaction.

The Electrolysis of Brine is Done by the Chlor-alkali Industry

1) The products of the chlor-alkali process are used for all kinds of things.
2) For example, the hydrogen gas is used to make ammonia (in the Haber process) and margarine.
3) The chlorine is used to disinfect water, to make plastics (e.g. PVC), solvents or hydrochloric acid.
4) The sodium hydroxide is used to make soap, or can be reacted with chlorine to make household bleach.
5) All of these uses of the products of the electrolysis of brine makes the chlor-alkali industry very important to the economy — lots of new products can be made and lots of jobs are created.

Salt — it's not just for chips any more...

Wowzers — that's an awful lot to learn about salt. Better get cracking, you need to know all of it.

Revision Summary for Module C2

The only way that you can tell if you've learned this module properly is to test yourself. Try these questions, and if there's something you don't know, it means you need to go back and learn it. Even if it's all those equations for the reactions of acids. Don't miss any questions out — you don't get a choice about what comes up on the exam so you need to be sure that you've learnt it all.

1) What is the lithosphere?
2) Briefly describe the inner structure of the Earth.
3) Explain how scientists investigate what lies underneath the Earth's crust.
4) Describe the evidence that backs up Wegener's theory of continental drift.
5) What is meant by 'subduction'?
6) Sketch a labelled diagram showing how a volcano forms.
7) How is an eruption of silica-rich rhyolitic lava different from an eruption of iron-rich basaltic lava?
8) Draw a diagram to show how metamorphic rocks form.
9) Give an example of a metamorphic rock and say what the material it formed from is.
10) Which material is hardest, granite, limestone or marble?
11) How is glass made?
12) How is cement made? What about concrete?
13) Why is reinforced concrete better than non-reinforced concrete as a building material?
14) List three environmental impacts of extracting rocks from the Earth.
15) Draw and label the apparatus used to purify copper. Label the anode, the cathode and the electrolyte.
16) During the purification process, which electrode gets bigger — the cathode or the anode? Write down the equation for the reaction at the anode, and the equation for the reaction at the cathode.
17) Give an example of a large-scale use of each of the following: brass, solder, amalgam.
18) What two metals is brass made from? How are its physical properties different from those metals?
19) Give an example of a smart alloy. What is it used for?
20) Write down the word equation for the corrosion of iron.
21) Explain why a car parked on the Brighton seafront rusts more than a car parked in hot, dry Cairo.
22) Why doesn't aluminium corrode when it's wet?
23) Give two advantages of using aluminium instead of steel for car bodywork.
24) Polypropylene fibres are cheap and hard-wearing. What might they be used for when building a car?
25) What are acids and bases? What is an alkali?
26) What type of ions are always present when: a) acids, and b) alkalis dissolve in water?
27) Write the equation of a neutralisation reaction in terms of these ions.
28)* Write a word equation for the reaction between phosphoric acid and potassium hydroxide.
29)* Write a balanced symbol equation for the reaction between sulfuric acid and sodium carbonate.
30) Write a balanced symbol equation for the reaction between nitric acid and ammonia.
31) Name three essential elements in fertilisers.
32) How does nitrogen increase the growth of plants?
33) Name two fertilisers which are manufactured from ammonia.
34) Describe what can happen if too much fertiliser is put onto fields.
35) Describe how you could produce ammonium nitrate in the lab.
36) Explain why 450 °C is used as the operating temperature for the Haber process.
37) What effect does the catalyst have on the Haber process reaction?
38) Give five factors that affect the cost of producing a chemical on an industrial scale.
39) Describe two ways that salt can be mined.
40) What are the three main products of brine electrolysis?

* Answers on page 132.

Using the Sun's Energy

The Sun is very hot and very bright — which means it's kicking out a lot of energy.

The Sun is the Ultimate Source of Loads of Our Energy

1) Every second for the last few billion years or so, the Sun has been giving out loads of energy — mostly in the form of heat and light.
2) Some of that energy is stored here on Earth as fossil fuels (coal, oil and natural gas). And when we use wind power, we're using energy that can be traced back to the Sun (the Sun heats the air, the hot air rises, cold air whooshes in to take its place (wind), and so on).
3) But we can also use the Sun's energy in a more direct way — with photocells and solar heating.

Fossil fuels are the remains of plants and animals that lived millions of years ago.

You Can Capture the Sun's Energy Using Photocells

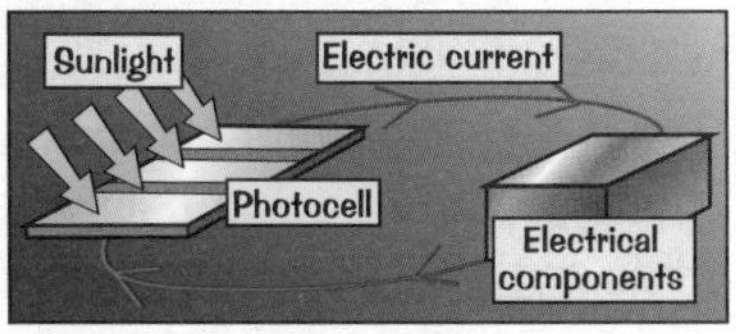

1) Photocells (solar cells) generate electricity directly from sunlight.
2) They generate direct current (DC) — the same as a battery. Direct current just means the current flows the same way round the circuit all the time — not like mains electricity in your home (AC), which keeps switching direction (see page 110).
3) Photocells are usually made of silicon — a semiconductor. When sunlight falls on the cell:
   i) the silicon atoms absorb some of the energy, knocking loose some electrons,
   ii) these electrons then flow round a circuit — which is electricity.
4) The current and power output of a photocell depends on:
   - its surface area (the bigger the cell, the more electricity it produces),
   - the intensity of the light (brighter light = more electricity),
   - the distance from the light source (the closer the cell, the more intense the light hitting it will be).

Photocells have lots of advantages:

There are no moving parts — so they're sturdy, low maintenance and last a long time.
You don't need power cables or fuel (your digital calculator doesn't need to be plugged in/fuelled up).
Solar power won't run out (it's a renewable energy resource), and it doesn't pollute the environment.

But there's one major disadvantage — no sunlight, no power.
So they're rubbish at night, and not so good when the weather's bad.

Curved Mirrors can Concentrate Energy from the Sun

1) Curved mirrors focus the Sun's light and heat.
2) A single curved mirror can be used as a solar oven.
3) Large curved mirrors (or a combination of lots of smaller mirrors) can be used to generate steam to produce electricity.

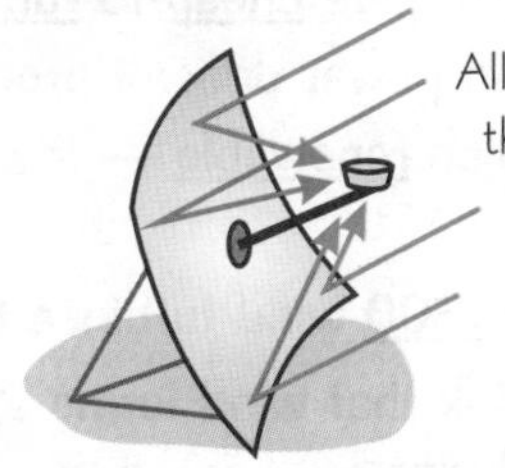

All the radiation that lands on the curved mirror is focused right on your pan.

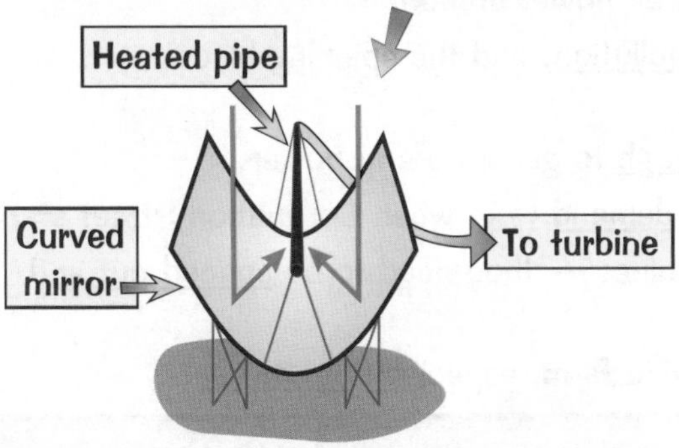

4) All devices that collect energy from the Sun (mirrors, solar cells and solar panels) are most efficient if they track the Sun's movement across the sky.
5) If collectors are pointed directly at the Sun then they can capture the maximum amount of light and heat.

Don't let the Sun go down on me — I hate cold dinners...

Although initial costs can be high with solar power, once you're up and running the energy is free and running costs are almost nil. It's even better if you live somewhere that's sunny most of the time. Not Britain then.

Solar and Wind Power

The Sun's going to be around for a long, long time and as long as there's the Sun there'll also be wind. Time to figure out how to make the most of all that free energy...

Passive Solar Heating — No Complex Mechanical Stuff

1) Passive solar heating is when energy from the Sun is used to heat something directly.
2) You can reduce the energy needed to heat a building if you build it sensibly and think about passive solar heating — e.g. it can make a big difference which way the windows face.
3) Glass lets in heat and light from the Sun, which is absorbed by things in a room, heating them up.
4) The light from the Sun has a short wavelength, so it can pass through the glass into a room.
5) But the heated things in a room emit infrared radiation of a longer wavelength, which can't escape through the glass — it's reflected back instead, just like in a greenhouse.
6) So this 'greenhouse effect' works to heat, and keep heat, inside a building.
7) Solar water heaters use passive solar heating too — the glass lets heat and light from the Sun in which is then absorbed by the black pipes and heats up the water (which can be used for washing or pumped to radiators to heat the building).

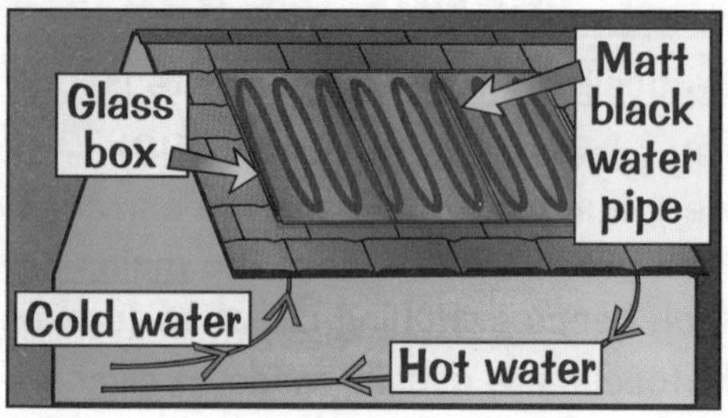

Wind Farms — Lots of Little Wind Turbines

The Sun is the reason we have wind — it's also the reason we have wind farms.

1) Wind power involves putting lots of wind turbines up in exposed places — like on moors, the coast or out at sea.
2) Energy from the Sun heats the atmosphere which causes convection currents (see p. 54), which produce wind.
3) Wind turbines convert the kinetic energy of moving air into electricity. The wind turns the blades, which turn a generator.

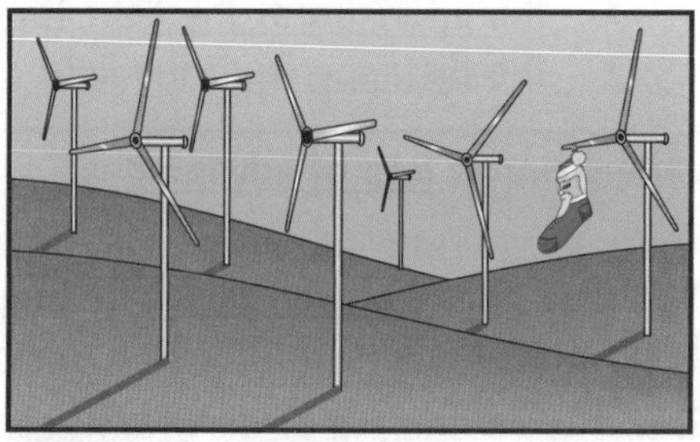

Wind is a Renewable Resource

Wind turbines, like any energy source, have advantages and disadvantages which you need to learn:

ADVANTAGES

1) Wind turbines are quite cheap to run — they're very tough and reliable, and the wind is free.
2) Even better, wind power doesn't produce any polluting waste.
3) Wind power is also renewable — the wind's never going to run out.

DISADVANTAGES

1) You need about 1500 wind turbines to replace one coal-fired power station.
2) Some people think that wind farms spoil the view (visual pollution) and the spinning blades cause noise pollution.
3) Another problem is that sometimes the wind isn't fast enough to generate any power.
4) It's also impossible to increase supply when there's extra demand (e.g. when Coronation Street starts).
5) It can be difficult to find a suitable place to build wind turbines — they need to be spaced out and built in places that are windy enough.
6) And although the wind is free, it's expensive to set up a wind farm, especially out at sea.

I love the feeling of wind in my hair...

Perhaps I should build a miniature wind farm into a hat, then I wouldn't need batteries to listen to music anymore. I'm sure there's a market for PowerHats™. I'll be rich, I tell you, rich! Anyway, before I go off and make my millions you need to make sure you know all about the advantages and disadvantages of wind power.

Producing and Distributing Electricity

In the UK, most electricity is generated in power stations and then distributed via the National Grid.

The National Grid Connects Power Stations to Consumers

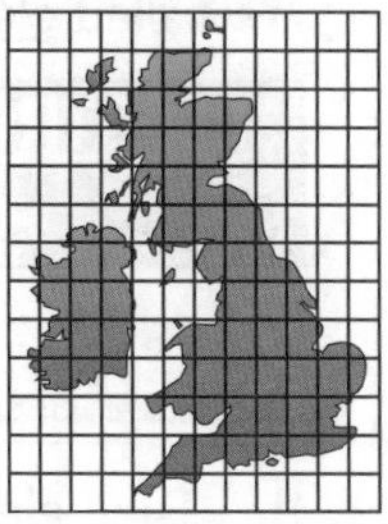

The National Grid.

1) The National Grid is the network of pylons and cables which covers the whole country.
2) It takes electricity from power stations to just where it's needed in homes and industry.
3) It enables power to be generated anywhere on the grid, and then supplied anywhere else on the grid. (See also page 111.)

All Power Stations are Pretty Much the Same

1) The aim of a power station is to convert one kind of energy (e.g. the energy stored in fossil fuels, or nuclear energy contained in the centre of atoms) into electricity. Usually this is done in three stages...

① The first stage is to use the fuel to produce heat which then generates steam — this is the job of the boiler.

② The moving steam drives the blades of a turbine...

③ ...and this rotating movement from the turbine is converted to electricity by the generator (using electromagnetic induction — see the next page).

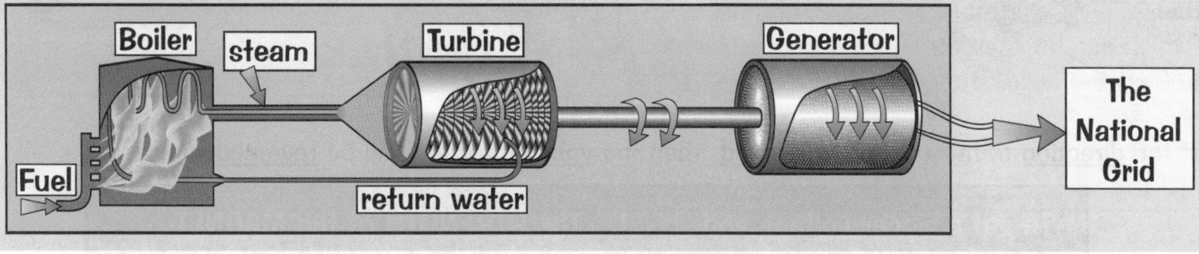

2) Most power stations are terribly inefficient — usually more than half the energy produced is wasted as heat and noise (though the efficiency of the power station depends a lot on the power source).

Different Power Sources Have Advantages and Disadvantages

You need to learn the advantages and disadvantages of different types of power source:

FOSSIL FUELS Fossil fuels are burnt to release their heat energy. At the moment, these fuels are readily available, and they're a concentrated source of energy (a little bit of coal gives a lot of heat). But burning fossil fuels causes acid rain and produces carbon dioxide (a greenhouse gas — see p. 113). Also, we buy most of our fossil fuels from other countries — which means we don't have control of the price or supply. (Plus they're running out, of course.)

BIOMASS Biomass is stuff from plants (like wood and straw) or animals (their manure) that can be burnt directly, or fermented to produce methane that's also burnt. Biomass is renewable — we can quickly make more by growing more plants and rearing more animals. Burning methane does produce carbon dioxide, but this is CO_2 that the plants took out of the atmosphere when they were growing — the process is 'carbon neutral' overall. Recently, we've started to use more biomass in the UK. You do need a lot of biomass to replace one lump of coal, and it takes a lot of room to grow it. But we don't need to import straw and poo from other countries.

NUCLEAR POWER Nuclear power stations use the heat released by uranium (or plutonium) atoms as they split during a nuclear reaction. There's more on the pros and cons of nuclear power on page 117.

PHOTO CELLS Photocells absorb energy from the Sun and convert it into electricity. There's more about the positives and negatives of photocells on page 107.

WIND POWER Wind turbines convert energy from the movement of the wind into electricity. The pros and cons of wind power are on page 108.

You could be asked to compare things like availability and environmental issues.

Power stations — nothing to get steamed up about...

Steam engines were invented as long ago as the 17th century, and yet we're still using the idea to produce most of our electricity today, over 300 years later. I doubt any of my ideas will last as long as that...

The Dynamo Effect

Generators use a pretty cool piece of physics to make electricity from the movement of a turbine. It's called electromagnetic (EM) induction — which basically means making electricity using a magnet.

ELECTROMAGNETIC INDUCTION: The creation of a VOLTAGE (and maybe current) in a wire which is experiencing a CHANGE IN MAGNETIC FIELD.

The Dynamo Effect — Move the Wire or the Magnet

1) Using electromagnetic induction to transform kinetic energy (energy of moving things) into electrical energy is called the dynamo effect. (In a power station, this kinetic energy is provided by the turbine.)
2) There are two different situations where you get EM induction:
   a) An electrical conductor (a coil of wire is often used) moves through a magnetic field.
   b) The magnetic field through an electrical conductor changes (gets bigger or smaller or reverses).

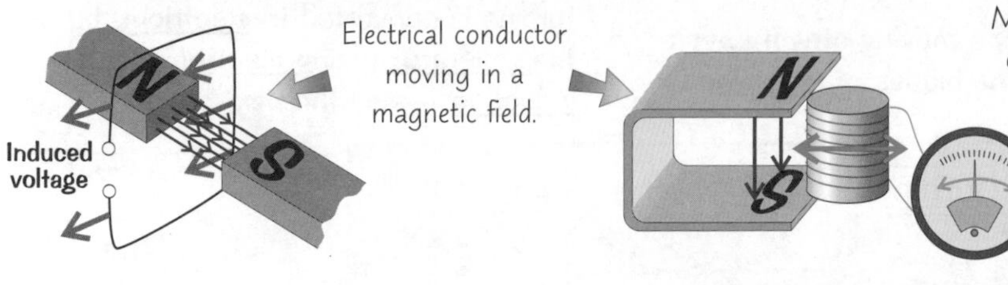

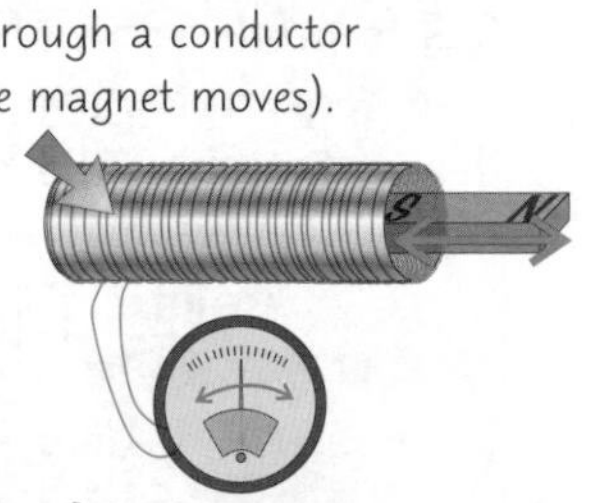

3) If the direction of movement is reversed, then the voltage/current will be reversed too.

To get a bigger voltage and current, you can increase...
1. The STRENGTH of the MAGNET
2. The number of TURNS on the COIL
3. The SPEED of movement

Generators Move a Coil in a Magnetic Field

Generators can work by rotating a magnet in a coil instead — the same principles still apply.

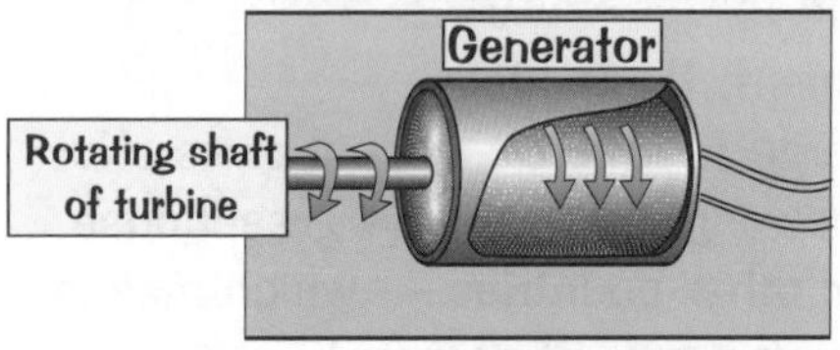

1) Generators rotate a coil in a magnetic field.
2) Every half a turn, the current in the coil swaps direction. (Think about one part of the coil... sometimes it's heading for the magnet's north pole, sometimes for the south — it changes every half a turn. This is what makes the current change direction.)
3) This means that generators produce an alternating (AC) current. If you looked at the current (or voltage) on a display, you'd see something like this...
   Turning the coil faster produces not only more peaks, but a higher voltage and current too.

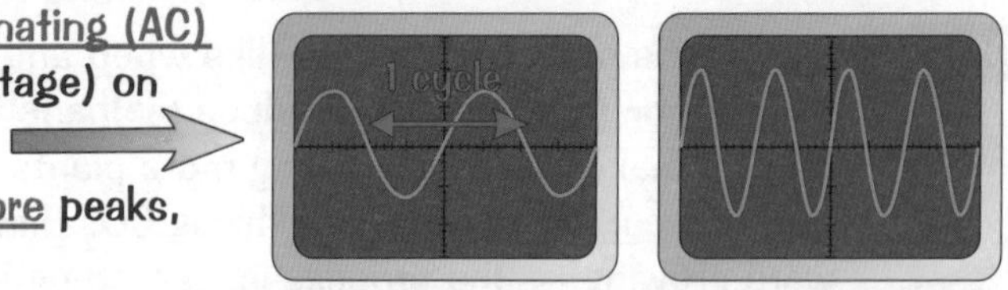

4) The frequency of AC electrical supplies is the number of cycles per second, and is measured in hertz (Hz). In the UK, electricity is supplied at 50 Hz (which means the coil in the generator at the power station is rotating 50 times every second).
5) Remember, this is completely different from the DC electricity supplied by batteries and photocells. If you plotted that on a graph, you'd see something more like this...

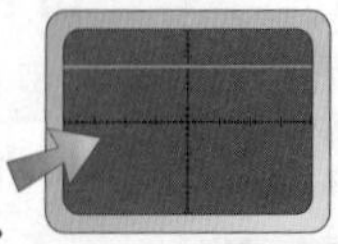

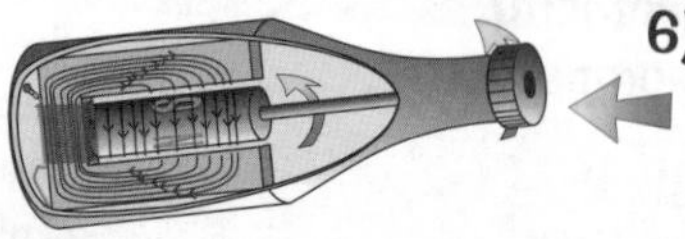

6) Dynamos on bikes work slightly differently — they usually rotate the magnet near the coil. But the principle is exactly the same — they're still using EM induction.

A conductor moving in a field — must be an open-air concert...

EM induction sounds pretty hard, but it boils down to this — if a magnetic field changes (moves, grows, shrinks... whatever) somewhere near a conductor, you get electricity. It's a weird old thing, but important — this is how all our mains electricity is generated. Not with hamsters then — I was wrong about that.

Supplying Electricity Efficiently

Sending electricity round the country is best done at high voltage.
This is why you probably weren't encouraged to climb electricity pylons as a child.

Electricity is Transformed to High Voltage Before Distribution

1) To transmit a lot of electrical power, you either need a high voltage or a high current. But... a higher current means your cables get hot, which is inefficient (all that heat just goes to waste).

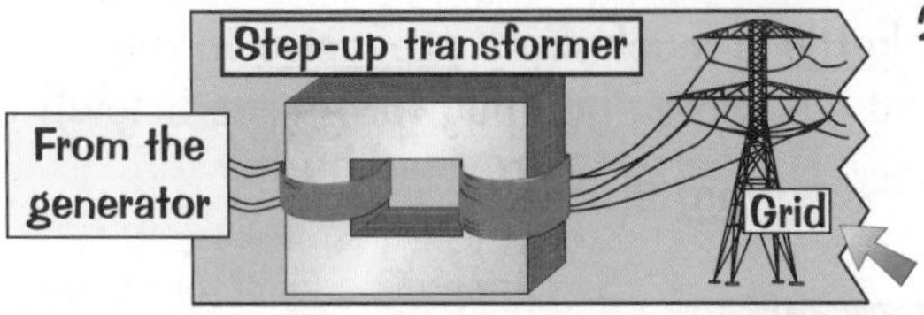

2) It's much cheaper to increase the voltage. So before the electricity is sent round the country, the voltage is transformed to 400 000 V. (This keeps the current very low, meaning less wasted energy because heating of the cables is reduced.)
3) To increase the voltage, you need a step-up transformer.

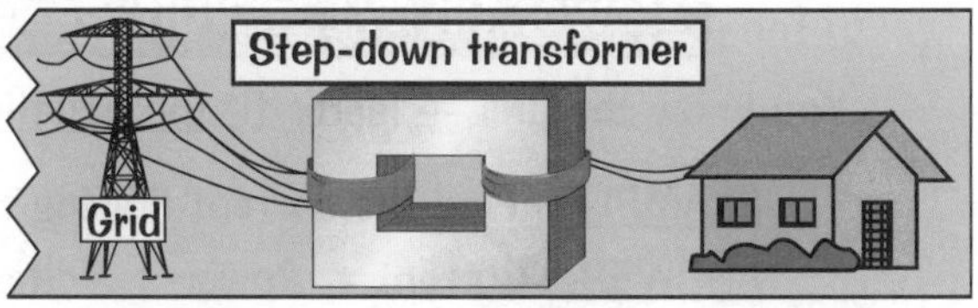

4) Even though you need big pylons with huge insulators (as well as the transformers themselves), using a high voltage is the cheapest way to transmit electricity.
5) To bring the voltage down to safe usable levels for homes, there are local step-down transformers scattered round towns — for example, look for a little fenced-off shed with signs all over it saying "Keep Out" and "Danger of Death".
6) This is the main reason why mains electricity is AC — so that the transformers work. Transformers only work on AC.

Power Stations aren't Very Efficient

1) The process of generating and supplying electricity isn't massively efficient.
2) Unfortunately most power stations produce a lot of waste energy (e.g. heat lost to the environment) as well as energy we can make use of. Basically the energy in each bit of fuel is broken down into two parts — the 'useful bit' and the 'wasted bit'. Learn this equation...

TOTAL Energy Input = USEFUL energy output + WASTE energy output

3) There's an equation for working out efficiency as well... yep, learn this one too:

$$\text{Efficiency} = \frac{\text{USEFUL Energy OUTPUT}}{\text{TOTAL Energy INPUT}} (\times 100\%)$$

Here's the formula triangle for the efficiency equation. As always, cover up the thing you want to find out — what you can still see is the formula that'll tell you how to get it.

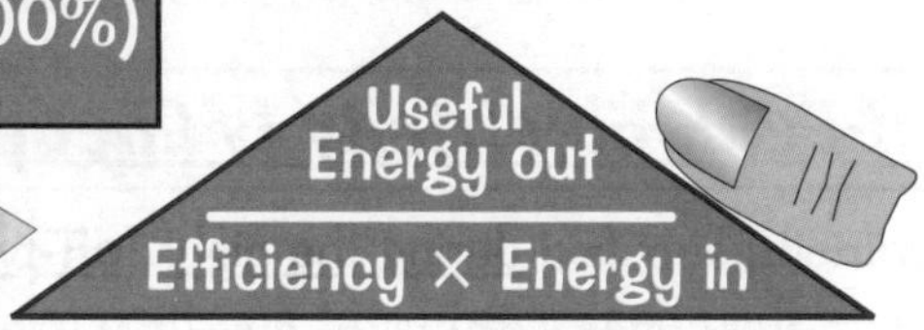

EXAMPLE: A coal-fired power station generates 200 MJ (200 000 000 J) of electrical energy per second. 450 MJ of energy is wasted per second as heat and noise.
Calculate: a) the energy used by the power station in a second,
b) the efficiency of the power station.

ANSWER: a) Energy used (energy input) = useful energy output + energy wasted
= 200 MJ + 450 MJ = 650 MJ
b) Efficiency = useful energy output ÷ total energy input = 200 ÷ 650 = 0.3077
Convert efficiency to a percentage by multiplying by 100, so 0.3077 = 30.77%

You can also calculate the efficiency as a decimal instead of a percentage — just don't do the '× 100%' bit.

All that energy — straight down the grid...

Once you've generated all that electricity, you don't want to waste it by heating up miles and miles of power cables when you're distributing it. So keep the current in the power cables low, and make the voltage high. Then the good folk of John o' Groats can still afford to boil the kettle. Problem solved.

Power

Electrical power is the amount of energy converted per second. It's a hoot.

Running Costs Depend on an Appliance's Power Rating

1) Power's measured in watts (W) or kilowatts (kW) — where 1 watt means 1 joule per second.
   For example, a light bulb with a power rating of 100 W uses 100 J of electrical energy every second. And a 2 kW kettle converts electrical energy at the rate of 2000 J per second. Easy.

2) If they're both on for the same amount of time, the kettle is much more expensive to run than the bulb, because it consumes more energy (and it's energy you pay for — see below).
3) The power rating of an appliance depends on the voltage and the current it uses.
   Equation time...

   Power (in W) = Voltage (in V) × Current (in A)

   So to transmit a lot of power, you need either a high voltage or a high current — see p. 111.

   You know the drill — learn: (i) the equation, and (ii) how to rearrange it.

EXAMPLE: Find the current flowing through a 100 W light bulb if the voltage is 230 V.
ANSWER: Current = Power ÷ Voltage = 100 ÷ 230 = 0.43 amps

Kilowatt-hours (kWh) are "UNITS" of Energy

Your electricity meter records how much energy you use in units of kilowatt-hours, or kWh.

A KILOWATT-HOUR is the amount of electrical energy converted by a 1 kW appliance left on for 1 HOUR.

The higher the power rating of an appliance, and the longer you leave it on, the more energy it consumes, and the more it costs. Learn (and practise rearranging) this equation too...

ENERGY SUPPLIED (in kWh) = POWER (in kW) × TIME (in hours)

And this one (but this one's easy): **COST = NUMBER OF UNITS × PRICE PER UNIT**

EXAMPLE: Find the cost of leaving a 60 W light bulb on for 30 minutes if one kWh costs 10p.
ANSWER: Energy (in kWh) = Power (in kW) × Time (in hours) = 0.06 kW × ½ hr = 0.03 kWh
Cost = number of units × price per unit = 0.03 × 10p = 0.3p

Off-Peak Electricity is Cheaper

Electricity supplied during the night (off-peak) is sometimes cheaper. Storage heaters take advantage of this — they heat up at night and then release the heat slowly throughout the day. If you can put washing machines, dishwashers, etc. on at night, so much the better.

ADVANTAGES of using off-peak electricity

1) Cost-effective for the electricity company — power stations can't be turned off at night, so it's good if there's a demand for electricity at night.
2) Cheaper for consumers if they buy electricity during the off-peak hours.

DISADVANTAGES of using off-peak electricity

1) There's a slightly increased risk of fire with more appliances going at night but no one watching.
2) You start fitting your routine around the cheap rate hours — i.e. you might stop enjoying the use of electricity during the day.

Watt's the answer — well, part of it...

Get a bit of practice with the equations in those lovely bright red boxes, and try these questions:

1) A kettle draws a current of 12 A from the 230 V mains supply. Calculate its power rating.
2) With 0.5 kWh of energy, for how long could you run the kettle?

Answers on p. 132.

The Greenhouse Effect

The atmosphere keeps us warm by trapping heat.

Some Radiation from the Sun Passes Through the Atmosphere

1) The Earth is surrounded by an atmosphere made up of various gases — the air.
2) The gases in the atmosphere filter out certain types of radiation from the Sun — they absorb or reflect radiation of certain wavelengths (infrared).
3) However, some wavelengths of radiation — mainly visible light and some radio waves — pass through the atmosphere quite easily.

The Greenhouse Effect Helps Regulate Earth's Temperature

1) The Earth absorbs short wavelength EM radiation from the Sun. This warms the Earth's surface up. The Earth then emits some of this EM radiation back out into space — this tends to cool us down.
2) Most of the radiation emitted from Earth is longer wavelength infrared radiation — heat.
3) A lot of this infrared radiation is absorbed by atmospheric gases, including carbon dioxide, methane and water vapour.
4) These gases then re-radiate heat in all directions, including back towards the Earth.
5) So the atmosphere acts as an insulating layer, stopping the Earth losing all its heat at night.

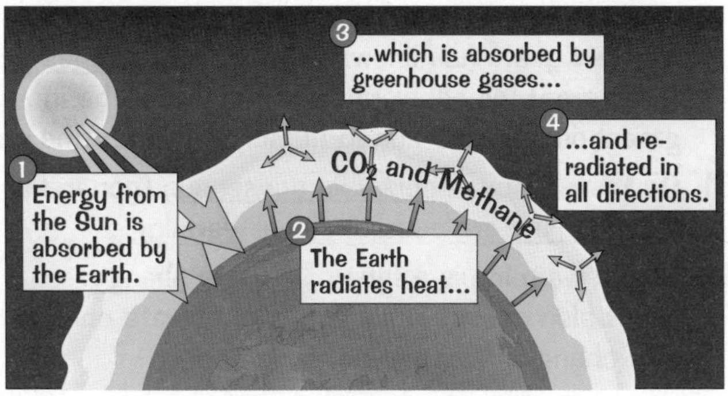

6) This is known as the 'greenhouse effect'. (In a greenhouse, the sun shines in and the glass helps keep some of the heat in.) Without the greenhouse gases (CO_2, methane, water vapour) in our atmosphere, the Earth would be a lot colder.

Humans are Causing an Increase in the Amount of Greenhouse Gases

Over the last 200 years or so, the concentration of greenhouse gases in the atmosphere has been increasing. This is because some of the sources of them are increasing, so more gases are being released:

Carbon Dioxide

People use more energy (e.g. travel more in cars) — which we get mainly from burning fossil fuels, which releases more carbon dioxide.

More land is needed for houses and food and the space is often made by chopping down and burning trees — fewer trees mean less CO_2 is absorbed, and burning releases more CO_2.

CO_2 also comes from natural sources — e.g. respiration in animals and plants, and volcanic eruptions can release it.

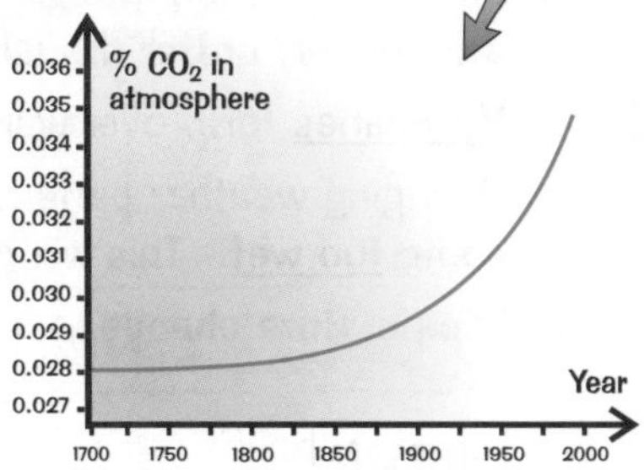

Methane

Cattle farming has increased to feed the growing population — cattle digestion produces methane, so the amount of methane is increasing.

Decaying waste in landfill sites produces methane — the amount of waste is increasing, causing, you guessed it, an increase in methane.

Methane is released naturally by volcanoes, wetlands and wild animals.

You might have to interpret data on greenhouse gases — there's more on interpreting data on p. 6-8.

Water Vapour

Most water vapour comes from natural sources — mainly oceans, seas, rivers and lakes.

As global temperature increases (see next page), so could the amount of water vapour.

Power stations also produce water vapour, which can affect the amount in the local area.

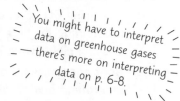

A biologist, a chemist and a physicist walk into a greenhouse...

...it works out badly. You need to know what greenhouse gases are and where they come from. Learn it well.

Global Warming and Climate Change

Without any 'greenhouse gases' in the atmosphere, the Earth would be about 30 °C colder than it is now. So we need the greenhouse effect — just not too much of it...

Upsetting the Greenhouse Effect Has Led to Climate Change

1) Since we started burning fossil fuels, the level of carbon dioxide in the atmosphere has increased (see previous page).
2) The global temperature has also risen during this time (global warming). There's a link between concentration of CO_2 and global temperature.
3) A lot of evidence has been collected that shows the rise in CO_2 is causing global warming by increasing the greenhouse effect.
4) For example, climate models can be used to explain why the climate is changing now. We know that the Earth's climate varies naturally (see below). But climate modelling over the last few years has shown that natural changes don't explain the current 'global warming' — and that the increase in greenhouse gases due to human activity is the cause.
5) So there's now a scientific consensus (general agreement) that humans are causing global warming.
6) Global warming is a type of climate change. But it also causes other types of climate change, e.g. changing weather patterns.

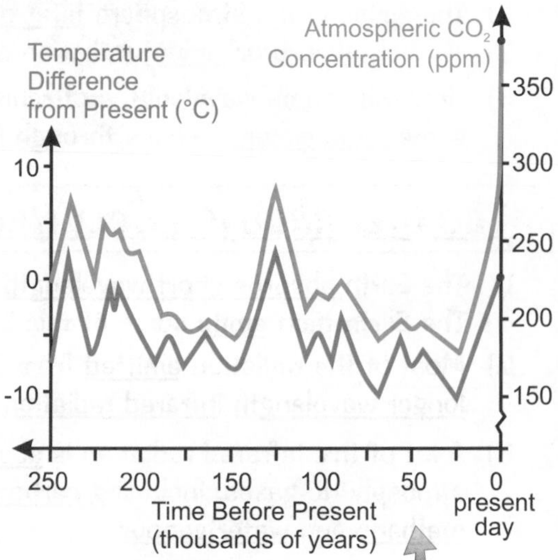

You might be asked to interpret evidence for natural or man-made global warming and climate change in the exam — make sure you look for the evidence and ignore opinions that aren't supported by data. See p. 8.

Changes to the Weather can have Human and Natural Causes

1) The climate is very complicated — conditions in the atmosphere, oceans and land all affect one another.
2) Changes in temperature can have large effects on the weather.
3) For example, many regions will suffer more extreme weather because of global warming, e.g. longer, hotter droughts.
4) Hurricanes form over warm water — so with more warm water, you'd expect more hurricanes.
5) Changing weather patterns also affect food production — some regions are now too dry to grow food, some too wet. This will get worse as temperature increases and weather patterns change more.
6) Temperature change, and so changes to the weather, can have both human and natural causes:

HUMAN

1) The rising CO_2 level caused by humans is affecting the greenhouse effect and causing global warming (see above).
2) Soot and gases produced by factories can reflect heat from cities back down to Earth, which can cause increases in local temperature.

NATURAL

1) Ash and gases thrown into the atmosphere by volcanoes can reflect radiation from the Sun back into space, causing the Earth to cool down.
2) Changes in our orbit round the Sun can cause ice ages.

Be a climate model — go on a diet...

'Global warming' could mean that some parts of the world cool down. For instance, as ice melts, lots of cold fresh water will enter the sea and this could disrupt ocean currents. This could be bad news for us in Britain — if the nice warm currents we get at the moment weaken, we'll be a lot colder.

Nuclear Radiation

Sometimes the nucleus of an atom can (for no immediately obvious reason) spit out nuclear radiation.

Nuclear Radiation Causes Ionisation

1) When an unstable nucleus decays, it gives off one or more kinds of nuclear radiation.
2) Radioactive materials give out nuclear radiation over time.
3) The three kinds of radiation are alpha (α), beta (β) and gamma (γ).
4) All three kinds of radiation can cause ionisation — the radiation causes atoms to lose or gain electrons, turning those atoms into ions.
5) Positive ions are formed when atoms lose electrons.
6) Negative ions are formed when atoms gain electrons.
7) Ionisation can also initiate (start) chemical reactions between different atoms.
8) When radiation enters human cells it can ionise molecules and damage DNA. This can cause mutations in the cell that could lead to cancer.
9) Very high doses of radiation can kill cells completely.
10) The ionising power of each kind of radiation is linked to how far it can penetrate materials. The further the radiation can penetrate before hitting an atom, the less ionising it is.

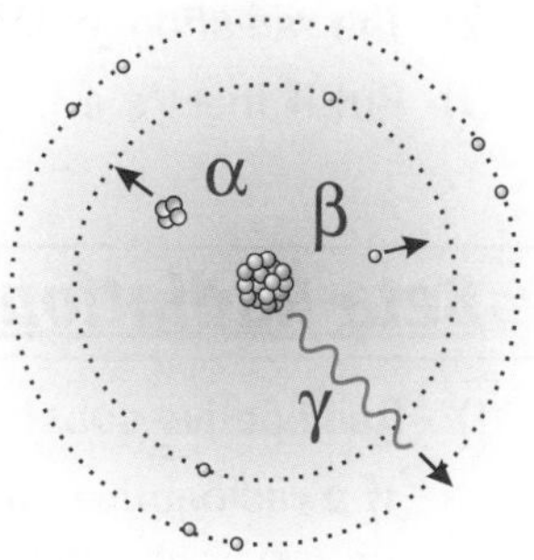

Alpha Particles are Big and Heavy

1) Alpha particles (α) are relatively big, heavy and slow moving (they're 2 protons and 2 neutrons).
2) Because of their size they're stopped quickly — they don't penetrate far into materials. Alpha particles can be stopped by paper or skin.
3) This means they're strongly ionising — they bash into loads of atoms and knock electrons off them before they slow down.

Beta Particles are Electrons

1) Beta particles (β) are just electrons — so they're small, and they move quite fast.
2) Beta particles penetrate moderately (further than α-particles) before colliding, so they're moderately ionising. But they can still be stopped by a thin sheet of metal — a few millimetres of aluminium, say.

Gamma Rays are Very High Frequency Electromagnetic Waves

1) After spitting out an α- or β-particle, the nucleus might need to get rid of some extra energy. It does this by emitting a gamma ray (γ) — a type of EM radiation.
2) Gamma rays have no mass and no charge. They can penetrate a long way into materials without being stopped — meaning they're weakly ionising (they tend to pass through rather than collide with atoms). But eventually they do hit something and do damage.
3) They can be stopped using very thick concrete or a few centimetres of lead.

You can Identify the Type of Radiation by its Penetrating Power

You can tell which kind of radiation you're dealing with by what blocks it.
E.g. place a sheet of paper between the radiation source (some radioactive material) and a detector (a Geiger counter): If no radiation reaches the detector, then it must be alpha. If radiation is still reaching the detector then it could be beta or gamma. Swap the paper for aluminium — if no radiation reaches it now, it must be beta. But if radioactivity still gets through, it must be gamma. Simples.

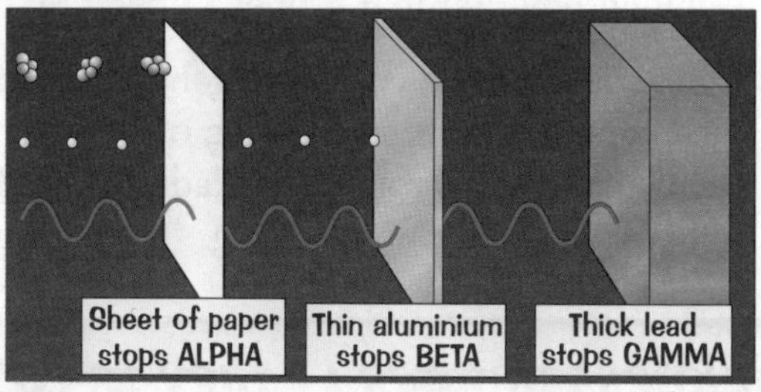

I'm tired out from all this activity...

When an atom spits out alpha or beta radiation it changes into a different type of atom in the process. Neat.

Uses of Nuclear Radiation

Nuclear radiation can be very dangerous. But it can be very useful too. Read on...

Alpha Radiation is Used in Smoke Detectors

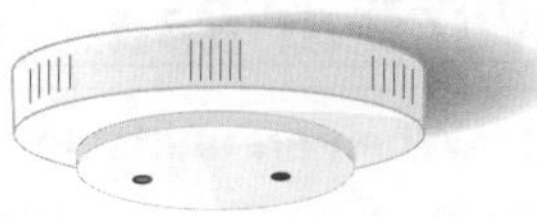

1) Smoke detectors have a weak source of α-radiation close to two electrodes.
2) The radiation ionises the air and a current flows between the electrodes.
3) But if there's a fire, the smoke absorbs the radiation — the current stops and the alarm sounds.

Beta Radiation is Used in Tracers and Thickness Gauges

1) Radioactive substances have medical uses as tracers:

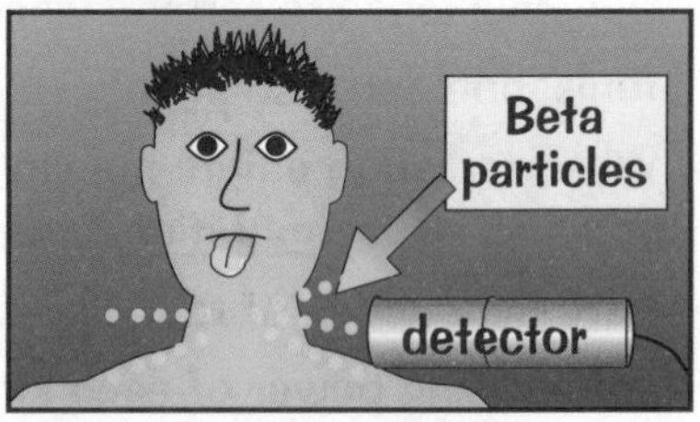

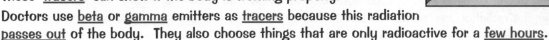

If a radioactive source is injected into a patient (or swallowed), its progress around the body can be followed using an external radiation detector. A computer converts the reading to a TV display showing where the strongest reading is coming from. These 'tracers' can show if the body is working properly.
Doctors use beta or gamma emitters as tracers because this radiation passes out of the body. They also choose things that are only radioactive for a few hours.

2) Beta radiation is also used in thickness control. You direct radiation through the stuff being made (e.g. paper or cardboard), and put a detector on the other side, connected to a control unit.

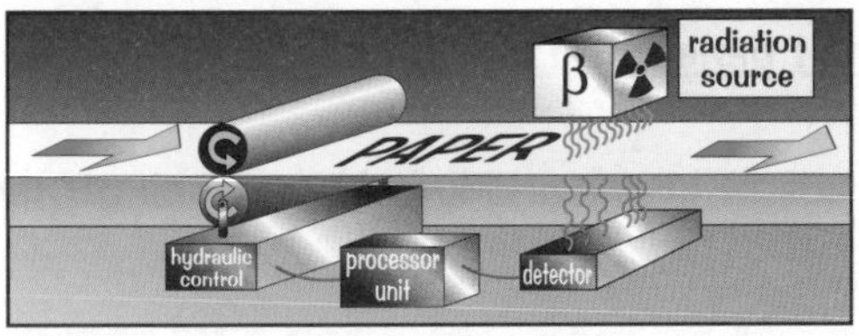

When the amount of detected radiation goes down, it means the paper is coming out too thick, so the control unit pinches the rollers up to make it thinner.
If the reading goes up, the paper's too thin, so the control unit opens the rollers out a bit.

For this use, your radioactive substance mustn't decay away too quickly, otherwise its strength would gradually fall (and the control unit would keep pinching up the rollers trying to compensate).
You need to use a beta source, because then the paper or cardboard will partly block the radiation.
If it all goes through (or none of it does), then the reading won't change at all as the thickness changes.

Gamma Radiation Has Medical and Industrial Uses

1) High doses of gamma rays will kill all living cells, so they can be used to treat cancers.
The gamma rays have to be directed carefully at the cancer, and at just the right dosage so as to kill the cancer cells without damaging too many normal cells.

2) Gamma rays are also used to sterilise medical instruments — by killing all the microbes.
This is better than trying to boil plastic instruments, which might be damaged by high temperatures.
You need to use a strongly radioactive source that lasts a long time, so that it doesn't need replacing too often.

3) Several industries also use gamma radiation to do non-destructive testing. For example, airlines can check the turbine blades of their jet engines by directing gamma rays at them — if too much radiation gets through the blade to the detector on the other side, they know the blade's cracked or there's a fault in the welding. It's so much better to find this out before you take off than in mid-air.

Thickness gauges — they're called 'exams' nowadays...

Knowing the detail is important here. For instance, swallowing an alpha source as a medical tracer would be very foolish — alpha radiation would cause all sorts of chaos inside your body but couldn't be detected outside, making the whole thing pointless. So learn what each type's used for and why.

Nuclear Power

Another use of nuclear radiation — nuclear power. Some people think nuclear power is the best way to reduce CO_2 emissions, but others think it's just too dangerous.

Nuclear Power Uses Uranium as Fuel

1) A nuclear power station is mostly the same as the one on page 109, but with nuclear fission producing the heat to make steam. The difference is in the boiler.
2) In nuclear fission, atoms in the nuclear fuel (e.g. uranium) are split in two, releasing lots of heat energy.
3) Water is used as a coolant to take away the heat produced by the fission process. This heat is used to produce steam to drive a turbine and generator.

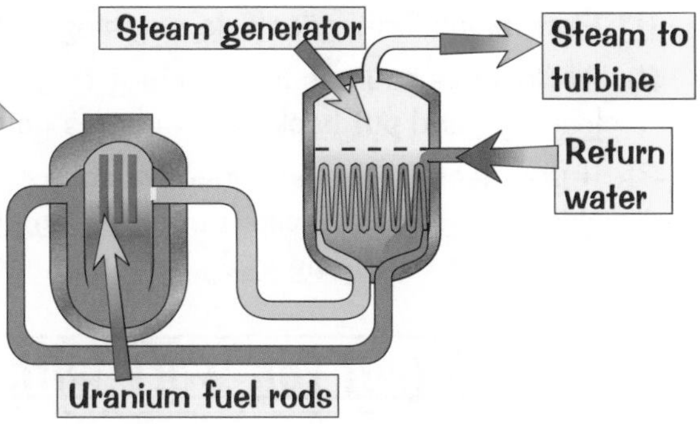

Nuclear Power Doesn't Produce Carbon Dioxide

Time for some advantages and disadvantages of using nuclear power:

ADVANTAGES

1) Nuclear power stations can make lots of energy without releasing lots of CO_2 into the atmosphere (which contributes to global warming — see page 114).
2) Nuclear reactions release a lot more energy than chemical reactions (such as burning), so it takes a lot less uranium to produce the same amount of power as fossil fuel.
3) Nuclear fuel (i.e. uranium) is relatively cheap.
4) There's still plenty of uranium left in the ground (although it can take a lot of money and energy to make it suitable for use in a reactor).

DISADVANTAGES

1) Nuclear power stations are expensive to build and maintain.
2) It takes longer to start up nuclear power stations than fossil fuel power stations.
3) Processing the uranium before you use it causes pollution.
4) And there's always a risk of leaks of radioactive material, or even a major catastrophe like the Chernobyl disaster. (Radioactive material can cause cancer and radiation sickness.)
5) A big problem with nuclear power is the radioactive waste that you always get — it's very dangerous and difficult to reprocess or dispose of.
6) When they're too old and inefficient, nuclear power stations have to be decommissioned (shut down and made safe) — that's expensive too.
7) Although there's plenty left, uranium is a non-renewable resource — so it will eventually run out.

See next page for more about nuclear waste.

Nuclear Fuel is Also Used to Make Nuclear Weapons

1) The used uranium fuel from nuclear power stations can be reprocessed. This is one way of dealing with some of the radioactive waste that would otherwise have to be stored.
2) After reprocessing, you're left with more uranium and a bit of plutonium.
3) You can reuse the uranium in your nuclear power station.
4) The plutonium can be used to make nuclear bombs.

Fission — also the starting orders of a fishing competition...

Current nuclear power stations work because of nuclear fission (where atoms split apart to release energy). In the future it may be possible to use nuclear fusion (where atoms are forced together) to produce power. Nuclear fusion produces more energy and less waste, but so far it's been very hard to get it to work.

Danger from Radioactive Materials

Radioactive stuff certainly has its uses — curing cancer, killing bacteria and generating electricity. But if you don't want to irradiate yourself, you have to know how to handle it safely.

You Should Always Protect Yourself...

1) First things first... don't do anything really stupid — like eating your smoke alarm.
2) Radioactive sources need to be stored safely. They should be kept in a labelled lead box and put back in as soon as you can to keep your exposure time short.
3) If you need to use a radioactive source, always handle it with tongs — never allow skin contact. And keep it at arm's length (so it's as far from the body as possible). Also, keep it pointing away from you and avoid looking directly at it.

...Especially If You Work with Nuclear Radiation

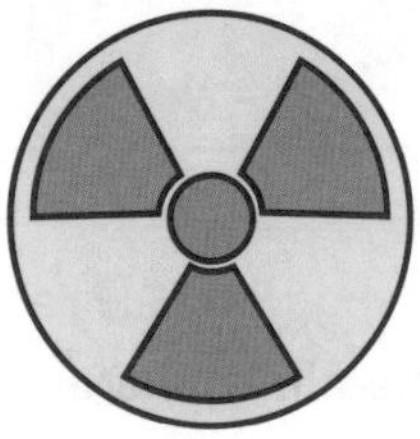

1) Industrial nuclear workers wear full protective suits to prevent tiny radioactive particles being inhaled, or lodging on the skin or under fingernails, etc.
2) Lead-lined suits and lead/concrete barriers and thick lead screens shield workers from gamma rays in highly radioactive areas. (α-radiation and β-radiation are stopped much more easily.)
3) Workers use remote-controlled robot arms to carry out tasks in highly radioactive areas.

Radioactive Waste is Difficult to Dispose of Safely

1) Most waste from nuclear power stations and hospitals is 'low-level' (only slightly radioactive). Low-level waste is things like paper, clothing, gloves, syringes, etc. This kind of waste can be disposed of by burying it in secure landfill sites.
2) High-level waste is the really dangerous stuff — a lot of it stays highly radioactive for tens of thousands of years, and so has to be treated very carefully. It's often sealed into glass blocks, which are then sealed in metal canisters. These could then be buried deep underground.
3) However, it's difficult to find suitable places to bury high-level waste. The site has to be geologically stable (e.g. not be prone to earthquakes), since big movements in the rock could disturb the canisters and allow radioactive material to leak out. If this material gets into the groundwater, it could contaminate the soil, plants, rivers, etc., and get into our drinking water.
4) Even when geologists do find suitable sites, people who live nearby often object. So, at the moment, most high-level waste is kept 'on-site' at nuclear power stations.
5) Not all radioactive waste has to be chucked out though — some of it is reprocessed to reclaim useful radioactive material (see previous page). But even reprocessing leaves some waste behind.
6) Nuclear power stations and reprocessing plants are generally pretty secure — they have high fences and security checks on the people going in and out. But they might still be a target for terrorists — who could use stolen radioactive material to make a 'dirty bomb', or attack the plant directly.
7) There are strict regulations about how waste is disposed of. But the rules could change as we find out more about the dangers of radiation, and the pros and cons of storing waste in different ways. E.g. what's classed as low-level now might be considered high-level in the future.

Radioactive sources — don't put them on your chips...

Most of the UK's nuclear power stations are quite old, and will have to be shut down soon. There's a debate going on over whether we should build new ones. Some people say no — if we can't deal safely with the radioactive waste we've got now, we certainly shouldn't make lots more. Others say that nuclear power is the only way to meet all our energy needs without causing catastrophic climate change.

The Solar System

When I were a lad I was taught that there were nine planets in our Solar System. But in 2006 some pesky astrobods decided that Pluto wasn't really a proper planet, so now there's only eight — for now...

Planets Reflect Sunlight and Orbit the Sun in Ellipses

Our Solar System consists of a star (the Sun) and lots of stuff orbiting it in slightly elongated circles (called ellipses).

Closest to the Sun are the inner planets — Mercury, Venus, Earth and Mars.

Then the asteroid belt — see next page.

Then the outer planets, much further away — Jupiter, Saturn, Uranus, Neptune.

You need to learn the order of the planets, which is made easier by using the little jollyism below:

Mercury,	Venus,	Earth,	Mars,	(Asteroids),	Jupiter,	Saturn,	Uranus,	Neptune
(Mad	Vampires	Eat	Mangoes	And	Jump	Straight	Up	Noses)

1) You can see some planets with the naked eye. They look like stars, but they're totally different.
2) Stars are huge, very hot and very far away. They give out lots of light — which is why you can see them, even though they're very far away.
3) The planets are smaller and nearer and they just reflect sunlight falling on them.
4) Planets often have moons orbiting around them. Jupiter has at least 63 of 'em. We've just got one (see page 121 for more about our Moon).

The Solar System is Held Together by Gravitational Attraction

1) Things only change direction when a force acts on them — if there were no force, they'd move in a straight line (or stay still). Since planets go round and round, there must be a force involved.
2) When it comes to big things in the Solar System and the rest of the Universe (like planets, asteroids, comets, meteors, and so on), there's only really one force it could be — gravity (gravitational attraction).
3) Gravity pulls everything in the Universe towards everything else. The effect is tiny between 'small' things (e.g. between you and a car, or between a house and a hat) — so tiny you don't notice it.
4) But when you're talking about things as big as stars and planets, the pull of gravity can be huge (the bigger the 'thing', the bigger its pull). So it's gravity that makes planets orbit stars, and moons orbit planets. Gravity keeps satellites, comets and asteroids in their orbits, and so on. Get the idea...
5) The pull of an object gets smaller the further away you go. This is why you're pulled strongly towards the Earth and don't hurtle towards the Sun, for example. And this is why the Earth orbits the Sun, rather than some other much bigger star further away.

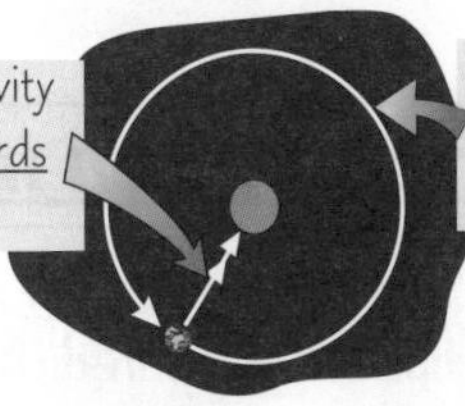
The pull of gravity is directly towards the Sun...
...but the motion of the Earth is around the Sun.

6) If the Earth wasn't already moving, it would be pulled by gravity directly towards the Sun. But what gravity normally does is make things that are already moving change their course — often into circular or elliptical orbits.

Circular motion is always caused by a force (pull) towards the centre of the circle. For planets, moons, etc. in an orbit, this force is provided by gravity.

A force that causes a circular motion is called a centripetal force.

Pull yourself together — get this stuff learnt...

Brilliantly, the moons of some planets in our Solar System are so small that although there is enough gravity to keep you standing on them, if you jumped hard you'd fly off into outer space and never come back down. Head to Deimos (orbiting Mars) next time you're passing and give it a go. Weeeee...

Asteroids and Comets

There's more than planets out there in the Solar System — aliens, space probes, but mostly just other rocks.

There's a Belt of Asteroids Orbiting Between Mars and Jupiter

1) When the Solar System was forming, the rocks between Mars and Jupiter didn't form a planet — the large gravitational attraction of Jupiter kept interfering.
2) This left millions of asteroids — piles of rubble and rock measuring up to about 1000 km in diameter. They orbit the Sun between the orbits of Jupiter and Mars.
3) Asteroids usually stay in their orbits but sometimes they're pushed or pulled into different ones...

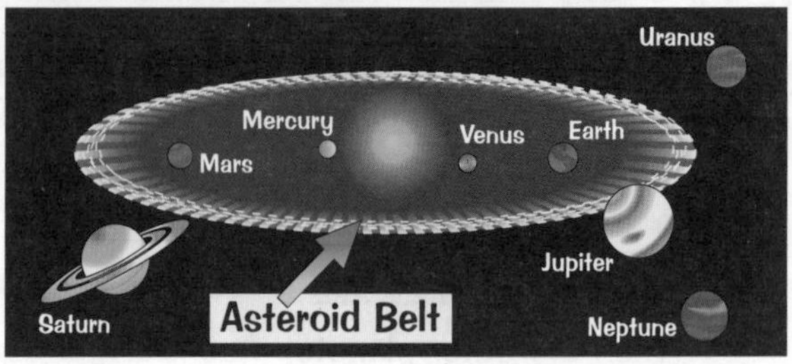

Not to scale.

Meteorites are Rocks That Have Crashed Down to Earth

1) Meteors are rocks or dust that enter the Earth's atmosphere. As they pass through the atmosphere they burn up, and we see them as 'shooting stars'.
2) Sometimes, not all of the meteor burns up and part of it crashes into the Earth's surface as a meteorite. This only happens rarely, but when large meteors do hit us, they can cause havoc...
3) They can start fires, and throw loads of hot rocks and dust into the air. They also make big holes in the ground (craters, if we're being technical).

4) The dust and smoke from a large impact can block out the sunlight for many months, causing climate change — which in turn can cause species to become extinct.
5) For example, about 65 million years ago an asteroid about 10 km across struck the Yucatán peninsula in Mexico. The dust it kicked up caused global temperatures to plummet, and over half the species on Earth subsequently died out (including maybe the last of the dinosaurs).
6) We can tell that asteroids have collided with Earth in the past. There are the big craters, but also:
   - layers of unusual elements in rocks — these must have been 'imported' by an asteroid,
   - sudden changes in fossil numbers between adjacent layers of rock, as species suffer extinction.

Comets Orbit the Sun in Very Elliptical Orbits

1) Comets are balls of rock, dust and ice which orbit the Sun in very elongated ellipses, often in different planes from the planets.
2) They come from objects orbiting the Sun way beyond the planets.
3) As a comet approaches the Sun, its ice melts, leaving a bright tail of gas and debris which can be millions of kilometres long. This is what we see from the Earth.
4) Comets speed up as they approach the Sun, because the Sun's gravitational pull increases as you get closer.

Comet in an elliptical orbit (red line).

I remember that asteroids looked different in 1979...

They were definitely more angular and collisions could be solved simply by shooting them or 'warping' to another part of space*. Comets looked the same in 1066 though — Halley's comet is shown on the Bayeux tapestry.

*computer game history lesson no. 4

NEOs and the Moon

As you read this, there are thousands of hefty lumps of rock just whizzing about in space — and one of them might be coming straight at you.

Near-Earth Objects (NEOs) Could Collide with Earth

1) Near-Earth objects (NEOs) are asteroids or comets which might be on a collision course with Earth.
2) Astronomers use powerful telescopes and satellites to search for and monitor NEOs.
3) When they find one they can calculate the object's trajectory (the path it's going to take) and find out if it's heading for us.
4) NEOs can be difficult to spot because they're small, dark and may have unusual orbits.
5) Small NEOs would burn up harmlessly in the atmosphere if they hit the Earth, but larger ones could cause explosions more powerful than nuclear weapons.
6) If we got enough warning about an NEO coming our way, we could try to deflect it before it hit us.
7) If you exploded a bomb really close to (or on or in) the NEO when it was far away from us, you might 'nudge' it off course. (That'd probably make quite a good plot for a film.)

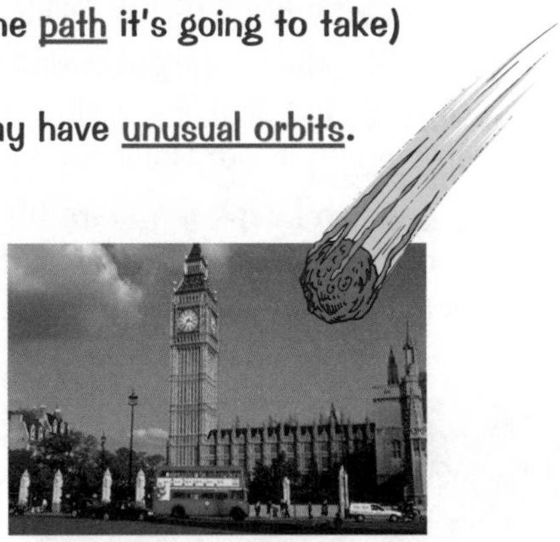

Even Bruce Willis gets it wrong sometimes.

The Moon May Have Come from a Colliding Planet

Scientists can use what they know about the Earth and the Moon to come up with believable theories about where the Moon came from in the first place.
It's pretty amazing.

1) Scientists think that 'our' Moon was formed when another planet collided side-on with Earth.
2) The theory is that some time after the Earth was formed, a smaller Mars-sized object crashed into it.
3) In the heat of the collision, the dense iron cores of these two planets merged to form the Earth's core.
4) The less dense material was ejected as really hot dust and rocks — which orbited around the Earth for a while and eventually came together to form the Moon.
5) There's quite a bit of evidence for this theory. For example:

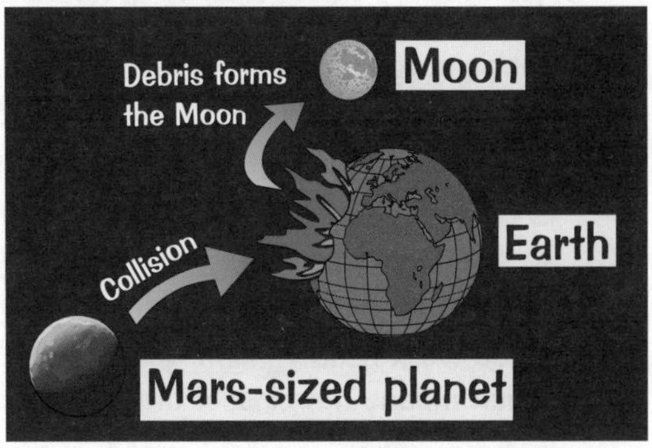

A chocolate-bar sized planet collides with Earth and forms the Moon.

- The Moon has a lower density than the Earth and doesn't have a big iron core, whereas Earth does.
- Moon rocks contain few substances which evaporate at low temperatures — suggesting that the Moon formed from hot material (all the water, etc. was boiled away, as would happen in a collision).

Sadly the Moon isn't made of cheese...

Time for some exciting Moon facts — don't say I never treat you... There's no evidence of mice (or other life) on the Moon. Sad. When humans landed on the Moon they were worried that the surface wouldn't be solid enough and the landing craft would sink — not because they actually thought it was made of cheese though.
The Moon is also known as Luna, after the Roman goddess of the Moon. Astrobods call the planet that hit the Earth 'Theia' after the mother of the ancient Greek moon goddess Selene.

Beyond the Solar System

There's all sorts of exciting stuff out there... Our whole Solar System is just part of a huge galaxy. And there are billions upon billions of galaxies. You should be realising now that the Universe is huge...

We're in the Milky Way Galaxy

1) Our Sun is just one of many billions of stars which form the Milky Way galaxy. Our Sun is about halfway along one of the spiral arms of the Milky Way.
2) The distance between neighbouring stars in the galaxy is usually millions of times greater than the distance between planets in our Solar System.
3) The force which keeps the stars together in a galaxy is gravity, of course. And like most things in the Universe, galaxies rotate — a bit like a Catherine wheel.

The Whole Universe Has More Than a Billion Galaxies

1) Galaxies themselves are often millions of times further apart than the stars are within a galaxy.
2) So even the slowest among you will have worked out that the Universe is mostly empty space and is really really BIG.

Scientists Measure Distances in Space Using Light Years

1) Once you get outside our Solar System, the distances between stars and between galaxies are so enormous that kilometres seem pathetically small for measuring them.
2) For example, the closest star to us (after the Sun) is about 40 000 000 000 000 kilometres away (give or take a few hundred billion kilometres). Numbers like that soon get out of hand.
3) So scientists use light years instead — a light year is the distance that light travels through a vacuum (like space) in one year. Simple as that.
4) If you work it out, 1 light year is equal to about 9 460 000 000 000 kilometres. Which means the closest star after the Sun is about 4.2 light years away from us.
5) Just remember — a light year is a measure of DISTANCE (not time).

Stars Can Explode — and They Sometimes Leave Black Holes

1) When a really big star has used up most of its fuel, it explodes. What's usually left after the explosion is really dense — sometimes so dense that nothing can escape its strong gravitational attraction. It's now called a black hole.
2) Black holes have a very large mass, small volume and a very high density.
3) They're not visible — even light can't escape their gravitational pull (that's why it's 'black', d'oh).
4) Astronomers have to detect black holes in other ways — e.g. they can observe X-rays emitted by hot gases from other stars as they spiral into the black hole.

See p. 125 for more about the death of stars.

Spiral arms — would you still need elbows...

A lot of people say it's a small world. I'm not sure... it's always seemed pretty big to me. Anyway... you never hear anybody say the Universe is small. Not nowadays, anyway. Weirdly though, the Universe used to be tiny (see p. 124). That was a while ago now though. Before my time.

Exploring the Solar System

If you want to know what it's like on another planet, you have three options — peer at it from a distance, send a robot to have a peek, or get in a spaceship and go there yourself...

We Can Explore Space Using Manned Spacecraft...

1) The Solar System is big — so big that even radio waves (which travel at 300 000 000 m/s) take several hours to cross it. Even from Mars, radio signals take at least three minutes.
2) But sending a manned spacecraft to Mars would take at least a couple of years (for a round trip).
3) The spacecraft would need to carry a lot of fuel, making it heavy — and expensive.
4) And it would be difficult keeping the astronauts alive and healthy for all that time...
   - the spacecraft would have to carry loads of food, water and oxygen (or recycle them),
   - you'd need to regulate the temperature and remove toxic gases from the air,
   - the spacecraft would have to shield the astronauts from radiation in space,
   - long periods in low gravity causes muscle wastage and loss of bone tissue,
   - spending ages in a tiny space, with the same people, is psychologically stressful.

Space travel can be very stressful.

...but Sending Unmanned Probes is Much Easier

First, build a spacecraft. Then build and program loads of instruments — to record data and send it back to Earth (probably by radio). Finish the job by packing the instruments on board, turning on the computer and launching your probe. Like I said... easy.

1) 'Fly-by' missions are simplest — the probe passes close by an object but doesn't land. It can gather data on loads of things, including temperature, magnetic and gravitational fields and radiation levels.
2) Sometimes a probe is programmed to enter a planet's atmosphere. It might be designed to burn up after a while, having already sent back lots of data.
3) Some probes are designed to land on other planets (or moons, asteroids...). They often carry exploration rovers that can wander about, taking photos and sample, etc.

Advantages of Unmanned Probes

- They don't have to carry food, water and oxygen.
- They can withstand conditions that would be lethal to humans (e.g. extreme heat, cold or radiation levels).
- With no people taking up room and weighing the probe down, more instruments can be fitted in.
- They're cheaper — they carry less, they don't have to come back to Earth, and less is spent on safety.
- If the probe does crash or burn up unexpectedly it's a bit embarrassing, and you've wasted lots of time and money, but at least no one gets hurt.

Disadvantages of Unmanned Probes

- Unmanned probes can't think for themselves (whereas people are very good at overcoming simple problems that could be disastrous).
- A spacecraft can't do maintenance and repairs — people can (as the astronauts on the Space Shuttle 'Discovery' had to do when its heat shield was damaged during take-off).

The Information Collected Needs to be Sent Back to Earth

Whether a spacecraft is manned or unmanned, the information it collects needs to be sent back to Earth. How it's sent back depends on how far it's travelled and the type of information (e.g. samples or data).

1) Distant objects (e.g. further away than Mars) — data needs to be 'beamed' back (e.g. using radio waves) as it would take too long (or be too difficult) for the spacecraft itself to travel back to Earth.
2) Nearer objects — probes or people could collect samples and physically bring them back to Earth.

Probes — a popular feature of alien abduction stories...

The first ever space probe was called Sputnik 1, which orbited the Earth for 3 months and went 'beep'.

The Origin of the Universe

How did it all begin... Well, once upon a time, there was a really Big Bang.
(That's the most convincing theory we've got for how the Universe started.)

The Universe Seems to be Expanding

As big as the Universe already is, it looks like it's getting even bigger.
All its galaxies seem to be moving away from each other. There's good evidence for this...

Light from Distant Galaxies is Red-Shifted

1) When we look at light from distant galaxies we find that the frequencies are all lower than they should be — they're shifted towards the red end of the spectrum.
2) This red-shift is the same effect as a car horn sounding lower-pitched when the car is travelling away from you. The sound drops in frequency.
3) Measurements of the red-shift suggest that all the distant galaxies are moving away from us very quickly — and it's the same result whichever direction you look in.

More Distant Galaxies Have Greater Red-Shifts

1) More distant galaxies have greater red-shifts than nearer ones.
2) This means that more distant galaxies are moving away faster than nearer ones. The inescapable conclusion appears to be that the whole Universe is expanding.

There's Microwave Radiation from All Directions

This is another observation that scientists made. It's not interesting in itself, but the theory that explains all this evidence definitely is.

1) Scientists can detect low frequency microwave radiation coming from all directions and all parts of the Universe.
2) It's known as the cosmic background radiation.
3) For complicated reasons this background radiation is strong evidence for an initial Big Bang (see below). As the Universe expands and cools, this background radiation 'cools' and drops in frequency.

This Evidence Suggests the Universe Started with a Bang

So all the galaxies are moving away from each other at great speed — suggesting something must have got them going. That 'something' was probably a big explosion — the Big Bang. Here's the theory...

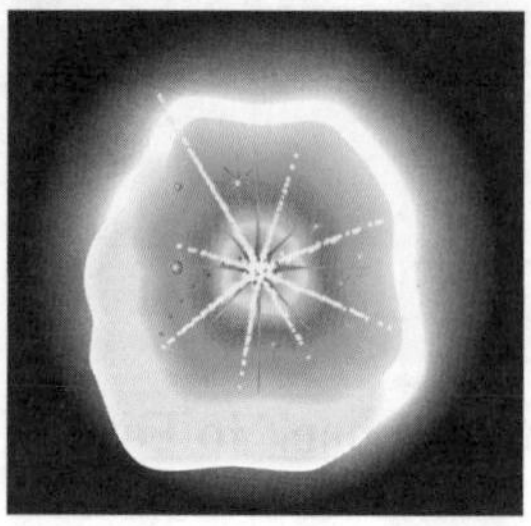

1) Initially, all the matter in the Universe occupied a very small space (that's all the matter in all the galaxies squashed into a space much much smaller than a pinhead — wowzers). Then it 'exploded' — the space started expanding, and the expansion is still going on.
2) The Big Bang theory lets us guess the age of the Universe. From the current rate of expansion, we think the Universe is about 14 billion years old.
3) But estimates of the age of the Universe are very difficult because it's hard to tell how much speed of the expansion has changed since the Big Bang.

In the beginning, there were — no exams...

'How it all began' is quite a tricky problem. Some religious people say that God created the world. Among scientists, the theory of a 'big bang' to get things started is now generally accepted, because that's what the evidence suggests. But we're still rather hazy about if/when/how it's all going to end...

The Life Cycle of Stars

Stars go through many traumatic stages in their lives — just like teenagers.

1) Stars initially form from clouds of DUST AND GAS.

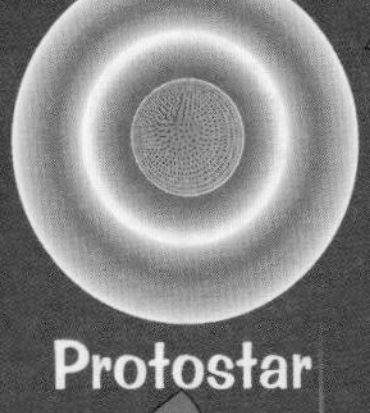

2) The force of gravity makes the gas and dust spiral in together to form a protostar. Gravitational energy has been converted into heat energy, so the temperature rises.

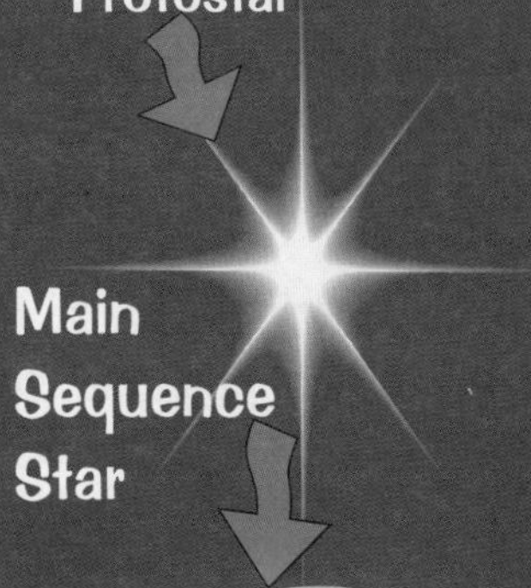

3) When the temperature gets high enough, hydrogen nuclei undergo thermonuclear fusion to form helium nuclei and give out massive amounts of heat and light. A star is born. It immediately enters a long stable period where the heat created by the nuclear fusion provides an outward pressure to balance the force of gravity pulling everything inwards. In this stable period it's called a MAIN SEQUENCE STAR and it typically lasts several billion years. (The Sun is in the middle of this stable period — or to put it another way, the Earth has already had half its innings before the Sun engulfs it!)

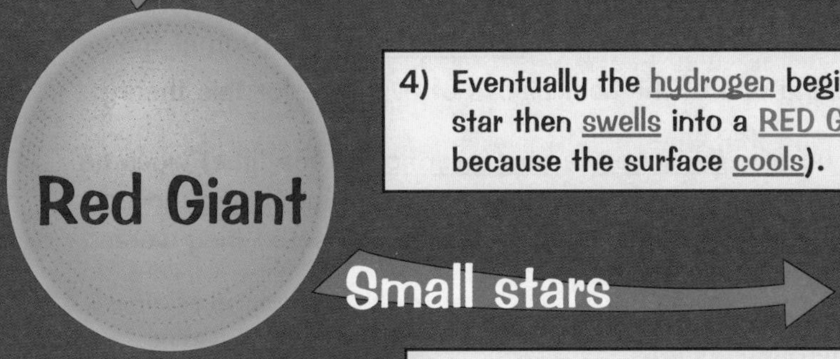

4) Eventually the hydrogen begins to run out and the star then swells into a RED GIANT (it becomes red because the surface cools).

5) A small-to-medium-sized star like the Sun then becomes unstable and ejects its outer layer of dust and gas as a planetary nebula.

6) This leaves behind a hot, dense solid core — a WHITE DWARF, which just cools down and eventually fades away. (That's going to be really sad.)

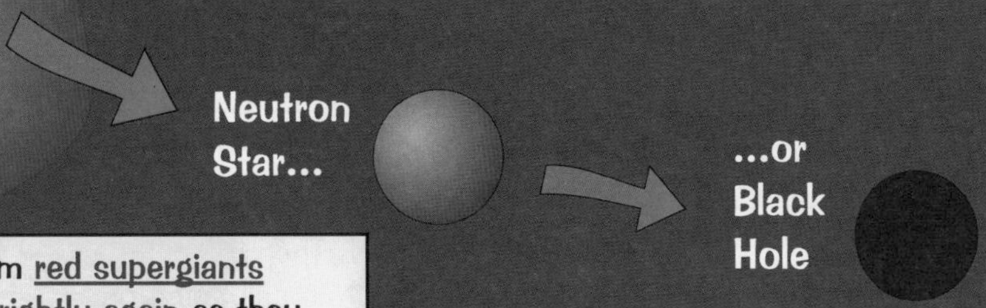

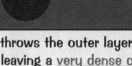

7) Big stars, however, form red supergiants — they start to glow brightly again as they undergo more fusion and expand and contract several times, forming heavier elements in various nuclear reactions. Eventually they'll explode in a SUPERNOVA.

8) The exploding supernova throws the outer layers of dust and gas into space, leaving a very dense core called a NEUTRON STAR. If the star is big enough this will become a BLACK HOLE (see p. 122).

Red Giants, White Dwarfs, Black Holes, Green Ghosts...

Erm. Now how do they know that exactly... Anyway, now you know what the future holds — our Sun is going to fizzle out, and it'll just get very very cold and very very dark. Great.
On a brighter note, the Sun's got a good few years in it yet, so it's still worth passing those exams.

Galileo and Copernicus

We're pretty sure we know what the Solar System is like now, but we haven't always thought it was like this...

Ancient Greeks Thought the Earth was the Centre of the Universe

1) Most ancient Greek astronomers believed that the Sun, Moon, planets and stars all orbited the Earth in perfect circles — this is known as the geocentric model or Ptolemaic model.
2) The Ptolemaic model was the accepted model of the Universe from the time of the ancient Greeks until the 1500s. It was only in the 1600s that it began to be replaced by the Copernican model...

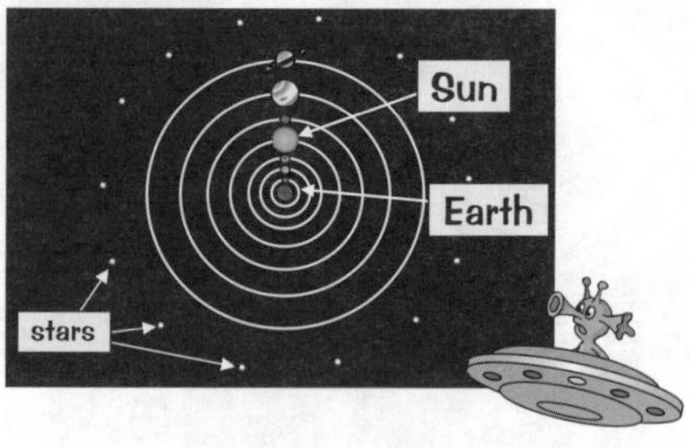

Copernican Model — Sun at the Centre

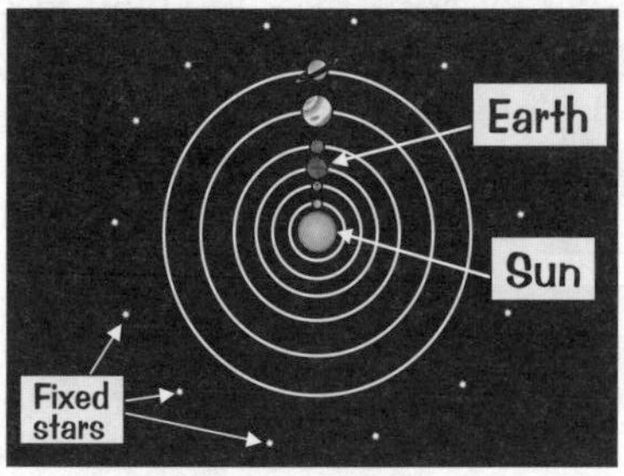

The Copernican model.

1) The Copernican model states that the Earth and planets all orbit the Sun, which is at the centre of the Universe, in perfect circles.
2) The idea had already been around for 2000 years, but the model was first introduced in a book by Copernicus in 1543.
   This book showed astronomical observations could be explained without having the Earth at the centre of the Universe.
3) The Copernican model is also a heliocentric model (Sun at the centre).
4) Galileo found one of the best pieces of evidence for this theory:

Around 1610, Galileo was observing Jupiter using a telescope (a new invention at the time) when he saw some stars in a line near the planet. When he looked again, he saw these stars never moved away from Jupiter and seemed to be carried along with the planet — which suggested they weren't stars, but moons orbiting Jupiter.
This showed not everything was in orbit around the Earth — evidence that the Ptolemaic model was wrong.

Theories change with technological advances — like the invention of the telescope.

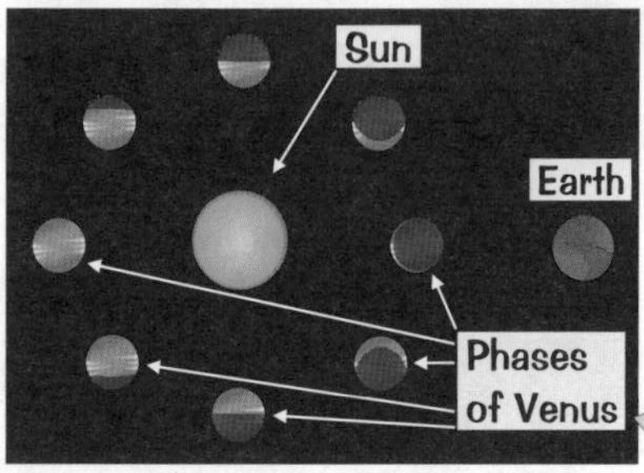

The phases of Venus as it orbits the Sun, as seen from Earth.

5) In the autumn of 1610, Galileo noticed that Venus has phases — where the amount of the planet that's lit by the Sun seems to change over time.
6) If the Ptolemaic model was right then these changes would be very small because Venus would always be in front of the Sun.
7) But if the Copernican model was right, Venus could move in front of and behind the Sun and so the changes in the amount Venus was lit would be really big — just like Galileo saw.
8) Copernicus' ideas weren't very popular at that time because the current models had been around for a long time.
9) The model was also condemned by the church. They claimed that the model went against the Bible, which said the Earth was at the centre of the Universe.
10) Gradually, evidence for the Copernican model increased thanks to more technological advances.
11) The current model still says that the planets in our Solar System orbit the Sun — but that these orbits are actually elliptical rather than circular and the Sun isn't really at the centre of the Universe.

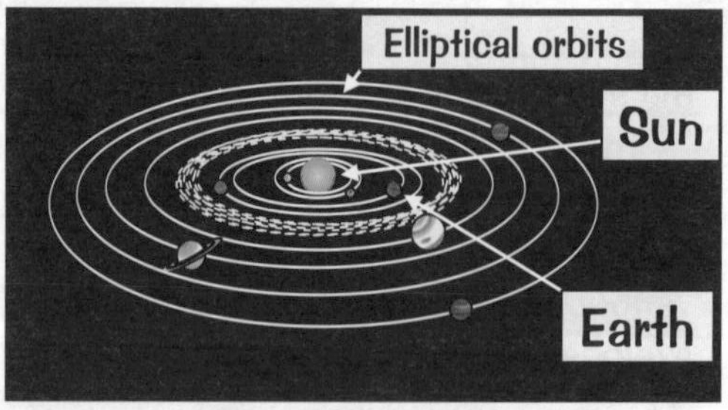

Our current view of the Solar System.

Copernicus — not a brand of metal underwear...

It's taken thousands of years for us to reach our current model of the Solar System. Although these models turned out to be wrong, they played a really important part in helping us reach the model we have today. And unsurprisingly, there's loads and loads that scientists still don't know about our Solar System.

Revision Summary for Module P2

Just what you were waiting for — a whole list of lovely questions to try. You know the routine by now... try the questions, then look back and see what you got right and what you got wrong. If you did get any wrong, you're not ready for the exam — so do more revision and then try the questions again.

1) Give one advantage and one disadvantage of using photocells to generate electricity.
2) Explain how wind turbines convert energy from the Sun into electricity.
3) Briefly describe how a typical power station works.
4) Give one advantage and one disadvantage of using: a) fossil fuels; b) biomass, to generate power.
5) Define electromagnetic induction. What factors affect the size of the induced voltage and current?
6) Describe how a generator works.
7) Explain why a very high electrical voltage is used to transmit electricity in the National Grid.
8) Write down the formula for calculating the efficiency of power stations.
9) *a) How many units of electricity (in kWh) would a kettle of power 2500 W use in 3 minutes?
   *b) How much would that cost, if one unit of electricity costs 12p?
10) Briefly describe how the greenhouse effect keeps the Earth warm.
11) How has human activity affected weather patterns?
12) Name the three types of radiation and describe their ionising powers.
13) Explain which types of nuclear radiation are used, and why, in each of the following:
    a) medical tracers, b) treating cancer, c) smoke detectors.
14) Give one advantage and one disadvantage of nuclear power.
15) Describe the precautions you should take when handling radioactive sources in the laboratory.
16) Briefly explain why it's difficult to dispose of high-level radioactive waste safely.
17) What shape are the orbits of the planets in the Solar System?
18) What force keeps planets and satellites in their orbits?
19) What are asteroids and where are they found? How are they different to meteorites?
20) Briefly describe the evidence that led scientists to think that the Moon may be the result of another planet colliding with Earth.
21) What's a light year?
22) Briefly describe the problems with sending a group of astronauts to Neptune.
23) Give two advantages and two disadvantages of manned space travel.
24) What type of radiation is found everywhere in the Universe?
25) Briefly describe the 'Big Bang' theory for the origin of the Universe.
26) List the steps that lead to the formation of a main sequence star (like our Sun).
27) Describe Copernican's model of the Universe.
28) Explain the evidence that Galileo produced that supported Copernicus' theory.

*Answers on p. 132.

The Perfect Cup of Tea

The making and drinking of tea are important life skills. It's not something that will crop up in the exam, but it is something that will make your revision much easier. So here's a guide to making the perfect cuppa...

1) Choose the Right Mug

A good mug is an essential part of the tea drinking experience, but choosing the right vessel for your tea can be tricky. Here's a guide to choosing your mug:

Some bad mugs:

No handles.
Too fancy (and saucers are for grannies).
Too flimsy and too 80s.
Too many handles.

The perfect mug:

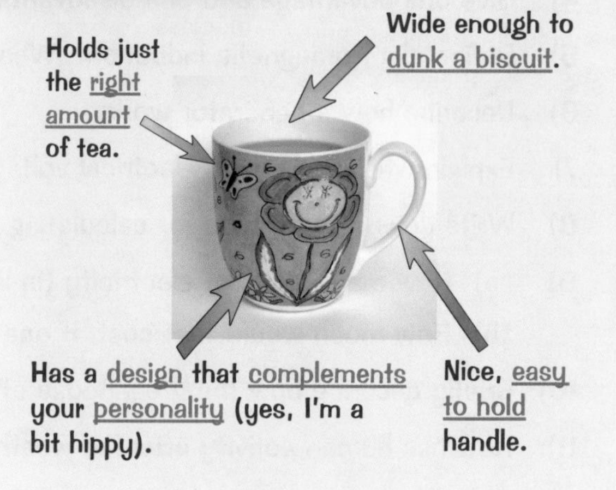
Holds just the right amount of tea.
Wide enough to dunk a biscuit.
Has a design that complements your personality (yes, I'm a bit hippy).
Nice, easy to hold handle.

2) Get Some Water and Boil It

Top tea tip no. 23: why not ask your mum if she wants a cup too?

For a really great brew follow these easy step-by-step instructions:

1) First, pour some water into a kettle and switch it on. (Check it's switched on at the wall too.)
2) Let the kettle boil. While you're waiting, see what's on TV later and check your belly button for fluff. Oh, and put a tea bag in a mug.
3) Once the kettle has boiled, pour the water into the mug.
4) Mash the tea bag about a bit with a spoon. Remove the tea bag.
5) Add a splash of milk (and a lump of sugar or two if you're feeling naughty).

Note: some people may tell you to add the milk before the tea. Scientists have recently confirmed that this is nonsense.

3) Sit Back and Relax

Now this is important — once you've made your cuppa:

1) Have a quick rummage in the kitchen cupboards for a cheeky biscuit. (Custard creams are best — steer clear of any ginger biscuits — they're evil.)
2) Find your favourite armchair/beanbag. Move the cat.
3) Sit back and enjoy your mug of tea. You've earned it.

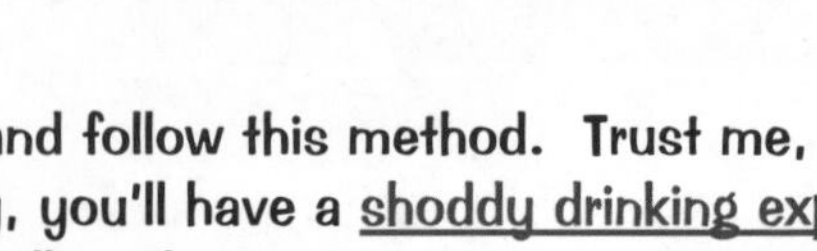

Phew — time for a brew I reckon...

It's best to ignore what other people say about making cups of tea and follow this method. Trust me, this is the most definitive and effective method. If you don't do it this way, you'll have a shoddy drinking experience. There, you've been warned. Now go and get the kettle on. Mine's milk and two sugars...

Index

Index

Index

Answers

Revision Summary for Module B1 (page 29)

2) a) Non-smokers. Group B have higher blood pressures so they are likely to be the smokers because smoking increases your blood pressure.

b) 2.

c) E.g. quit smoking, cut alcohol intake, do more exercise, reduce stress levels, lose any excess weight, have a more balanced diet.

30)

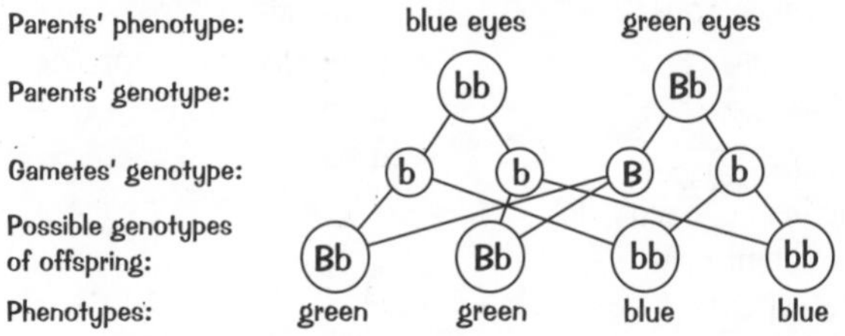

Revision Summary for Module C1 (page 51)

1) 14 H and 6 C

2)

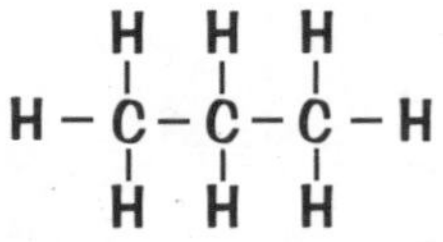

4) $2Na + 2H_2O \rightarrow 2NaOH + H_2$

34) E.g. $C_2H_6 + 3O_2 \rightarrow CO + CO_2 + 3H_2O$

Revision Summary for Module P1 (page 73)

2) Energy = Mass × Specific Heat Capacity (SHC) × Temperature Change (Temp. Ch.),
so SHC = Energy ÷ (Mass × Temp. Ch.)
= 5000 ÷ (0.05 × 40)
= 2500 J/kg/°C

4) Energy = Mass × Specific Latent Heat (SLH)
= 0.5 × 2 260 000
= 1 130 000 J

8) Efficiency = Useful energy output ÷ Total energy input,
so Useful = Efficiency × Total energy
= 0.2 × 200 000
= 40 000.
Wasted energy = Total energy input – Useful energy output
= 200 000 – 40 000
= 160 000 J

Revision Summary for Module C2 (page 106)

28) phosphoric acid + potassium hydroxide → potassium phosphate + water

29) $H_2SO_4 + Na_2CO_3 \rightarrow Na_2SO_4 + H_2O + CO_2$

Power (page 112)

1) Power = Voltage × Current
= 230 × 12
= 2760 W
= 2.76 kW

2) Energy = Power × Time,
so Time = Energy ÷ Power
= 0.5 kWh ÷ 2.76 kW
= 0.18 hours
= 10.8 or 10.9 mins

Revision Summary for Module P2 (page 127)

9) a) Energy = Power × Time
= 2.5 kW × 0.05 h
= 0.125 kWh

b) Cost = Cost per unit × number of units
= 12 × 0.125
= 1.5 p